FIGHTING THE
SULTAN'S WAR

FIGHTING THE SULTAN'S WAR

THE MEMOIR OF A BRITISH INFANTRY OFFICER IN OMAN'S DHOFAR WAR, 1974–1976

DAVID FREEMAN

INTRODUCED BY CALVIN H. ALLEN
FOREWORD BY MAJOR PETER WILLDRIDGE

Greenhill Books

Fighting the Sultan's War
First published in 2026 by
Greenhill Books,
c/o Pen & Sword Books Ltd,
George House, Units 12 & 13
Beevor Street, Off Pontefract Road,
Barnsley, S. Yorkshire S71 1HN

www.greenhillbooks.com
contact@greenhillbooks.com

ISBN: 978-1-80500-225-3

No part of this book may be reproduced, transmitted, downloaded, decompiled or reverse engineered in any form or by any means, electronic or mechanical including photocopying, recording or by any information storage and retrieval system, without permission from the Publisher in writing.
NO AI TRAINING: Without in any way limiting the Author's and Publisher's exclusive rights under copyright, any use of this publication to 'train' generative artificial intelligence (AI) technologies to generate text is expressly prohibited. The Author and Publisher reserve all rights to license uses of this work for generative AI training and development of machine learning language models.

All rights reserved.
© Estate of David Freeman, 2026
Introduction © Calvin H. Allen, 2026

The right of David Freeman to be identified as author of this work has been asserted in accordance with Section 77 of the Copyrights, Designs and Patents Act 1988.

The Publisher's authorised representative in the EU for product safety is Authorised Rep Compliance Ltd., Ground Floor, 71 Lower Baggot Street, Dublin D02 P593, Ireland.
www.arccompliance.com

CIP data records for this title are available from the British Library

Designed and typeset by Donald Sommerville

Printed and bound in the UK by CPI Group (UK) Ltd, Croydon, CR0 4YY.

Typeset in 11.5/13.8 pt Adobe Garamond Pro Regular

Contents

	List of Illustrations and Maps	vii
	Glossary	ix
	Dramatis Personae	xiii
	Introduction *by Calvin H. Allen, Jr.*	xvii
	Foreword *by Peter Willdridge*	xxxi
Chapter 1	Arrival	1
Chapter 2	Settling In	3
Chapter 3	White City and Medina al-San	15
Chapter 4	Hagaif	23
Chapter 5	A Dual Command	33
Chapter 6	Miscellany	57
Chapter 7	The Darbat Picquet	65
Chapter 8	Tawi Atair: June–August 1975	77
Chapter 9	Tawi Atair: September–December 1975	119
Chapter 10	Tawi Atair: January–March 1976	168
Chapter 11	Arzat	176
	Epilogue	199
Appendix 1	Letter to Lieutenant Colonel John McKeown	201
Appendix 2	Timeline: War in Dhofar	211
	Index	221

Illustrations and Maps

Plates

Major David Freeman, OC C Company, KJ, 1975–6, Dhofar.
Men of C Company, KJ, post-Khareef 1975; CSM Hajji Bilal; Lieutenant Charki, OC 10 Platoon, C Company, KJ, 1976.
Staff Sergeant Ahmed Dur Mohammed, OC 9 Platoon, C Company, KJ, KIA 9 August 1975; Peter Willdridge on patrol, Jebel ash Shawr; Lieutenant Badil Mohammed, OC 11 Platoon, C Company, KJ; David Freeman on patrol, Jebel ash Shawr.
Sangar overlooking Wadi Darbat, 1976; Baluch GPMG gunner, Dhofar 1975.
Resupply by Skyvan; Sergeant Gulam Hussein, Platoon Sergeant, 11 Platoon, C Company.
Brian Spice and Peter Willdridge in the mud at Tawi Atair, August 1975; Lalu the cook, making chapattis on the Jebel 1975; C Company helping Jordanian engineers build a road.
C Company building sangars, 1976; David Freeman's sangar, Tawi Atair, 1975.
Range day at Tawi Atair. Peter Willdridge and CSM Bilal watching; Firqa Tawai personnel, including Ahmed Said, 1976.
David Freeman on patrol 1975; ubiquitous rats, September 1975.
The harsh terrain of the Jebel seen from the air; Yanusz Heath and Yarpy Wardle, Jibjat 1976.
Christmas 1975. The Freeman family duck hunting; schoolchildren in Tawi Atair.
25-pounder gun, Eastern Dhofar 1975; Strikemaster in action 1975.
C Company on patrol, Jebel ash Shawr; two Strikemasters pass low over Tawi Atair, 1975.
C Company Land Rover on patrol above Wadi Darbat; *firqa* leader Ahmed Said searching for weapons in caves east of Tawi Atair; dawn stand-to. Wadi Hinna 20 December 1975.
Captain Jummah Hussein, Omani Artillery; Sergeant Jelal, 10 Platoon; Rajah Masoud al-Amri, leader of the Adoo in the Eastern Area until July 1976; Peter Willdridge and the battalion shooting team, 1976.

Saladin armoured car. Peter Willdridge, David Freeman, Staff Sergeant John Perkins.

Illustrations in Text

KJ Order of Battle	page xxxii
Jebali girls at a watering hole north of Tawi Atair.	34
C Company's Land Rover at Tawi Atair.	66
Brian Spice, CSM Bilal and *firqa* fighters, Tawi Atair.	81
Peter Willdridge and David Freeman, 1975.	95
Donkey racing.	131
Trish Sole at the well at Tawi Atair, 1975.	155
Firqa guides, David Freeman, Peter Willdridge, and others, overlooking Mirbat, 1976.	191
Lieutenant Charki, OC 10 Platoon, on the Jebel above Mirbat, 1976.	194
Jerry Blatch and John Gordon-Taylor.	200

All photographs © David Freeman estate, Peter Willdridge or Trish Sole. All rights reserved.

Maps

Southern Arabia	page xvi
The Eastern Area	14
Tawi Atair Area	64
Action on 9 August 1975	102

Glossary

Adoo From the Arabic *adu*, meaning 'enemy'.
AK-47 Soviet assault rifle. 7.62-mm calibre.
Askar Arabic: soldier, but used to mean old armed retainer. '*Jundee*' was the term used for a regular soldier.
Babu Hindi: clerk. Used by the Baluch as a term of respect, by the British as one of contempt.
Barasti Palm-frond huts of Northern Oman.
Bayt Arabic: house (plural *buyoot*).
Boom Arab sailing vessel. Sometimes referred to in error as a dhow.
Burmail Large plastic drum for water.
Carl Gustav Swedish anti-tank recoilless rifle. In service with the British Army.
Chinko Corrugated iron.
Claymore The M18A1 Claymore, a directional anti-personnel mine.
Defender Light twin-engine STOL transport plane, made by Britten-Norman.
Eid Muslim festival.
Falaj Arabic: Water channel (plural '*aflaj*').
Farrash Arabic: bedroll.
Firqa Arabic: regiment. In Dhofar a unit of tribal irregular troops of any size. Many of the *firqa* were ex-Adoo who changed sides when Sultan Qaboos bin Sayyid came to the throne in 1970.
FN Fabrique Nationale 7.62-mm self-loading rifle.
FOO Forward Observation Officer. Gunner controlling the fire of a battery.
Gatn Spine of the mountains in Dhofar.
GPMG The L7A2 General Purpose Machine Gun (GPMG) is a general purpose machine gun that could be used as a light weapon and in a sustained fire (SF) role.
Halal The Islamic ritual method of slaughtering animals and by extension the meat prepared in this way. The Faithful may only eat meat killed in this manner.
Khanjar Arabic: curved Omani dagger.
Khareef Wet season in Dhofar. Late June–September.
KJ al-Kateeba al-Janoobia. The Southern Regiment.

Jaysh   Arabic: army.
Jebel/Jebali   Arabic: hill or mountain. Hillman.
Jundee   Arabic: soldier.
LZ   Landing zone.
M16   US made 5.56-mm calibre automatic rifle.
Mulazzim   Arabic: lieutenant.
Murcha   Shelter made of stone with overhead cover.
Naqeeb   Arabic: staff sergeant.
PDRY   The Peoples' Democratic Republic of the Yemen.
Picquet   Hill or outcrop. Also used as a verb for the tactic of guarding such places.
Raa'ees   Arabic: captain.
Raa'id   Arabic: major.
Ramadan   Islamic month of fasting and pilgrimage.
Rial   The currency of Oman, at this period exchangeable at a fixed rate of 1 rial = US$2.895
RPG-7   Soviet made anti-tank rocket. A portable, reusable, unguided, shoulder-launched, anti-tank rocket-propelled grenade launcher. The ruggedness, simplicity, low cost, and effectiveness of the RPG-7 has made it the most widely used anti-armour weapon in the world. The RPG has been used in almost all conflicts across all continents since the mid-1960s from the Vietnam War to the early 2010s War in Afghanistan.
SAF   The Sultan's Armed Forces.
Saladin   British-made six-wheeled armoured car mounting a 76-mm gun. Nicknamed 'Doobuba' by Baluch soldiers because of its distinctive bubbling exhaust sound.
Sangar   Circular wall of rock erected as protection against small-arms fire.
Sarbe   Pocket-size automatic distress radio used by aircrew and, in Dhofar, by ground troops. Emits homing bleep to guide in aircraft.
Seeyasee   Arabic: political officer. In Dhofar, used to mean intelligence officer.
SEP   Surrendered Enemy Personnel.
Shimaag   Headcloth worn turban-style in Oman.
Shimaal   North wind blowing out of the Empty Quarter in winter.
Skyvan   Transport aircraft, made by Shorts of Belfast.
SOAF   The Sultan of Oman's Air Force.
SON   The Sultan of Oman's Navy.
Suk   Arabic: market.
Strikenaster   Light attack aircraft, made by BAC.
Tawi   Arabic: well.
Wadi   Arabic: dry watercourse, valley.
Wahiba   Desert region of Eastern Oman.

GLOSSARY

Wali   Arabic: ruler.

Waqeel   Arabic: sergeant major.

Yarpy   Originally an Afrikaans term for a 'country boy', later also a derogatory name for a white South African or Rhodesian.

Dramatis Personae

Arab/Baluch Personnel

Abdul Qadir   Captain, KJ. Transport officer.
Ahmed Dur Mohammed   Staff Sergeant, C Company, KJ. Platoon Commander 9 Platoon. Killed in action August 1975.
Ahmed Said   Leader Firqa al-Amri, Tawi Atair till October 1975, then Firqa Jebel Ali.
Ali Matook   Adoo paymaster in Eastern Area. Killed by C Company in August 1975.
Alum Khan   Corporal, 12 Platoon, C Company, KJ.
Badil Mohammed   Lieutenant, KJ. Platoon Commander 11 Platoon, C Company, KJ.
Charki Faqir Mohammed   CSM, C Company, KJ, till March 1975. Then platoon commander.
Faqir Mohammed   Staff Sergeant, C Company, KJ. Company Quartermaster Sergeant till March 1976, then CSM.
Habib Ullah   Soldier, C Company, KJ.
Hajji Bilal   Acting Sergeant-Major, C Company, KJ.
Hatim Ali   Captain, KJ. OC recce platoon.
Ibrahim Abdullah   Corporal, 12 Platoon, C Company, KJ.
Imam Din   Sergeant, KJ. C Company mortar NCO.
Jelal   Sergeant, Platoon Commander 10 Platoon, C Company, KJ.
Karim Bux   Major, KJ. OC Headquarters Company.
Lai Bux   Sergeant, 10 Platoon, C Company, KJ.
Mohammed Daan   NCO, Firqa al-Amri till October 1985, then Firqa Jebel Ali.
Mohammed Said   Sergeant Major, Firqa al-Amri, then leader from October 1975.
Mohammed Salim   Lieutenant, KJ. Platoon Commander 11 Platoon, C Company till mid-1975.
Mohim Khan   Soldier, C Company Headquarters, KJ.
Murad Jan   Captain, KJ. Air Movements officer.

Rajah Masoud al-Amri.   Leader of the Adoo in the Eastern Area until July 1975.
Saleh Mohammed   Corporal, C Company, KJ. Signaller.
Salim Musalim   Leader, Firqa Khalid Walid, White City.
Shahbaz Khan   Sergeant, 12 Platoon, C Company, KJ.
Sher Mohammed   Captain, KJ. Quartermaster March 1975– c. March 1976.
Suleiman   Lieutenant, KJ. Platoon Commander 12 Platoon, C Company.

British Personnel

John Akehurst   Brigadier, Commander Dhofar Brigade.
Jerry Blatch   Captain, KJ. Ex-Queen's Regiment.
David Bills   Captain, KJ. OC B Company, April 1975–June 1976. RAF Regiment.
Keith Brett   Major, KJ. Second-in-Command till March 1975. Murdered in 1976 in Oman.
Tim Burls   Captain, The Parachute Regiment.
George Burns   Captain, KJ. Quartermaster till March 1975.
Ian Cartwright   Major. Staff Officer, Dhofar Brigade HQ (DAA & QMG).
Hugh Cross   Captain, KJ. Adjutant till early 1975. RAF Regiment.
Tim Creasey   Major General, Commander Sultan's Armed Forces.
Harry Fecitt   Captain, KJ. OC C Company till April 1975.
John Gordon-Taylor   Lieutenant Colonel, KJ. Commanding Officer.
John Gorman   Captain, KJ. Adjutant from late 1975.
Yanusz Heath   Captain, Operations Officer, KJ.
Geoff Hill   Captain. Staff Officer, Dhofar Brigade HQ (Staff Captain 'A').
Michael Jacks   Captain, KJ. Ex-Parachute Regiment.
Ashley Loxton   Captain, Oman Artillery. FOO, Tawi Atair, mid-1975. Royal Artillery
Douglas McCully   Major, KJ. Second-in-Command, from March 1975. Queen's Regiment.
Ernie Marchant   Captain, KJ. Quartermaster from November 1975. Ex-Scots Guards.
Mike Martin   Taylor Woodrow employee.
John Moody   Captain, KJ. Second-in-Command, B Company. Queen's Royal Irish Hussars.
Peter Packham   Major. Staff Officer, Dhofar Brigade HQ (Brigade Major). Queen's Regiment.
Geoff Ritson   Major, KJ. Commander B Company till April 1975. Ex-Parachute Regiment. Wounded April 1975.
Martin Robb   Official Civil Aid Department.
Mike Rose   Major, KJ. Wounded November 1974.

DRAMATIS PERSONAE

Jim Shepherd   Lieutenant Colonel, the Desert Regiment. Commanding Officer.
Whimpy Waite   Sergeant, armoured car squadron.
Ian (Yarpy) Wardle   Captain, KJ. Intelligence Officer. Ex-Rhodesian Army.
Peter Willdridge   Captain, KJ. Second-in-Command, C Company. Royal Anglian Regiment.
Hugh Willoughby   Major, KJ. Commander D Company. Coldstream Guards.

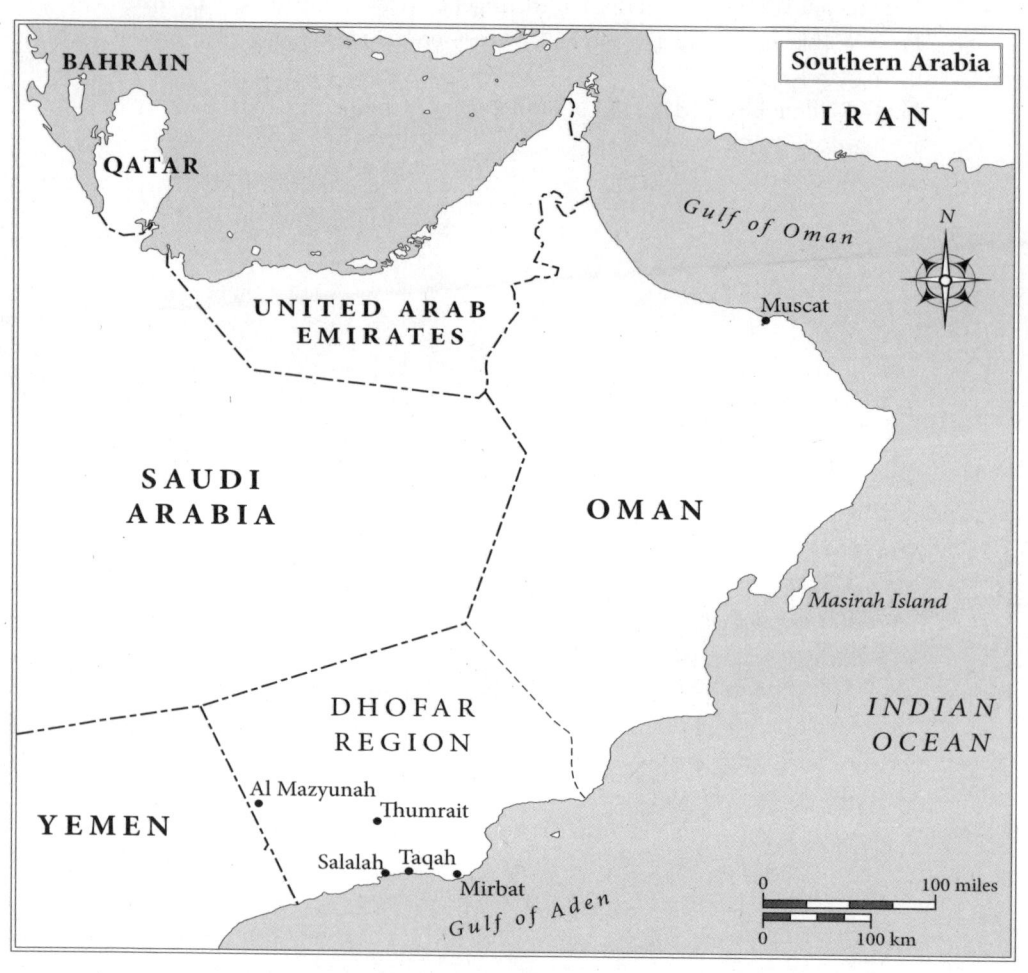

Introduction

by Calvin H. Allen, Jr.

Major David Freeman's account of his eighteen months of service in the armed forces of the Sultanate of Oman joins a relatively short list of memoirs about the Dhofar insurgency against the government of Oman.[1] The Dhofar War (1965–76) was one of the many Cold War era 'small wars' that ostensibly pitted Western democracy against Soviet bloc communism, although, in reality, they often had more to do with anti-colonialism and nationalism.[2] All also tended to be overshadowed by the American 'small war' in Vietnam. The importance of Freeman's memoir is that, unlike those of staff officers who dominate the literature, he gives us the perspective of a field officer, having served as Officer Commanding (OC) a rifle company involved in the day-to-day operations of the conflict.

Oman is an Arab, Islamic country, but the majority form of Islam in Oman is Ibadism, the third major division within the faith after Sunnism and Shi'ism. The distinctive feature of Ibadism is its principle that the community be governed by an imam who is selected by a process of *shura* (consultation) among the religious and community leaders. The selection of imams began in the eighth century and continued into the twentieth century. The current ruling family, the al-Bu Said, traces its legitimacy to the selection of Ahmad bin Said al-Bu Said as imam in 1749. In theory, the imamate is not hereditary. In practice, the ideal has often been ignored, and imamates have morphed into dynasties.[3]

Such was the case with the al-Bu Said who dropped their ties to the imamate to focus on the creation of a commercial empire in the Western Indian Ocean. Those efforts reached their peak under Sayyid (Lord) Said bin Sultan al-Bu Said (1806–56), whose territorial claims spread from Gwadar in modern-day Pakistan, to various ports along the coasts of Iran, and to East

Africa. Midway through his reign Said even transferred his capital from Muscat to Zanzibar to be closer to his East African territories.[4]

Said's aspirations brought Oman into contact with the rising British Empire in India. Said's father had concluded a commercial treaty with Great Britain in 1798, and Said allied with the British in fighting piracy in the Gulf in the 1810s. The British reciprocated by assisting Sayyid Said in his conflict with the Bani Bu Ali tribe in south-eastern Oman in 1820. However, the British soon began to encroach on Omani interests with an 1822 treaty that restricted the lucrative Indian Ocean slave trade and an 1839 revision of the 1798 commercial treaty that limited the duty Oman could levy on British goods, granted British extraterritorial rights over its subjects (including those from India) in Oman, and permitted British warships to board Omani vessels suspected of trading in slaves. British interference in Omani affairs ultimately led to the demise of Said's maritime empire as, following his death in 1856, the British mediation of a dispute between two of Said's sons resulted in the 1861 Canning Award, which created separate Sultanates of Muscat and Zanzibar. The separation included terms requiring that the Sultan of Zanzibar pay an annual subsidy. When the Sultan of Zanzibar proved unable to keep up the payments, the British government assumed the responsibility, which gave considerable financial leverage over the rulers of Muscat.

There then followed more than half a century of turmoil in Oman as in 1866 the Ibadis, desiring the re-establishment of an imamate and dissatisfied with British influence over the sultans, selected Azzan bin Qais al-Bu Said, a member of a collateral branch of the al-Bu Said family, as imam and temporarily occupied Muscat. With British support Turki bin Said, a son of Said bin Sultan, restored the Sultanate in 1872 but ruled over only Muscat and the Omani coast. Ibadi opposition to the sultanate continued, resulting in periodic attacks on Muscat. Britain remained active in Omani affairs, and in response to Sultan Faisal bin Turki's efforts to establish closer ties with France, it imposed a secret article to a revised commercial treaty in 1891 that prohibited the sultan from ceding, selling, mortgaging, or in any way permitting the occupation of any part of his possessions except to Britain. Oman, or at least those parts ruled by the al-Bu Said sultans, became a virtual British protectorate.

Ibadi tribal opposition to the Sultanate continued to rise, culminating in the 1895 occupation of the port. Although the British did not intervene directly, the presence of a British warship in Muscat harbour encouraged the rebellious tribes to withdraw. British influence increased even more in 1912, when, concerned by Muscat's recently developed role as a centre of the Indian Ocean arms trade, they convinced Sultan Faisal bin Turki effectively to end the trade in exchange for a new subsidy that increased the British financial hold on the Sultanate. The end of the arms trade also served to increase tribal opposition to the al-Bu Said, resulting in the May 1913 election of Salim bin Rashid al-Kharusi as imam. The new Imamate quickly established control in Oman and expressed its intentions to occupy Muscat and depose Sultan Faisal.

While Imamate forces consolidated control in Oman the situation in Muscat deteriorated. Sultan Faisal bin Turki died in October 1913. The British backed the new government of Sultan Taimur bin Faisal by pledging to continue their financial support and, more importantly, providing direct military intervention with British ships shelling Imamate forces along the coast and British-Indian troops being stationed in Muscat. Those troops easily repulsed a January 1915 attack by the tribal forces of the imam. There followed several years of negotiations involving the sultan, imam, and British, resulting in the 1920 Treaty of Seeb which effectively divided Oman between the Sultanate of Muscat and Oman controlling Muscat and the coast and the Imamate controlling the interior of the country.

The Treaty of Seeb brought peace and some stability to Taimur bin Faisal but also served to launch a period of increased British control over Muscat's affairs. British-imposed reforms compelled the sultan to establish the Muscat Infantry (MI), a small military force comprised of Baluchi mercenaries commanded by British officers, first from India and later, after Indian independence, from Great Britain. Additional reforms included a new council of ministers which included a British financial advisor who dominated its affairs. Sultan Taimur proved to be a compliant if reluctant ruler who spent as much time as possible away from Muscat, leaving affairs in the hands of his son Said and the British until the British finally acceded to his desire to abdicate in 1932.

Sultan Said bin Taimur al-Said[5] (1932–70) initially enjoyed nearly twenty years of peace and stability, and spent most of that time trying to escape his British overlords. An early victory came when he refused to accept a British financial advisor, although the Government of India Political Agent (until 1948) or the British Ambassador (after Indian independence) continued to exert considerable influence over the sultan. Sultan Said's success at balancing Muscat's budget also helped to lessen his financial dependence on the British. However, Said's decision to spend as much time as possible in Salalah in Dhofar as opposed to Muscat provides the most visible example of his efforts to escape the British.

Dhofar, extending south from Oman proper, is geographically and culturally distinct from Oman. While most of the region is an arid, mountainous, largely uninhabited territory, Dhofar benefits from the annual monsoon (known locally as the *Khareef*), which brings sufficient rains from late June through September to support agriculture, including the frankincense tree for which the region is so famous and that made it an important trade centre in ancient and medieval times, and animal husbandry, most especially cattle rather than the camels that predominate in northern Oman. Linguistically, while Arabic is spoken along the coast, the population, known as *Jebalis* ('mountaineers'), of the surrounding region speak dialects of Mahri languages related to ancient South Arabian. Religiously, the population of Dhofar is Sunni rather than Ibadi Muslim.

Up until the reign of Sultan Said bin Taimur the al-Bu Said had not been particularly active in the region. Sayyid Said bin Sultan intervened briefly in a conflict among Dhofari tribes in 1829 but did not exercise any Omani control thereafter. In 1879 Sultan Turki bin Said formally annexed Dhofar and appointed a resident governor. However, Omani rule proved difficult to maintain and a series of revolts over the next fifteen years resulted in periodic al-Bu Said withdrawals from the territory. By 1900, with British assistance, Sultan Faisal bin Turki had established Muscati control under a governor. The al-Bu Said tended to treat Dhofar as a private estate rather than an integral part of the Sultanate; Said bin Taimur even went so far as to issue separate coinage for the province. Sultans rarely travelled to the area until Sultan Said began extended visits in the 1930s and made it his summer residence beginning in the 1940s.

In the 1950s Sultan Said bin Taimur's tranquil rule began to weaken, victim to the world's need for petroleum, the Cold War, and the rise of nationalism and anti-colonialism. Sultan Said developed an interest in the possibility of the wealth that the production of oil in Oman could bring him early in his reign, and in 1937 awarded a concession covering all of Oman, including Dhofar and those territories under the administration of the imam, to the British-owned Iraq Petroleum Company, whose Oman subsidiary eventually became known as Petroleum Development Oman (PDO). PDO explorations extended into Imamate territory and benefited Sultan Said both by providing much-needed income to the government and by increasing the Sultan's influence among the tribes in negotiations about the granting of PDO access to their territories. It also brought conflict with the imam and his tribal supporters who saw exploration as an encroachment on their domain.

INTRODUCTION

In addition to the domestic situation, oil exploration also had international repercussions. In 1952 Saudi Arabia, at the instigation of its own oil concession holder, the Arabian-American Oil Company (ARAMCO), occupied the Buraimi Oasis, claiming it as Saudi territory and opening it up to oil exploration. Both the sultan and imam disputed the Saudi claim, arguing that three of the nine villages in the oasis belonged to Oman. The Sheikh of Abu Dhabi joined in, asserting *his* claim to the other six villages. Sultan Said gathered his forces, including the Muscat Infantry and tribal levies, to stage an attack on the Saudis. The imam supported the endeavour by sending his tribal supporters. The army gathered in Sohar and prepared to march on Buraimi. However, the British intervened, ordering Said to abandon military action in favour of arbitration. Said, embarrassed by the British, fled to Salalah.

While Buraimi festered, Said began to turn his attention to expanding his military forces. The process began with a reorganisation of the Muscat Infantry in 1953, followed by the formation of the Batinah Field Force (BFF), charged with defending Muscat's coastal territories. Unlike the Baluchi-manned Muscat Infantry, the BFF drew its troops from the Omani Hawasina tribe, but Britain continued to provide its officers and staff. A third unit, the Muscat and Oman Field Force (MOFF), soon followed. PDO financed MOFF, with the unit's charge being to defend oil company operations, including its plans to move into the Fahud area. MOFF recruited its forces from a wide range of Omani tribes but, like MI and BFF, Britain provided its officers.

The next several years witnessed heightened tensions as PDO activities disrupted the tribal equilibrium established by the Treaty of Seeb. Fahud lay within the tribal territory of the Duru, whose sheikhs generally leaned toward the Imamate but who now saw the potential of oil wealth and were more amenable to a relationship with the sultan, if not outright independence. The death of Imam Muhammad al-Khalili and the election of Ghalib bin Ali al-Hinai exacerbated the political situation. A compromise candidate who lacked the backing of rival tribal leaders, Imam Ghalib only weakened his position by courting Saudi support. The Duru responded by reaching an agreement with PDO allowing exploration of Fahud in exchange for an annual payment. In turn Imam Ghalib occupied the town of Ibri, in the centre of Duru territory. PDO joined in, without the sultan's approval but with the encouragement of the Duru, by sending MOFF forces to Ibri in September 1954. The imam took no further action.

There followed a brief quiet, but in October 1955 Sultan Said agreed to join the British in military action against the Saudis in Buraimi. MOFF occupied several more towns in interior Oman en route to Buraimi and drove the Saudis from the village of Hamasa in Buraimi. Emboldened by MOFF's success, Sultan Said decided to unite the country under his rule. On 13 December 1955 Said's forces set out from Fahud towards Nizwa. They met virtually no resistance, and on 15 December occupied the town. Imam Ghalib had fled to the al-Hinai tribal stronghold of Ghafat, only to be placed under house arrest by the leader of his tribe. The BFF secured control of the area around the strategic town of Rustaq, where the imam's brother Talib bin Ali al-Hinai led somewhat stiffer resistance before fleeing to Saudi Arabia. Sultan Said travelled overland from Salalah, arriving in Nizwa on 24 December to receive the proclamations of loyalty from the principal tribal leaders, and then proceeded on a tour of his newly unified country.

Sultan Said enjoyed a short period of peace. Imamate supporters staged periodic attacks on PDO operations. A planned uprising in May 1957 fizzled out, but by July Talib bin Ali had returned from Saudi Arabia, other tribal leaders began to gather with him in Jebel Akhdar, and Ghalib bin Ali escaped his house arrest and proclaimed the restoration of the Imamate. MOFF's efforts to suppress the restoration failed miserably. They withdrew to Fahud as the imam's forces came out of the mountains and occupied the territory around Nizwa. Britain sent reinforcements, in the form of regular British Army units, and the Royal Air Force (RAF) began providing air support. Thus fortified, by mid-August MOFF had succeeded in driving the rebels back into Jebel Akhdar, from where they continued a guerilla war against the sultan.

Britain withdrew its forces from Oman, although the RAF continued to attack Imamate positions in the Jebel. Said also reorganised his defeated army, disbanding MOFF and BFF to form the Northern Frontier Regiment (NFR). Following a failed NFR assault on Jebel Akhdar in late August 1957, Sultan Said found himself compelled to seek more direct British assistance to defeat the insurrection. A July 1958 'Exchange of Letters' between Britain and Muscat and Oman promised British financial assistance in exchange for British-supervised Omani military reorganisation and a civil development programme. Despite decades of efforts to secure his independence, Sultan Said found himself under even greater British control, and in April 1958, in the midst of the negotiations over the 'Exchange of Letters', the sultan moved permanently to Salalah to escape his British overlords.

INTRODUCTION

Under the command of Colonel David Smiley, the MI, the NFR, and newly formed Sultan's Navy, and Sultan's Air Force comprised the Sultan's Armed Forces (SAF). Despite the reorganisation and an influx of supplies and money from Britain, SAF proved incapable of expelling Imamate forces from Jebel Akhdar, and rebel attacks became even more aggressive, strengthened by increased Saudi military supplies. The situation once again required direct British intervention. Thus reinforced, SAF proved successful by October in surrounding Jebel Akhdar and cutting off Imamate forces from their Saudi supply lines. After a failed cease-fire, a squadron of the Special Air Service (SAS) arrived from Malaya. By the end of January resistance had ended, although Imam Ghalib, his brother Talib, and several of their allies succeeded in escaping to Saudi Arabia from where they conducted a political campaign against Sultan Said, including bringing the 'Oman Question' before the United Nations. Despite periodic terrorist attacks in Oman and against Omani overseas interests, military resistance now ended, and the Imamate ceased to be a threat.

With the end of the war, Said remained in Salalah while in Muscat a small group of family members and friends managed affairs with British oversight. A British-funded development project began to expand transport, agriculture, education, and health facilities in northern Oman. PDO continued its explorations, those efforts finally attaining success in September 1962 with the discovery of oil. Exports began five years later in September 1967, offering Sultan Said substantial wealth and the hope of freedom from the British.

Meanwhile, little changed in Dhofar, treated as Sultan Said's private fief. Some development did occur, with the opening of a school and hospital in Salalah, but those efforts did not extend to the rest of the province. Said paid some attention to the defence of his estate, however. Following a Saudi incursion in northern Dhofar in early 1954, he created the Dhofar Force (DF), comprised of *Jebali* recruits with British officers. DF remained under the sultan's direct command even after the reorganisation of SAF in 1958.

Social conditions in Dhofar deteriorated under Sultan Said's malevolent rule. When the *Jebalis* were slow to pay the exorbitant taxes the sultan imposed on their cattle and fishing activities, he imposed blockades on all trade with the coast. This served only to exacerbate the already grinding poverty of the region, forcing many to migrate to better opportunities in Saudi Arabia and other Gulf States, in their oilfields or armed forces. There they came into contact with others working in opposition to Sultan Said and with broader philosophies of Arab nationalism and Marxism. Organising began as early as 1962 when exiles united around Dhofari and/or Arab nationalist ideologies began forming groups such as the Dhofar Benevolent Society and the Dhofar Branch of the Movement of Arab Nationalists.

Opposition also began organising in Dhofar, and one such group under the leadership of Musallim bin Nufl al-Kathiri, of the prominent Bait Kathir tribe, began attacking oil company and SAF vehicles in 1962. Said responded with even more repression, arresting insurgents, including Musallim who eventually escaped and continued to be active in fighting Sultan Said, and destroying water wells. The repression failed to suppress the opposition. In June 1965 various anti-Sultanate groups met in central Dhofar to form the Dhofar Liberation Front (DLF) and began military operations, an act that marked what is usually regarded as the start of the Dhofar war.[6] DLF attacks from their base of operations in the Arzat region north-west of Salalah, focused mainly on the Salalah–Thumrait (Midway) road and the coastal villages of Taqah and Mirbat and continued for the next three years. One of their more daring operations occurred in April 1966 when DLF members of the DF unsuccessfully attempted to assassinate Sultan Said. SAF proved somewhat successful at limiting DLF activities by intercepting arms shipments coming both overland and by sea from Saudi Arabia.

With the British withdrawal from Aden and the rest of the Federation of South Arabia and the emergence in November 1967 of the independent Marxist state of the People's Republic of South Yemen (after 1970 the People's Democratic Republic of Yemen – PDRY, but commonly referred to as South Yemen), fortunes changed dramatically for the Dhofari insurgency. The DLF moved its headquarters to Hawf, in South Yemen. Now part of the Cold War struggle between the Soviet bloc and the West, the movement also began to take on a much more leftist orientation and received moral and material support from the Soviet Union, China, Cuba, Egypt, Iraq, and Libya. The ideological shift resulted in a split in 1968 when the Marxist faction formed the Popular Front for the Liberation of the Occupied Arabian Gulf (PFLOAG) and took control of the insurrection. The DLF continued to exist but assumed a secondary role in the opposition to Sultan Said.

With a steady supply of armaments, PFLOAG adopted a much more aggressive military strategy, dividing Dhofar into Western and Eastern Zones, divided by the Midway Road (the PFLOAG Red Line), and a Central Zone around Salalah. By late winter 1970 PFLOAG controlled

INTRODUCTION

nearly two-thirds of Dhofar, including the towns of Madhub and Rakhyut in western Dhofar, with SAF forces largely limited to Salalah and the coastal towns to its east. The DF proved incapable of combatting the PFLOAG threat and when Sultan Said disbanded the unit after the 1966 assassination attempt, he had no choice but to bring in SAF to defend his territory. SAF defenders were no more successful, especially because they withdrew from the mountains during the *Khareef* season each year, abandoning any gains they might have made during the preceding months. As in 1957 and 1958, the British decided to intervene directly. In February 1970 Brigadier Hugh Oldman, who had replaced Colonel Smiley as commander of SAF in April 1961, became Sultan Said's Defence Secretary and initiated plans to expand SAF with new infantry units, including a Baluchi-manned Southern Regiment (often known as KJ after its Arabic name al-Katibah al-Janubiyah). Brigadier John Akehurst, the new commander of SAF, advised that the war could not be won by force of arms alone, and in March John Watts, the Commanding Officer of 22 SAS, arrived in Dhofar to evaluate the situation and proposed a five-point 'hearts and minds' campaign, including bringing schools, clinics, veterinary services, and water wells to the *Jebalis* as a complement to military operations. Sultan Said rejected the whole idea.

Meanwhile, opposition to Sultan Said continued to grow in northern Oman. Many prominent Omanis, most notably the sultan's brother Sayyid Tariq bin Taimur al-Said, had fled the country in 1962 and become openly opposed to Said's continued rule. In 1969 a group of Omani exiles in Iraq formed the National Democratic Front for the Liberation of Oman and the Arabian Gulf, and in June 1970 the opposition took on a more violent turn when a small group of activists unsuccessfully attacked the SAF base at Izki in northern Oman. Information gathered from those captured during the attack led authorities to arms caches in Sur, Matrah, and elsewhere in Oman, which served to confirm the level of opposition to Sultan Said's authoritarian rule.

The British government in London, British personnel in the Omani armed forces, and Sayyid Qaboos bin Said, the sultan's son who had been held in virtual house arrest in Salalah since 1964 following his return to Oman after his graduation from the British military academy at Sandhurst, a year of duty in the British Army, and a world tour, were all in agreement of the need for a change in leadership. The very loosely organised group, with Buraik bin Hamud al-Ghafiri, the son of Said's governor of Dhofar and one of Sayyid Qaboos' few Omani associates, among the key conspirators, took action on 23 July 1970. A small band of

Omani soldiers led by Buraik entered the palace and after a short exchange of fire between Said and the soldiers, in which Said shot himself in the foot, the sultan surrendered and signed an abdication paper, making way for Qaboos to become sultan.

Former Sultan Said flew off to London, where he died two years later. New Sultan Qaboos spent the initial month of his reign consolidating his position by visiting his capital Muscat for the first time, forming a new government, establishing relationships with the principal tribal leaders, and touring the country to make himself visible to the people of the newly proclaimed Sultanate of Oman.

Once in power Sultan Qaboos and his British advisors implemented a comprehensive military, political, diplomatic, and economic plan of action. A first step came with the centralisation of the war effort under the Dhofar Brigade, comprising the Baluchi Southern (KJ) and the Frontier Regiments and two of SAF's northern Oman regiments, rotating through Dhofar. The government also purchased helicopters and Short Skyvans to provide greater mobility and supply capabilities to the mountains and ordered fast patrol boats to gain control of the coast and reduce PFLOAG supply capabilities. Qaboos also invited the SAS to return to a direct involvement. SAS personnel operated under the label British Army Training Team (BATT) and took control of the 'hearts and minds' campaign first proposed by John Watts, rejected by Sultan Said, but accepted by Qaboos. This included operating as Civilian Action Teams (CAT) that provided civil services first to areas under government control around Salalah and later to newly liberated areas in the mountains.

Qaboos also accepted another Watts proposal, that *Jebalis* be incorporated into the SAF whenever possible. A general amnesty issued in August 1970 to any rebel who surrendered to the government brought early success when Musallim bin Nufl and other leaders of the DLF, including Yusuf bin Alawi, a future Minister for Foreign Affairs under Qaboos, abandoned the rebellion and turned themselves in. However, the success of the 'hearts and minds' campaign depended even more on securing the support of actual *adu* (enemies, the term used to describe the rebel fighters, usually given as Adoo in British accounts) than to obtaining the loyalty of political leaders.

The *firqa*, irregular, home guard units each made up of about 100 *Jebalis* who had surrendered to the new government, were given military training by the SAS, armed, and sent into action against PFLOAG. The first, Firqa Salah al-Din, formed in January 1971, followed PFLOAG practice of ignoring tribal affiliations (in PFLOAG's case in line with Marxist philosophy about social structures). While Firqa Salah al-Din proved successful, and played an important role in the retaking of the town of Sadah, tribal differences were difficult to overcome and often led to tensions in the units. Future *firqa*, among them Firqa Khalid bin al-Walid, were formed along tribal lines and deployed to their home territories. Although often criticised for lax military standards, the *firqa* were critical to the success of the war as their inclusion provided a clear demonstration of Sultan Qaboos' trust in Dhofaris in contrast to Said's general disdain. Furthermore, the *firqa* appealed to traditional Dhofari religious and social values in contrast to PFLOAG's anti-Islam and anti-tribal ideology.

Despite these efforts, the situation on the ground saw very little improvement during the first year as PFLOAG remained on the offensive and succeeded in gaining full control over the Midway Road. As usual, SAF withdrew from the mountains during the *Khareef*. However, in October 1971 the government launched its first offensive, Operation Jaguar, which succeeded in capturing the towns of Medina al-Haq (known as White City) and Jibjat and establishing the Leopard Line designed to cut PFLOAG supply lines into eastern Dhofar. SAF also established a base in Medina al-Haq, its first in the mountains to remain manned through the *Khareef*. Then, in April 1972, SAF turned its attention to western Dhofar with Operation Simba and occupied the town of Sarfait, along the coast near the South Yemen border. Simba did not succeed in its wider goal of completely blocking PFLOAG supplies from South Yemen but SAF's permanent occupation of Sarfait served as an important symbol of SAF resilience. PFLOAG continued with its offensive, staging a dramatic but failed assault on the coastal town of Mirbat in July 1972.

Despite SAF and SAS advances, by late 1972 the need to expand international support against PFLOAG had become very apparent, and that is where Sultan Qaboos' diplomatic efforts began to impact the war effort in Dhofar. Under Sultan Said, Oman had been completely isolated in the world, maintaining diplomatic relations only with Britain and India – Said allowed Britain to handle the rest of his foreign relations. Once in power, Qaboos launched an active campaign to reverse that, applying to join the Arab League and the United Nations and fully integrate the Sultanate into world affairs. On a country-to-country basis, Qaboos focused his attention on Saudi Arabia and Iran. The Saudis had been early supporters of the insurgency, and Musallim had been closely associated with the kingdom. Saudi backing ceased when PFLOAG took control of the rebellion, but they did not shift their support to Sultan Said. Qaboos' efforts to improve relations with Riyadh finally bore fruit in 1972 when the Saudis began providing financial and military aid as well as much-needed diplomatic support.

Iran, however, became perhaps the biggest international supporter. Aid began with military supplies, and more importantly, helicopters in late summer 1972. And then, in spring 1973, an Iranian special forces unit joined with SAF and a *firqa* unit to establish the Hornbeam Line, stretching from the coast at Mugsayl (west of Salalah) into the mountains. This operation disrupted, if not completely blocked, PFLOAG supply lines traversing western Dhofar and established a permanent government presence in the Jebel Qamar region. Even greater Iranian participation followed at the end of 1973 with the arrival of the 1,200-man Imperial Iranian Battle Group (IIBG) which then participated in securing the old Leopard Line and the region around Midway Road, further limiting PFLOAG in eastern Dhofar.

The creation of the Leopard and Hornbeam Lines, as well as a number of smaller defensive positions throughout Dhofar, contributed greatly to the political victory in the war. Once an area became secure, the SAS CATs moved into action, providing basic services to the local population. Once these were established CAT turned operations over to the government Civil Aid Department (CAD) which established centres in populated areas. These government centres featured wells and cattle-watering troughs, schools, medical and veterinary clinics, mosques, shops, and government offices to spread information to the *Jebalis* about government programmes and policies. CAD also built roads to link the government centres. As a result, the government no longer represented tax collections and repression but became a source of income and economic and social services, in marked contrast to PFLOAG's anti-Islam, anti-tribal rhetoric and promise only of continued warfare. 'Hearts and minds' contributed greatly to the war effort.

By mid-1974 victory seemed close at hand. PFLOAG military activities were greatly reduced and the organisation even acknowledged its diminishing goals by dropping any claims to broader revolution by becoming just the Popular Front for the Liberation of Oman (PFLO). SAF and its allies, now also including Jordan, undertook a series of military operations throughout Dhofar, occupying Tawi Atair through the *Khareef* for the first time. In December, SAF determined to strike a final blow to the insurgency with Operation Dharab, a direct attack on the PFLO's last

INTRODUCTION

major stronghold at the Shershitti cave complex near Rakhyut. Although an initial assault on the caves failed, the IIBG succeeded in capturing the port of Rakhyut in January 1975, thereby clearing the coast of PFLOAG. The operation continued into the mountains, ultimately establishing the Damavand Line, cutting off PFLO supply lines to South Yemen and establishing the government all along Dhofar's western border.

SAF, now bolstered by a Jordanian special forces battalion that relieved Omani forces guarding the Midway Road and King Hussein's gift of thirty Hawker Hunter fighter planes to the Sultan of Oman's Air Force, continued the pressure with a final push during 1975. Military operations focused on the South Yemen border area, where Sarfait continued to be bombarded, and South Yemen sent regular army units into Dhofar to assist PFLO activities along the Damavand Line. Operation Hadaf, launched in late October, secured this area. Minor operations in the Wadi Darbat area east of Midway Road sought to clear persistent small units of PFLO insurgents. CAD and its civil development projects became a much greater priority.

On 11 December 1975 Sultan Qaboos declared victory. Small groups of *adu* remained active, especially in eastern Dhofar, requiring continued military operations. In March 1976 South Yemen agreed to a ceasefire and ended its cross-border shelling and support for the PFLO. Eastern Dhofar remained a focus of anti-government activity with periodic attacks, principally against the KJ, reported until March 1980. Although British officers held the leadership positions in SAF through the 1980s, all foreign forces withdrew from Dhofar by the end of 1978.

David Freeman's account covers the last year (officially, at least) of the war in 1975 and the first six months of 1976 in the still active eastern sector of Dhofar. While this book will fall into the category of 'military history,' it is much more than that. Major Freeman is also, perhaps not by intention, a social historian, for this memoir reveals many of the micro-scale social conflicts, such as the divide between contract ('mercenaries') and seconded officers (British Army officers assigned to Oman) within the officer corps; tensions among British, Baluchi, and Dhofari (the *firqa*) army units; the ethnic and tribal divisions within Omani society; and the cultural differences between British officers and their Baluchi and Arab soldiers over religion and more mundane matters such as communication, food, personal hygiene, and inter-personal relations. Freeman's narrative at times may strike the 21st-century reader as insensitive, but at the same time the reader must be struck by his realisation of his own prejudices and admiration and respect for his 'brothers in arms'. His narrative provides rare insights into the complicated features of guerilla warfare in general and the Dhofar war in particular.

Calvin H. Allen, Jr. is the author of *Oman: Modernization of the Sultanate*, Boulder, CO/London: Westview Press/Croom Helm, 1987 (reissued Routledge: London, 2016) and *Oman*, Philadelphia: Chelsea Press, 2002, and co-author with W. Lynn Rigsbee, *Oman under Qaboos, From Coup to Constitution, 1970–1996*, London & Portland, OR: Frank Cass, 2000, as well as over forty articles on Oman and the Arabian Peninsula.

Notes to Introduction

1. Book-length memoirs include John Akehurst, *We Won a War: The Campaign in Oman 1965–1975*, Wilton: Michael Russell, 1982; David Arkless, *The Secret War: Dhofar 1971/72*, London: William Kimber, 1988; Ian Gardiner, *In the Service of the Sultan*, Barnsley: Pen & Sword Military, 2006; Tony Jeapes, *SAS Operation Oman*, Nashville: Battery Press, 1980 (with various later editions titled *SAS Secret War*); and Peter Thwaites, *Muscat Command*, London: Leo Cooper, 1995.
2. For an extensive list of the conflicts of the 1960s and 1970s see https://onwar.com/chronology/index.html.
3. On Ibadism see Valerie J. Hoffman, *The Essentials of Ibadi Islam*, Syracuse: Syracuse UP, 2021. John Wilkinson, *Ibadism: Origins and Early Development in Oman*, Oxford, OUP, 2010, focuses on Oman. Adam Gaiser, *Muslims, Scholars, Soldiers: The Origin and Elaboration of the Ibadi Imamate Traditions*, Oxford: OUP, 2010, discusses the general political tradition, and John Wilkinson, *The Imamate Tradition of Oman*, Cambridge, CUP, 1987, traces the imamate from its origins through the overthrow of the twentieth-century imamate in 1957.
4. Recent studies of the period of Omani history under discussion in this introduction include Jeremy Jones and Nicholas Ridout, *A History of Modern Oman*, Cambridge: CUP, 2015; Francis Owtram, *A Modern History of Oman*, London: I. B. Taurus, 2004; J. E. Peterson, *Oman's Insurgencies: The Sultanate's Struggle for Supremacy*, London: Saqi, 2007, and *Oman's Transformation after 1970*, Leiden: Brill, 2024; and Uzi Rabi, *The Emergence of States in a Tribal Society: Oman under Said bin Taymur, 1932–1970*, Eastbourne: Sussex Academic Press, 2006. All of these have excellent bibliographies that can direct the reader to more detail on Omani history in general or to specific topics contained herein.
5. Literally 'Family of Said'. The ruling family of Oman continues to come from the al-Bu Said tribe but distinguishes itself from the larger group by emphasising its descent from Said bin Sultan al-Bu Said.
6. The most detailed study of the Dhofar War is Peterson, *Oman's Insurgencie*s (n.4, above). See also Geraint Hughes, *Britain and the Dhofar War in Oman, 1963–1976: A Covert War in Arabia*, London: Palgrave Macmillan, 2024, and Abdel Razzaq Takriti, *Monsoon Revolution: Republicans, Sultans, and Empires in Oman, 1965–1976*, Oxford: OUP, 2013. Takriti's study is written much more from the perspective of the insurgents. As with the general historical accounts above, consult the bibliographies of these works for more information on the extensive literature on the war.

Foreword by Peter Willdridge

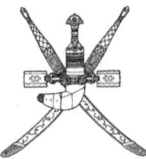

I was contacted in 2025, out of the blue, by Alex Freeman who told me his father David, who had died in 2016, had, unbeknown to me, left a diary. Alex told me that he had found a draft typewritten manuscript locked away in an old box. It had been transcribed by David Freeman in 1986 from his handwritten diaries of 1974–76. I was astonished when I read it and it brought back a flood of memories and feelings.

I was at David's side for most of the period covered by the diary and can vouch for its accuracy. Alex and I helped correct a few typographical errors, clarified some muddled dates and helped with simple editing like standardising the spelling of Arabic names. But we worked to the principle of keeping the diary as close to the original as possible. The diary covers two years of the Sultan of Oman's campaign to bring peace and prosperity to the province of Dhofar. The operations described were wild and dangerous at the time and, on reading the diary, still feel that way today.

This is a highly personal account of one man's attitudes, feelings and observations whilst at the same time it shows timeless principles of warfare, infantry tactics and skills. It also demonstrates the need to adapt fast when your plan is not working or when confronted by problems. It is not written as an army training manual in counter-insurgency, but it could well serve as one.

Peter Willdridge,
April 2025

al-Katibah al-Janubiyah – The Southern Regiment
1975–1976

Notes on Order of Battle
Ranks and appointments changed regularly due to casualties, postings and promotions. Some of the officers and NCOs shown held various positions at different times during 1974–6. Not all key positions are shown.

CO – Lt. Col. John Gordon-Taylor ('Black John')
2iC – Maj. Douglas McCully
QM – Capt Sher Mohammed/Capt. Ernie Marchant
Adjt. – Capt. Hugh Cross/Capt John Gorman
Ops. Offr. – Capt. Yanusz Heath
IO – Capt. Ian Wardle
Trg. Offr. – Capt. Jerry Blatch

A Company
OC – Maj. David Bills

B Company
OC – Maj. John Moody

C Company
OC – Maj. David Freeman
2iC – Capt. Peter Willdridge
CSM – WO2: Hajji Bilal
Medic – Brian Spice
Signaller – Cpl Saleh Mohammed

D Company
OC – Maj. Hugh Willoughby

HQ Company
C – Maj. Karim Bux

Recce Platoon
OC – Capt. Hatim Ali

---

9 Platoon
OC – Sgt. Ahmed Dur Mohammed (KIA)

10 Platoon
OC – Lt. Charki/Sgt Jalal
Pl. Sgt. – Sgt Lai Bux

11 Platoon
OC – Lt. Mohammed Salim
Pl. Sgt. – Sgt. Gulam Hussein

12 Platoon
OC – Lt. Suleiman/Lt Badil Mohammed
Pl. Sgt. – Sgt. Shahbaz Khan
Section Comd. – Cpl. Ibrahim/Cpl Alum Khan

Firqa
Leader – Ahmed Said Mohammed Said

Mortars
OC – Sgt. Imam Din

Chapter 1

Arrival

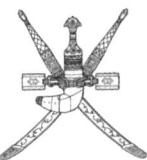

In early 1974 I was halfway through a very dreary tour in the Ministry of Defence when the news came through that my Battalion was posted to Northern Ireland for an eighteen-month tour. As a fairly senior captain the prospects of employment there did not seem too bright as there were several majors in the Regiment queuing up for appointments as Company Commanders, and all I could hope for was a couple of years cooling my heels in some humdrum captain's post. I had had enough of that over the past year or so in London but in the Sultan of Oman's army there was a good chance of getting a Company fairly quickly and with it, acting rank. If I was going to be shot at it seemed to me that it might as well be in a pleasant climate with a very much higher salary. In retrospect it was one of the best decisions I ever made, for after a few months as second-in-command to Harry Fecitt, a bluff ex-officer whom I had known as a subaltern in the Loyal Regiment, I took over C Company of the Southern Regiment (KJ – al-Katibah al-Janubiyah) and commanded it through almost a year and a half of the most exciting time of my life.

I had arrived at a good time. The Army's confidence was growing, and it was moving out of the defensive mentality which had dogged early efforts to defeat the rebellion. There was a worthwhile job to be done there, and after almost two years of frustration and boredom at the Ministry of Defence, I was eager to get on with it.

It was a grey, freezing November afternoon as the small local train pulled into Stroud station and the moment which had loomed closer and closer through my embarkation leave at last arrived. The time had come to say goodbye to my family for what seemed an eternity and all the easy bravado with which I had volunteered for an eighteen-month unaccompanied tour of duty in the Sultan of Oman's Armed Forces (SAF) evaporated in the sadness of parting.

We embraced one by one, Carol as usual putting on her brisk, 'Let's get it over with' manner although I knew that she was as miserable as I was with the prospect ahead of us. The train jolted and began to move off, and as I looked back longingly at the little group standing forlornly on the platform I felt close to tears and not a little guilty at leaving Carol to cope with the numerous problems of looking after two small boys and the complexities of a new house that was to absorb much time and money before it was completed to our satisfaction.

The six months until my first leave seemed a lifetime away, and I had not been exactly encouraged by a cheery, pencil written note from Harry Fecitt which had arrived the night before my departure. In it he had described the numerous horrific casualties that the Southern Regiment had suffered recently during its tour of duty on Simba, the hill fortress on the border with the People's Democratic Republic of the Yemen, and whilst I knew that I was in for an action-packed tour, I did not relish being told about it in quite such detail the night before leaving.

I gazed gloomily out of the train window at the scenery I had come to know so well during our short time in the village, trying to spot the lane winding down into the Golden Valley under the railway line and up to the Crown, and thought about the times that I had hurried down from the language school at Beaconsfield on dark Friday evenings, eager to be back with Carol and the boys after a week spent trying to get my tongue round the seemingly impossible vowel sounds of Arabic. The early winter darkness closed around and for the rest of the journey I huddled in my seat, trying to read and going over the same paragraph time and time again without seeing a single word of it.

By the time we reached Heathrow I was beginning to feel some of the old familiar excitement at the prospect of a long journey, and when I went into the departure hall there was no difficulty in identifying the check-in desk for the flight to Muscat. There was only one woman in the queue and the men were clearly a different breed of traveller from the other domesticated males standing about in family groups elsewhere in the airport. They had that look about them that comes from many years of being alone in the less comfortable parts of the world, and they were obviously either oilmen or soldiers of one sort or another. The journey was uneventful enough, though I remember the excitement of seeing the thin pink band over Bahrain heralding dawn in the clear air of the desert, a sight that was never to lose its beauty for me, although God knows it became familiar enough in the next couple of years.

ARRIVAL

Shortly after we landed the plane filled with noisy Arabs commuting down the Gulf, all chattering and gesticulating at one another without a thought for the hangovers that we gloomy Englishmen were nursing, and after another short stop in Dubai the gaunt grey peaks of the Musandam Peninsula came into sight under the starboard wing. We new boys craned our heads to catch a first glimpse of Muscat. The plane disgorged its motley collection of travellers into the bright sunshine at Seeb airport and as I stood in line waiting for customs and immigration clearance I remember being impressed by the immaculate Omani policemen who seemed to be everywhere. In due course I discovered that they were not quite as efficient as they looked, but in the whole of my time in Oman I never saw a scruffy policeman, and they were certainly better trained than most of their counterparts in the Arab world.

I had not expected anyone to meet me, but I spotted a craggy-looking individual in the smart red beret which I found out later was the badge of the Headquarters staff and he gave me a lift up to the new barracks which had just been completed near the airport and which went by the name of Muaskar al-Murtafaa. On the way he explained the setup in Northern Oman and promised to contact Army Headquarters to let them know that I had arrived. The rest of his off-the-cuff briefing consisted of a bewildering string of initials and names and I began to get the same feeling of being slightly stupid that I usually experience in similar situations. After kicking my heels for an hour or so in the extravagant new Officers' Mess I was picked up by an Arab soldier in a truck and driven to the Headquarters at Bait al-Falaj (House of the Water Channel) which was housed in an old *Beau Geste* style of fort huddled amongst the crowded buildings of Ruwi, a town close by Muscat. The drive lasted about forty minutes or so and on the way I decided that it was time to try out my Arabic on a real Arab. I ventured an opening pleasantry and was ignored, presumably because he had not realised that I was attempting to speak his language but was clearing my throat or perhaps talking to myself in that inexplicable way that foreigners, especially Ingleez, tend to do. I tried again, more loudly. This time he got my drift and we launched into the comfortable routine of greetings that the Arabs love so well. Encouraged by my success I essayed a more ambitious enquiry into the health of his family or some such banal matter. In reply I received a positive barrage of Arabic that defeated me completely. I smiled weakly and fell silent for the rest of the journey.

I should have been prepared for the sheer barren bleakness of the landscape for we had seen many slides and pictures of Oman during our time at Beaconsfield, but of course they tended to show the scenic bits in the early morning or late afternoon when the slanting sun put the colour back into the landscape. In the middle of the day the harsh bright light rebounded from the bare rocks in a dazzling glare and there was not a green blade of grass to be seen. The world seemed painted in shimmering shades of grey and brown and it was a daunting first prospect. All along the way building was in progress, especially as we neared Muscat – roads, schools and even a new town where large hoardings advertising houses at outlandish prices contrasted starkly with the humble *barastis* (palm-frond huts) of the Batinah Coast fisherfolk which could be glimpsed through the trees on either side.

No-one seemed to know or care very much about my arrival at Bait al-Falaj, but eventually I found the Mess and behind one of the outbuildings, a small ferrety ginger-haired man asleep on a lounger. I coughed politely. No response.

'Excuse me, I'm looking for the Mess Secretary.'

'You've found him.'

'My name's Freeman, I've just arrived in Muscat and I have to report to HQ SAF first thing in the morning. Do you have a bed for me?'

'Nope.'

'Well there's nowhere else I can stay so do you think you can help out?'

'Nope, I've never heard of you and that's that.'

By now I was beginning to get very angry. I was tired and dispirited from the total lack of interest that my arrival had evinced and it began to show. After another fairly terse exchange Ginger grudgingly rose from his siesta and gave me the number of a grubby little room which I found for myself tucked away at the back of the Mess with four beds crammed in so tightly that there was barely space to move between them. They all looked equally filthy and when I pulled back the covers to inspect them more closely, all the sheets were covered in blood spots. I sought out Ginger again and asked if there was a pair of clean sheets to be had, a request which he clearly viewed as utterly unreasonable. By now I had the feeling that I was becoming thoroughly unpopular but I persisted despite his irate assertion that the sheets had only just been changed and eventually a sour Pakistani waiter brought another set, dropped them on one of the beds and stalked out in a huff. It was all very discouraging and not a bit as I had imagined it would be. I sat down on one of the beds and wondered gloomily what I had let myself in for.

Chapter 2

Settling In

The next morning I was awoken early with a cup of tea brought by the same surly Pakistani whom I had met the night before. Without any preliminaries he put the tea on my small bedside locker, announced the time and left. It had been a long night during the course of which I had discovered the source of the blood spots covering all the sheets – the local mosquitoes thoroughly enjoyed a meal of blood fresh from England and they attacked me with the same gusto as they had doubtless attacked all my wretched predecessors in that room. Later in the day I was told that the remedy for this particular torment was to switch on the air conditioner and leave it on all night. There was only one small difficulty in adopting such an obvious course and that was that my room did not boast an air conditioner. I felt tired and scratchy, but in better spirits. For one thing despite the mosquitoes, I had succeeded in getting a few hours' sleep and for another, I had met a few friendly souls at dinner the previous evening who had given me a good deal more information. Being comparatively rested and relatively well informed I could face the day with equanimity.

I reported to Army Headquarters, a cool gloomy rabbit warren of a place with huge thick walls pierced by narrow low doors leading to a myriad of small crowded offices. Each office seemed to be overflowing with files and paper and each had its small complement of Pakistani clerks beavering away behind their littered desks. I filled in a number of questionnaires about myself, wondering why the Army always seems to need to renew its acquaintance with its officers every time they move from one posting to another, and I also discovered that I was to spend the next few days in Muscat before flying down to Dhofar to join what I was already beginning to think of as 'my' Regiment. I was issued with a few items of exotic military equipment, most of which I was never to use but all of which conjured up impossibly romantic visions of desert soldiering, and I spent my afternoons on the beach enjoying the warm winter sunshine and getting the first of a tan on my white sun-starved torso.

Late one afternoon, I visited the twin towns of Muscat and Muttrah clustered together under the bare crags of the mountains which come down to the sea on that part of the coast of Northern Oman. The *suk* in Muscat was a fascinating warren of a place and the smart neon-lit interiors of new shops built into the old structures came as something of a mild surprise. It was an Aladdin's cave of expensive gewgaws – cameras, tape recorders, transistor radios and a large variety of flashy watches. Only television sets were missing because, as yet, Oman had no national television network but within a year or so they too would follow. The old prison fortress of Jelali dominated Muscat harbour, and it enjoyed a fearsome and bloodthirsty reputation as a place of nameless cruelties even in the recent past, but in the soft indigo and pink shades of that evening it was hard to believe the stories of suffering and persecution that were told of it. Painted in whitewash on a steep granite rock face opposite were the names of Royal Navy warships that had visited Muscat in years gone by.

30 November 1974

On Saturday morning I went back to the airport and boarded the ancient Viscount for Salalah. I was eager to be on my way and by chance I sat next to an expatriate employee of the Omani Government who had flown out with me from England, and over the next hour or so I quizzed him about Dhofar. His answers were not very satisfactory partly because no mere words could properly describe such an unfamiliar place, and partly because most of the province was closed to him as a civilian. He was trying to draw a picture for me of a pattern of hills and valleys that he had only glimpsed from the plain below or from an aircraft flying high above the plateau.

As we flew on southwards the shimmering red and grey emptiness of the Wahiba stretched to the horizon in every direction. The darker stains of dry watercourses veining its surface served only to underline the harshness of one of the most inhospitable places on Earth. We began to descend over the slopes of the Qara mountains which flank the eastern edge of Dhofar proper. Although they were not as jagged as the peaks of the Jebel Akhdar, they were massive enough and I tried to imagine what walking over them would be like. At that season they looked bare and forbidding, and I began to wonder what had happened to the fabled land of greenery and water that everyone had been talking about in the North.

SETTLING IN

At Salalah the sunlight seemed even brighter but the air moved with an occasional ocean breeze that made the climate so much pleasanter than in the North where the heat could be stifling, especially in summer which even the Omanis called 'Wagd al-Qaidth' – 'The Time of the Oppression'. It took me a moment to recognise Harry Fecitt at the airfield in Salalah. He was heavier than I remembered him, and until he took off his dark glasses he was a total stranger. His manner seemed to have become even rougher than that which he affected as a subaltern, and almost at once I detected a cynicism and bitterness in his tone which was to become familiar over the next few months. He had enjoyed the reputation of being a wild man in the Loyals but it was soon clear that he had discarded what I had always suspected was something of a facade and was now a loner, keeping himself to himself and eschewing the company of the regular drinkers at the Mess bar.

As we drove the few miles from the airfield to the Southern Regiment at Arzat, Harry talked about soldiering in Dhofar in general and about C Company of the Southern Regiment in particular, and I hung on every word. The picture was rapidly becoming clearer, even though I found later that some of Harry's wilder allegations had to be modified a little in the light of experience. Harry was nothing if not a man of very forceful views and strong prejudices, and life in Dhofar tended to reinforce such attitudes of mind as I was to discover for myself.

We drove in through the battlemented gates of the camp and I was immediately struck by the haphazard, half-finished look of the place. A few permanent single-storey buildings were grouped around a large dusty square, but most of the camp accommodation was in tents, and very dilapidated tents at that. Administrative and headquarters staff were housed in the permanent accommodation whilst the rifle companies had to make do with the tents. There was an opulent, gleaming white new mosque, a humble Sergeants' Mess, and facing it across the square, a new Spanish-style single-storey Officers' Mess with a few straggly shrubs clinging desperately to life in front of it. I was allocated a small room in an annex at the back of the Mess, which was clean, spartan and aside from the smell of drains, a vast improvement on Bait al-Falaj.

I dropped my suitcases on the floor and made my way round to the main rooms of the Mess, where people were beginning to gather for lunch. Unusually, the whole Battalion was in Arzat together and within a short time I had met many of the other officers of the Regiment who all made me feel very welcome.

A stocky, older man with black hair and swarthy dark skin came into the anteroom and after a few minutes of conversation with one of the company commanders during which he ignored me, he turned and thrust out a hand in greeting.

John Gordon-Taylor, at that time the Commanding Officer of the Southern Regiment of the Sultan of Oman's Armed Forces, was nothing if not a showman. His carefully timed entrances, his displays of rage, and his flashes of expansive bonhomie were always calculated to achieve a particular result, and in this case it was to establish straight away the insignificance of the latest arrival in KJ. It was off-putting to say the least, and I was not encouraged to overhear him say a few moments later that only over his dead body would there be seconded officers as company commanders in his battalion.

There was clearly going to be a problem if I was not careful, and I had a distinct feeling that I had started off my new life in KJ with a debit balance in the account simply because I was a seconded officer and not on contract. At the time the distinction meant little to me but later it was to become very significant. Things got worse in the evening when it became apparent that the CO liked to take his drink with the full complement of British officers in attendance. Not that I would have minded that – it was a fairly common characteristic of a certain type of CO and one of the many small inconveniences of mess life to be borne almost without noticing – but he was uninterested in food and would sometimes go in to dinner as late as ten or eleven o'clock after five or six hours of fairly hard drinking. I enjoyed my pre-dinner gin and tonic, especially after a hot and dusty day's work, but I could not pretend that I was able or even wanted to keep pace with the CO at the bar, and after all, one of the reasons I had volunteered for SAF was to make money and not, in the Army's elegant phrase, to 'piss it all up against a wall'. Somehow, I would have to make it plain, if possible without giving offence, that I wished to follow my own preferences in the matter. Over the next few days I tried to do so by joining the group at the bar on the odd occasion, but more often than not, finding things to do in my room and then making my way straight into the dining room. Even so there were muttered criticisms from the CO on the subject directed at no-one in particular, but obviously intended for me, and I soon became impatient to get away into the hills.

Harry was due to go on leave before the Company moved up to its new dispositions in the eastern half of the Jebel theatre of operations, and he arranged for me to visit each of the three bases we would be occupying. The plan was for me to go to Ashinhaib, the most westerly of the three, by helicopter. I was then to return to Salalah and catch the regular Skyvan run to White City (Medina al-Haq). From there I would go by truck across the Gatn to Jibjat, the most easterly of the three, and the oldest of the Jebel positions.

The helicopter trip was an education in itself, for no-one had bothered to brief me on the method of entry and exit to and from the Jebel positions by chopper, so when we began to descend over Ashinhaib in a dizzy series of tight spirals that pushed me hard down onto the canvas bucket seat, I assumed that the worst had happened and that my hour had come. The only remotely comforting factor was that none of the other passengers seemed in the least bit perturbed by imminent death, and I could only think that they were either incredibly brave or totally without any imagination at all. In the face of such stoicism I could hardly make any fuss which was just as well, for we landed safely in a cloud of dust and in seconds we were clear of the chopper and making our way up to the wire and sandbags of the position.

Whatever I was expecting, it was not the prosaic ordinariness of Ashinhaib. The low squat stone-built *murchas* scattered in apparently random fashion inside the small perimeter formed by the barbed wire looked like nothing so much as a cluster of Stone Age huts set down for no obvious reason in the middle of nowhere. Some of the low scrub had been cleared around the wire, the red earth showed in raw patches where it had been excavated to fill sandbags, and here and there were sangars for riflemen or mortars. The base was set on a low rise high up on the Gatn close to the spine of the hills along which it was possible to drive from the Midway (Thumrait) road at Raven's Roost in the west to Jibjat in the east, and from the base there was a long, spectacular view over the rolling hills to the west.

I was given a short briefing on the area and the problems of Ashinhaib, chief of which seemed to be that so far no water had been found at the site although drilling had been going on for several weeks. This could have been serious in the long run, for the success of the policy of establishing bases on the Jebel depended above all else upon locating and maintaining a reliable source of water to attract the tribesmen and their cattle, and Ashinhaib was never to enjoy much success in this respect.

Late in the afternoon, I returned to Arzat, and early the next morning I took off again for White City, this time in one of the squat little Skyvans of the Sultan's Air Force which did most of the short haul work around Dhofar. Again, I was unprepared for a hair-raising landing on the short dirt airstrip, for we seemed to be running very quickly out of road as we tore uphill towards a large green tree at the end of the strip, but we roared to a halt in a cloud of red dust, and I began to get the message that flying around the Jebel was not quite the same as the civilised, organised little hops hither and thither that I had been used to.

Medina al-Haq, or White City as it had been dubbed by some irreverent soldier in the recent past, was an older settlement than Ashinhaib, and had a well-established community of tribesmen and their families as well as a garrison consisting of a battery of 25-pounder guns manned by Arab soldiers of the Oman Artillery. It had a well, a small mosque, a government shop and a school run by a long-suffering Egyptian teacher on loan. It also had two detachments of *firqa*, the Firqa Khalid Walid North and South, which was an ingenious way of getting the pay for two *firqa* lieutenants, two sergeant majors and two staff sergeants in the same base. It was not the only example in Dhofar of the *firqa* wringing perks out of the government by means of wheedling and on occasions, downright blackmail.

The base was somewhat larger than Ashinhaib and sprawled over several acres of grassland and hill. There was no continuous perimeter except around the artillery compound, which was poorly sited from a defensive point of view in the low ground between two hummocks, one occupied on an occasional basis by the *firqa*, and the other taken up by the turning circle at the top of the airstrip. There was a mountain of rubbish around the shacks occupied by the families of the *firqa*.

I met Salim Musalim, the leader of one of the *firqa* detachments, a thin, wiry little man with a grave manner and a curious, shushing way of enunciating his words. He was dressed in typical *Jebali* fashion in an old Army shirt, cotton kilt and sandals with the Omani turban wound carelessly round his head and an AK-47 rifle slung over his shoulder. He recounted a long list of problems and grievances to me in what was to become a familiar litany, and complained in particular about the daily burden of having to supply water by tanker lorry to Jibjat, something that did not come naturally to any *jebali*, particularly as the people in Jibjat were from another tribe. The problem was made worse by the fact that the well could not always be relied upon to produce enough water for White City let alone the daily consignment to Jibjat, and when the truck broke down, as it did frequently from a combination of Arab driving, atrocious tracks and lack of spares, complaints began coming at the wretched local Army commander from all directions. It was to be one of many headaches in the next few months.

SETTLING IN

We walked around the base area together and I met some of the other members of the *firqa*, the schoolteacher and the small detachment of artillerymen who were all dressed in the same way as the *firqa* and clearly in need of a little supervision.

In the early afternoon I got up into the open cab of the beaten-up old tanker and we bumped slowly northwards out of White City up the winding ridge track which led up onto the Gatn. Salim Musalim had assured me that the *firqa* maintained a 'sentry' post at the top of a narrow defile which led up onto the Gatn, but as we crawled into the bottom end of the gap, there was no evidence of them. The hills loomed close either side over the dusty white track, and my imagination began working overtime for it was just the place that I would have chosen to ambush a vehicle, and here we were on a regular daily run, just myself and an Arab driver alone in the world. It was a considerable relief when we came round the last corner out onto the relatively open stretch of road along the Gatn, and to the end of my time in Dhofar I could not work out why the Adoo never took such an excellent opportunity, for they carried out attacks from time to time within a few miles of that spot, and they mined the track about two miles from the top of the defile shortly after we took over at White City and Jibjat.

Another uncomfortable hour or so bumping over one of the many tracks that had been worn along the Gatn brought us within sight of Jibjat, and in that short distance the terrain altered dramatically as we made our way along the edge of the area of Dhofar affected by the monsoon. On our right the jebel stretched away in descending swoops of hills towards the sea, the valleys thick with tangled vegetation and the higher land silver with waving grass in the afternoon sun. On our left the vegetation died away abruptly within as little as a few hundred yards, giving way to a majestic panorama of bare yellow and grey cliffs riven with deep canyons leading away into the desert.

Perched around the edges of one of the most spectacular of these canyons lay the sprawling groups of huts and emplacements that made up Jibjat. All around the ground was bare and sandy, but within a mile were trees and the scrub which provided grazing for cattle and goats without which life at Jibjat would not have been possible. On arrival I was met by the three SAS soldiers at Jibjat who showed me the hole in the ground where I was to spend the night and for the next few hours I listened to a totally new point of view.

I was to meet and work closely with many members of the British Army Training Team, or BATT, as the SAS in Dhofar were universally known, and I found that like any organisation made up of human beings they had their faults as well as their more widely acclaimed and undisputed strengths. They could take the credit for getting SAF back onto the Jebel in Dhofar, for they spearheaded the assault, took heavy casualties, and got the *firqa* organisation under way. Many of them had fearsome stories to tell their grandchildren if they lived that long, and many young troopers carried responsibilities far beyond their rank and years. They were a closed elite, proven in battle, and they undoubtedly looked down upon the '*jaysh*' as they called the line infantry battalions of the Sultan's Army. The word simply means army in Arabic, but somehow on their lips it acquired a faintly pejorative ring. Often small detachments of troopers and junior NCOs were left out on their own for long periods, as at Jibjat, and it sometimes seemed to me that they lacked the broader judgement and insight that was necessary to cope with the complex problems that arose in dealings with the tribespeople and the *firqa*.

I certainly went to bed that night feeling that both in Jibjat and in White City there was a morale problem in relations with the *firqa*, and that I would have to come to grips with it. There was a host of reasons why things were not as they should be, not least of which was the fact that it had been comparatively peaceful in the area recently, and there was not enough for the *firqa* to do. If they were given a clear task and kept busy with patrols it should keep them out of mischief and maintain pressure on the enemy, who was still in the area, although not very active.

The next morning dawned cold and grey with rain clouds scudding across the hills and a light drizzle falling, but the clouds soon cleared and by mid-morning when the Britten-Norman Defender arrived to fly me back to Salalah the sun was shining out of a brilliant blue sky.

My basic education was completed a couple of days later by a trip along the coast road past the fishing village of Taqah and out onto the coastal plain under the shadow of the scarp, where the falls of the Wadi Darbat drop away in a magnificent curtain of rock a mile across and almost 400 feet high.

My guides were a couple of Baluch officers from the Dhofar Gendarmerie, and we set off from Arzat in two stripped-down Jebel Land Rovers armed with a fearsome array of .50-calibre Browning machine guns. For lunch we took a couple of tins of corned mutton (the sheep slaughtered according to the Muslim ritual of Halal, that is to say by having their throats cut and being therefore suitable for consumption by Muslims), a pile of chapatis and a couple of onions. It didn't look very appetising, but it turned out to be a most acceptable combination after

SETTLING IN

a long hot morning on patrol, though it may not have been very suitable for polite company. The trip was interesting, but enemy activity along the coast road was unlikely because the approaches to it across the gravel plain were too open and would provide little cover from avenging Strikemasters of the Sultan's Air Force in the event of a contact. Landmines were a different matter however, and the Adoo quite often planted them on dirt tracks closed to Taqah. The next year the government archaeologist was to be killed by a mine whilst visiting the ruins of the ancient city of Sumharam nearby.[1]

I now had a much better idea of what Dhofar was all about. I knew what kit I would need over the coming months and I had some ideas on what needed to be done in our new area. I was beginning to acquire a reasonable tan, although my lips blistered badly in the first few days, and I had bought myself a small camera as a Christmas present, for I was determined not to miss the chance of recording everything that happened. It looked as though the next eighteen months were going to be an interesting time.

---

1. This was Andrew Williamson, who was Director of Antiquities in Oman when he was killed in May 1975.

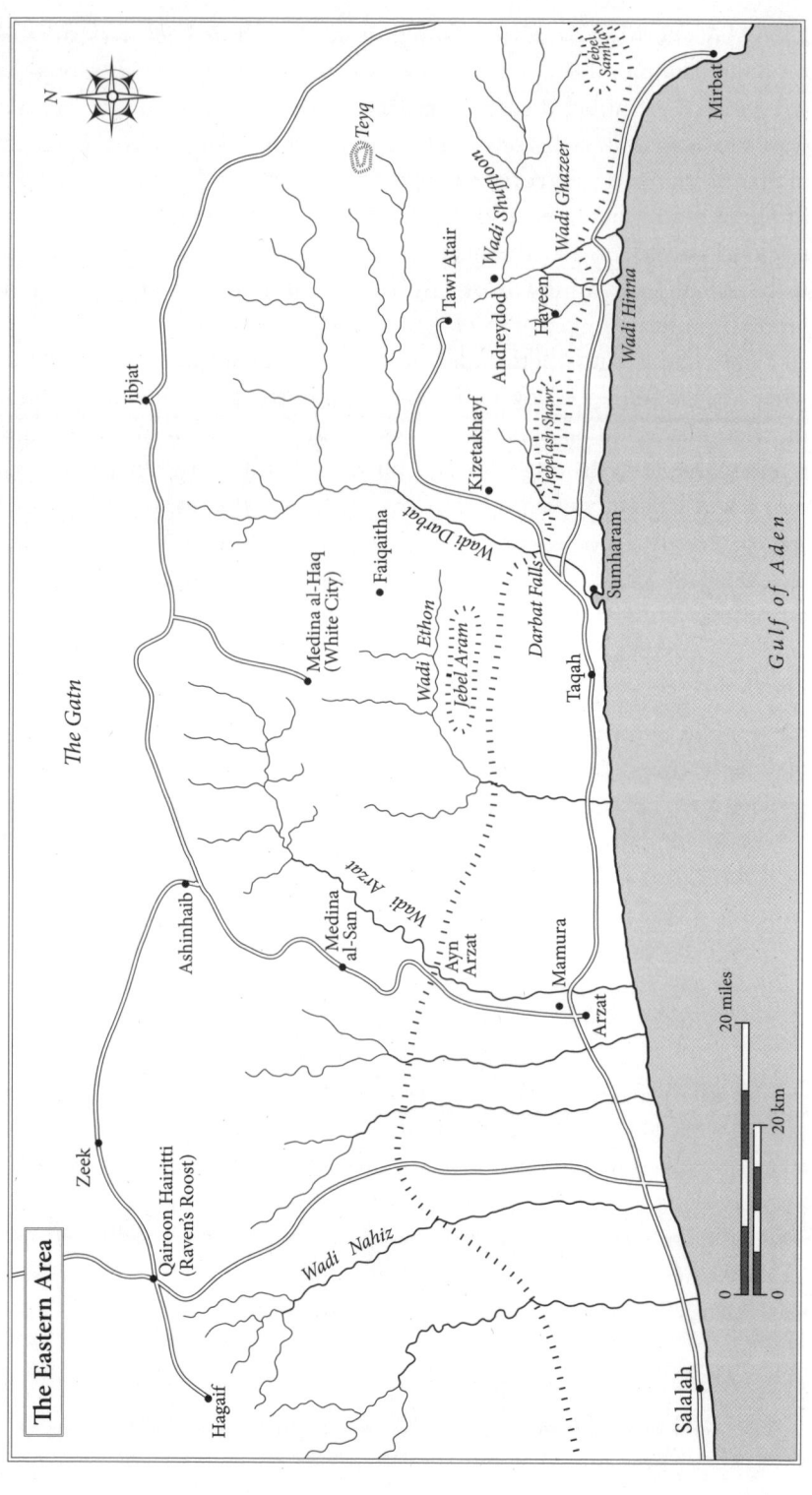

Chapter 3

White City and Medina al-San

16 December 1974

Harry Fecitt went off on leave to England with a cheery 'Don't get yourself killed before I get back' and I turned my attention to the problem of getting three lots of soldiers to three different places, with 12 Platoon under the command of Mulazzim (Lieutenant) Suleiman assigned to Jibjat, 9 and 11 Platoons under Mulazzimeen Mohammed Salim and Badil Mohammed assigned to White City with the Company Headquarters, and 10 Platoon under Naqeeb (Staff Sergeant) Jelal assigned to Ashinhaib. I was no expert on air movement but I was vaguely aware that it involved vast amounts of paper and some very elaborate planning whenever a unit moved by air in the British Army, and I had the uneasy feeling that I should have been doing all sorts of efficient things in preparation for our move. I approached the Adjutant for advice.

'Oh, don't worry about it,' he said nonchalantly.

'Well what about flight manifests and chalk numbers?' I asked, dredging up dimly remembered technical terms from the back of my mind.

'You won't need those,' he said 'Just get the blokes down to the airport and sling them on until each Skyvan is full. It all just happens somehow.'

It all seemed very casual and it contradicted completely the careful attention to detail which had been dinned into me since my first day at Sandhurst, but that is exactly what happened and it worked. We turned up very early the next morning at the airport and as the sun began to rise the first Skyvan revved up, the back door swung down and we began loading. The aircraft rapidly filled with soldiers, civilian cooks and camp followers who would be coming up to the Jebel with us. Besides the more obvious bits of military equipment such as weapons and the soldiers' *farrashes* there were cloth bundles containing the huge black pots and kettles that were the cooks' stock in trade, old suitcases tied up with string, and a small goat or two, and though an RAF loadmaster would have had heart failure at the loading plan, his Omani opposite didn't bat an eyelid.

Flying time to our positions was only a few minutes and after two lifts to deliver the platoon to Jibjat, we were on our way to White City. We spent a day or so getting ourselves organised, and the first subject I tackled was the siting of the compound. I walked around the perimeter with Badil and explained why I was worried and what changes I thought would have to be made. Badil looked baffled and tugged his beard.

'All these changes mean a lot of work Sahib' he said, unnecessarily.

'I know that Badil' I replied, 'But we can't just leave things as they are. What if we are attacked?'

He smiled incredulously. 'Adoo not attack us here.'

That may or may not have been so, but in any event, by the time I had finished a detailed reconnaissance of the place it was clear to me that poor though the present layout might be, all the other defensible positions in the immediate vicinity were occupied and short of moving out of White City altogether, which would have defeated the object of our being there in the first place, there was not much to be done about it.

I turned my attention to the next problem. 'Badil, where do the soldiers go for a shit?' He looked embarrassed and waved an arm vaguely in the direction of the southern perimeter and summoning up my courage, I went over to take a look. Description of the sight and smell which greeted me is superfluous, and I decided that to this problem at least, there was a standard and simple British Army answer – deep trench latrines. I explained what was required to Charki, my wizened little Sergeant Major, and he looked at me with the same melancholy disbelief that seemed to be the standard response to every simple suggestion that I had made since arriving on the Jebel. Nevertheless, the soldiers set to work and shortly I was pleased to see three neat lines of trenches taking shape in a suitably isolated downwind spot. Later in the morning I revisited the construction on site and was dismayed to see that almost no progress had been made.

I summoned Charki again. 'Charki, why have the soldiers stopped work?'

'Not stopped work Sahib, ground too hard.'

'Nonsense, bring me a pick.' Leadership by example, I thought to myself as I swung the pick vigorously. The shock wrenched my shoulders and arms as the point of the pick sank a full half inch into the iron-hard red soil. Charki was right.

Still, half a loaf was better than no bread, if that was an appropriate phrase in the circumstances. The soldiers had managed to sink the trenches a couple of feet into the ground, and it would do for a start until we could get hold of some explosives and make a better job of it. That night in my Company orders I explained carefully how the new latrines were to be used, and gave orders that henceforth random crapping in the bundu was to cease. More mournful looks all round. For a couple of days all seemed to be going well, but about three days later I was walking around the position with the Sergeant Major and in the best British Army fashion I decided to inspect the latrines. I peered cautiously over the tattered canvas screen at a scene of considerable squalor. My careful instruction had come to nought, and all I had succeeded in doing was concentrating the smell and flies in one small place. A radical rethink was obviously in order.

No-one else bothered too much about this particular disposal problem, and it didn't seem to make any difference to the health of the local people. Admittedly the smell in the immediate vicinity of the favoured spot was bad but it was localised, and there didn't seem to be too many flies around. The hot sun very quickly sanitised animal droppings of all sorts, wandering goats and cattle crushed them to a powder, and the wind did the rest. I told Charki to get the trenches filled in and we returned to the old system.

I took Badil's platoon and carried out my first patrol, a short daylight walk to a waterhole a few miles to the west of White City, and I discovered how unfit I was for this sort of terrain. Climbing in and out of the numerous wadis that we had to cross was very hard work and even though it was now the coolest season of the year, I was soon sweating heavily.

We also carried out an ambush at the head of the wadi where the track to Jibjat debouched onto the Gatn. As darkness was falling we dropped off the trucks and circled stealthily around a large patch of scrub which I had identified earlier as a good ambush site and settled into our positions. Light faded from a clear sky and the first bright stars appeared. Suddenly all around me a shuffling noise started up and when I went to investigate, I discovered about half the soldiers in prayer, their foreheads close to the ground, their feet bare, and their equipment and weapons discarded beside them. Despite my surprise at this unexpected turn of events, I knew enough not to interfere, but as soon as they were finished, I crawled across to Badil and asked him what on earth was going on.

'They pray, Sahib,' he said.

'Well I can see that, but don't they know this is supposed to be an ambush?' I whispered, trying to keep the anger out of my voice.

'They know, but they must pray.'

This was yet another little difficulty for which my Sandhurst training had not prepared me. I knew that many of my Baluch soldiers were devout Muslims, and in the circumstances their faith was about the only comfort that was available to them. The drawbacks that it entailed were probably outweighed by the one big advantage which was that alcohol was forbidden to them, so drunkenness would never be the problem that it might have been in any other army marooned in the hills for months on end. Although the Baluch were comparatively docile soldiers and would put up with almost any amount of discomfort, I had already been told that any attempt to interfere with their religious observances could provoke them to mutiny and it was some time before I found the answer to the problem posed by their need to pray on operations. By that time I knew who were the regular attenders at prayers in our base and one day when we went into the field I told Hajji Bilal, our self-appointed mullah and the acting Sergeant Major, to take the names of those who were praying and ensure that from then on they all turned up five times a day without fail at his prayer sessions. The numbers of the faithful dropped abruptly to an irreducible minimum.

25 December 1974

We moved a Muslim holiday back a day to coincide with Christmas day and my thoughts naturally turned to my family, but I had already schooled myself to think of it as just another day, so being in such a remote spot at that particular time did not unduly depress. In the morning we played a vigorous and undisciplined game of soccer on the dusty patch in the middle of our compound, then I bathed and put on my last pressed uniform. A goat was killed, and Christmas dinner consisted of stringy goat and rice with an Army issue tinned fruit pudding which I convinced myself tasted like the real thing. Just before lunch the brigade commander, Brigadier John Akehurst, arrived by helicopter with his wife Shirley to distribute mince pies, and in the afternoon the artillery loosed off a few rounds in the general direction of the Gatn at what was allegedly an Adoo patrol. My own view was that it was more probably a good excuse to celebrate the holiday in style and as the Gatn was virtually uninhabited, no harm was done. I collected a couple of the fine brass shell cases as souvenirs and I could see them flanking the fireplace at

WHITE CITY AND MEDINA AL-SAN

home in a couple of years' time providing an excellent excuse to bore my Christmas guests with Dhofar war stories.

Shortly after Christmas we were warned for an operation to set up a new base position a few miles south of Ashinhaib, close to the scarp overlooking Ayn Arzat at a place known as Medina al-San, which was immediately dubbed Medina Elsan. The task force would be a small BATT group, some sixty of the Firqa Salah al-Din from Ashinhaib, a forward observation officer (FOO) from the artillery battery at Taqah, and a platoon of C Company. The operation was to be under my command, but the SAS captain who came with us had a great deal more experience of the Jebel than I, so I listened closely to the advice he offered, and I made it quite clear that I would consult him whenever necessary.

27 December 1974

We concentrated at Ashinhaib, completed our plans, gave out orders to the various components of the little force, and moved out an hour or so after dusk. The column of men wound up and down the dark hillocks and wadis of the undulating countryside, and at one point we filed through a steep, thickly wooded wadi along a path fashioned of curiously flat, flag-like stones. Halfway along the wadi were the ashes of what had obviously been a cooking fire, and as we came out into open country the captain turned to me and whispered that it had been an Adoo camp, and we were the first '*jaysh*' to pass that way. I don't suppose that he meant to be patronising, but there was that word again, and it irritated me.

We reached our objective at about four o'clock in the morning and half the *firqa* promptly disappeared to socialise in nearby dwellings, whilst the other half sat around doing nothing in particular. We sited the position carefully, allocating sectors of responsibility to the BATT team, the platoon, and the *firqa*, and the soldiers set to building sangars for there was a possibility that the Adoo might decide to contest our move or at least let us know that they were around by firing on us when the dawn came up. After we had been hard at work for a couple of hours the *firqa* began wandering back onto the position, and for the next hour or so they squatted on their heels and watched us working. Suddenly they announced that the positions which they had been given were no good, and that they preferred a place about 500 yards away down the slope dominated by the picquet on which we were sitting. It was a bit too much for me and despite placatory noises being made by the BATT captain I told them that I was not going to move a perfectly sound tactical location. If they wanted to take themselves off that was their business, but I would see to my own defences, which I proceeded to do. The *firqa* set up their own camp further down the hill, and that is how the layout of Medina al-San turned out.

There was no reaction from the Adoo at dawn, and soon afterwards the first helicopter load of defence stores began to arrive. We had to be careful to carry the piles of corrugated iron ('chinko') out of range of the downwash of the chopper blades for the top three sheets on the first pile were caught by the blast of air and whirled away at head height like so many sheets of waste paper, and any one of them could decapitate a man in a split second.

Work went on all day, and by the time we stood to on the first evening we had a reasonable defensive position. We had done a couple of short-range clearing patrols and registered some artillery targets out on the surrounding hills. Our FOO passed a fire order to the guns by radio, giving what we all agreed were the map coordinates of a small wadi some 500 yards west of the position. At that time we were working from 1:100,000 maps which although they were accurate as far as they went, necessarily left out quite a bit of detail so that unless there was a clearly recognisable feature such as a large wadi junction, all map coordinates tended to be a bit approximate.

After a short pause, we heard the guns acknowledge the fire order and we all looked expectantly out towards the setting sun. There was a bang behind us, followed by the sound of the shell rushing through the air and a moment or so later, the distant boom of the gun going off far away at Taqah. Heads swung round in time to see a puff of smoke and dust drifting up from the hillside about 500 yards to the east. Out came the maps again, the estimate of the map coordinates was reconsidered and a fresh order went off to the gun line. At the time it seemed amusing, but a month or two later Phillip Mann, a young cavalry officer who did the Arabic course with me at Beaconsfield was to die as the result of a similar error, and after that I always added a thousand yards to the estimated target position when firing guns or mortars unless I was absolutely certain of the grid coordinates.

That night I had my first taste of the Shimaal, a cold dry wind which blows down the slopes of the Jebel from the north (hence the name, *shimaal* means 'north' in Arabic). Lower down towards the coast it was quite mild, but in the hills in December it was bitterly cold, and it blew clouds of choking dust into everything. Eyes and nostrils clogged, anything that was not firmly secured blew away and after a couple of days of it, tempers began to fray. Fortunately it tended to occur in a comparatively short season around the turn of the year, and was usually heralded by a still, crystal clear morning. Sometimes it blew so hard that it drowned out all other sounds, and I was told that in one contact a soldier was actually hit and killed before the rest of the patrol realised that they were under enemy fire. From the scarp, the brown haze raised by the wind blotted out the whole of the Salalah plain to a height of several hundred feet, and close to any settlement on the Jebel, the dust would be mixed with powdered cattle dung, which lent a particularly piquant flavour to the air one was forced to breathe.

Helicopter resupply was a very expensive and wasteful way of doing things, and it was important therefore to clear an airstrip and recce a road route through to Medina as soon as possible. It was only about seven or eight miles to the coast in a straight line, but the scarp was very steep at that point. I had done a brief helicopter recce a few days before the operation to see whether there was a way down the hill, and although I had spotted a possible route, it looked doubtful, and it was now necessary to go on foot and have a good look. I set out with a small patrol of soldiers and a couple of *firqa*, and after an hour or so I stood on the scarp overlooking Ayn Arzat and the KJ camp by the coast across the plain. I could see a way down a narrow spur angling away to my right, but whether a way could be cleared through the rocks of a small saddle behind me was another matter.

Below the scarp fell away steeply, the brown foothills tumbling one on another towards the flat grey gravel of the plain. Between them nestled the spring from which Ayn Arzat takes its name, and its clear waters stretched out shimmering in the afternoon sun like a strip of molten silver. Away to the left the horizon was dominated by a huge spur which loomed over the Ayn Arzat wadi, whilst on the right ridge after ridge stretched to the western horizon, each successive fold a paler, smokier blue than the one before. In the distance the sea lay like burnished pewter in the sun, its flat surface rippled dark here and there by faint sea breezes.

I turned away, reluctant to leave the peace and tranquillity of the scene, and I made my way back across the saddle to where the remainder of the patrol was waiting, scattered in a defensive position on the next small knoll. When I climbed up onto the picquet I was immediately accosted by a white-bearded old man who had been chatting to the *firqa* whilst I had been away. The old fellow was delighted that we had come to Medina al-San, and wished me to assure him that we would begin building the road right away. Would it be tomorrow or at the very latest next week, for the Sultan was a generous man, and surely he had the interests of the people of Medina al-San next to his heart? Patiently I explained, my lungs still heaving from the climb, that I too wished to build a road but I could not simply snap my fingers and order it to happen. He then launched into a long monologue on the situation in Dhofar in general, how much roads were needed, how generous the Sultan was compared to his father and a number of other related subjects. I made no attempt to stem the flow for I was grateful for a chance to get my breath back, and I was beginning to learn that part of the art of dealing with the *Jebalis* was to be a patient listener, for they loved to talk. In any case I could guarantee nothing, and if I made promises that could not be fulfilled it would do our cause no good at all.

We left the old man somewhat assured even if still a little indignant that a start was not to be made that very afternoon on his cherished road, and we started back up the grassy slope, arriving at Medina a little before sunset.

Chapter 4

Hagaif

January 1975

Whilst we were busy setting up Medina al-San, the rest of the Company was being shuttled around to fill up holes being left by the withdrawal of the Jebel Regiment which had been earmarked at short notice to take part in an operation in the far west of Dhofar.

A few weeks before the Iranian Brigade had been ordered to advance south down the slopes of the western part of Dhofar in a drive to reach the sea. They were to establish a new fortified line closer to the PDRY border in order to reduce enemy infiltration across the border and, it was hoped, capture the massive enemy supply dump and base complex in the caves at Shershitti (Operation Dharab). The Iranians, who had been sent to Dhofar as part of the Shah's grandiose scheme for policing the Gulf and containing Communism, did not enjoy much of a reputation for military prowess, and there had been a good deal of uncharitable and sometimes uninformed criticism of them in SAF messes around the country. They had suffered heavy casualties, many, it was alleged, inflicted by the undisciplined fire of their own troops, but all this was hearsay to me so I said nothing when the subject came up in discussion, being content to reflect that whatever their faults, they were probably on balance an asset to us.

For a number of reasons the latest Iranian operation ground to a halt without achieving its main objective, and it was decided that the Jebel Regiment would be sent in to complete the task.

The Shershitti caves had been the main supply base for the Adoo for a long time. They were continually being strengthened and enlarged, and they were difficult to attack from the air because they were protected by steep cliffs. The Iranian attack upon them had been halted by a small but determined enemy force, well sited in defensive positions and able to put down a heavy barrage of small-arms fire on anyone approaching the caves. After a short time for preparation and under the command of a new CO, the Jebel Regiment moved out from their camp at Umm al-Ghawarif near Salalah and onto the hills. Within a day of their advance beginning things began to go wrong and when Major General Tim Creasey, the SAF commander, visited the battalion, he found the luckless CO rather too far to the rear for his liking. After a short and reportedly stormy interview the officer was sacked from his job and within a few hours he was on his way back to England.

He departed in time to avoid worse that was to come. The following day the leading company missed its way in thick trees and in an attempt to retrieve the situation, the second company took over the advance. As it approached the high ground overlooking the caves, it came under a hail of fire from above. The Arab soldiers scattered, many dropping their weapons and equipment in their panic, and thirteen men died on the slopes including two British officers. Although operations continued around the caves, it was a humiliating defeat for SAF, which we all shared and felt keenly.

It was also a reminder that service in SAF was not the same as service with soldiers of one's own nation. There was a cultural, philosophical and religious gap between British officers and their Muslim soldiers that no amount of leadership could ever completely bridge. Many of us became devoted to our soldiers, and I like to think that the feeling was sometimes reciprocated, but when the chips were down there was always a nagging doubt as to whether they would risk their lives for us in the same way as we would for them and for each other.

Nevertheless, I was beginning to appreciate the rewards of commanding Baluch soldiers, for there were moments of pure sunshine when the warmth of a greeting, an unexpected wave or smile or a proffered dish of food instantly wiped out any irritation I might have been feeling with them at that moment. There was an enormous reservoir of goodwill and respect for the British and given the right sort of lead they would work for long periods without complaint, but two basic facts influenced their behaviour. First, the Baluch were mercenary soldiers and whilst many of them were natural warriors, they had joined the Sultan's Army to get away from a fairly wretched existence in their impoverished homeland and to make money, so it would have been vain to expect the same dedication to the task as one might expect from a British Army unit. Second, there was the influence of their religion which seemed to create division between

HAGAIF

Baluch and Briton in a way that language and race did not. The Baluch are for the most part devoted Muslims, and when it came to a clash between the demands of their job and those of their religion, the former tended to take second place.

Baluch officers all came up through the ranks so they tended to identify with their soldiers when unpopular decisions were handed down, and it was some time before I could unthinkingly assume the support of my sergeant major and my platoon commanders. Resistance to the zealous insistence of the infidel on inconvenient and uncomfortable military procedures together with the geographical isolation of our position tended to reinforce what has been called the loneliness of command, but it was good training and, as time went on, I gained experience and the relationship between me and my soldiers became more relaxed.

Early in January 1975 I was ordered to go to Hagaif, or Point 825 as it was known, to occupy the position on behalf of a company of the Jebel Regiment which had gone to take part in the operation at Shershitti, and there I was to meet Suleiman and his platoon who were to be moved across from Jibjat.

Point 825 occupied a low horseshoe of hills a few miles to the west of Raven's Roost on the Midway Road. The open part of the horseshoe faced north across undulating, sparsely covered ground towards the Gatn a few miles away, whilst the southern end looked out over the tumbled, wooded hills around the headwaters of the Wadi Nahiz. The *firqa* there numbered about half a dozen men and boys, and when I walked around the position I was disconcerted at the size of the perimeter that had to be watched. I was even more disconcerted when Charki, who had arrived a day or so before me with the rest of company headquarters, showed me my *murcha*. He had decided that I should live in splendid isolation on the highest pimple at the south of the horseshoe a suitable distance from the rest of the little garrison, close to the firing positions the Adoo were fond of using. The *firqa* already occupied the eastern leg of the horseshoe, and Suleiman's platoon were settling in on the steep slopes on the other side. They looked happy and secure in their numbers but although I felt a trifle exposed, I said nothing.

The other *murcha* on my pimple was occupied by the small BATT team allocated to Point 825, but they seemed to spend a good deal of their time away on other business. They had two 81-mm mortars on the position and a .50-calibre Browning machine gun which we used to spectacular effect during the stand-off attacks which the Adoo frequently made on the position.

Shortly after I arrived at Hagaif the BATT detachment, who had not taken part in the Shershitti operation, were visited by the CO of 22 SAS who had flown out from the UK when things were at their worst in the West, and I joined them to listen to his account of the action. We sat in silence as he dwelt on every tragic detail and to my astonishment he ended by saying to his soldiers: 'There are some good officers in SAF and some bloody awful ones, and is up to you to choose between them. You do not have to follow a chap who in your opinion is not up to his job.' I couldn't disagree with his assessment of the quality of SAF officers, but the rest of what he had said was a novel philosophy to me, and if it was accepted SAS policy then it partly accounted for the difficulty we sometimes had in working with BATT.

We quickly settled into a routine which consisted of small-scale patrolling and ambushing and we continued to work on defences of the position. Most of the *murchas* were only half finished when we moved in and there was a long perimeter fence that had to be completed as stores became available. A detachment of Jordanian engineers arrived to lay out the helicopter landing zone which involved clearing loose stones from a circular pad about forty yards across, and this Herculean task took them almost a month. During that time they resolutely refused to take any part in the defence of Hagaif, even to the extent of declining to stand to in the morning and evening, and I quickly became exasperated with them.

After a few weeks I was beginning to feel a bit like Robinson Crusoe, and one morning as I was walking back from some work I had been doing on my personal defences, I was surprised to see three white civilians, an older man and two cool pretty girls. They stared at the brown, half-naked savage coming round the corner of the hill with amazement and despite my pleasure at seeing new faces the only comment I could summon up at that moment was 'Good God!' It was not a good opening, but I quickly gathered my wits and offered them tea, and we sat for an hour or so chatting amicably in the warm winter sunshine. It turned out that they were civilian employees of a construction firm in Salalah who had strayed a mile or so from the relative safety of the Midway Road. I was sorry to see them go, for since the departure of the BATT team there had been no-one to talk to except the Baluch and the *firqa*.

But as time went on I found that I began to resent intruders into my little world, and this antisocial frame of mind became so pronounced that later in my tour I earned the soubriquet of The Old Man of Tawi Atair, and on occasion the CO had to order me down from the hills.

HAGAIF

As always in wars great and small there was a sharp division between front-line soldiers and those employed on the staff and we hillmen liked to think of ourselves as the only real combat soldiers bearing the heat and burden of the day with no thanks or gratitude from down below, whilst they undoubtedly regarded us as surly and awkward. There was some truth in both points of view, but the armchair tacticians in Dhofar occasionally exercised a baleful influence on our reputations, as I was to discover after an action fought a few months later.

The Wadi Nahiz is a very large, rugged feature with many hiding places, and it was reputed to be an Adoo stronghold. We received a number of stand-off sniping attacks from that direction, the first of which occurred whilst I was relaxing outside my *murcha* one afternoon. I had been reading and dozing on and off in the warm sun when there was a sharp crack overhead followed by a thud away to the south. It took a moment for the realisation to sink in that someone was actually trying to kill me, then I was off the chair and sliding down in a cloud of dust to grab my rifle. I poked my head back up out of cover but there was nothing to be seen or heard. Suleiman's men stood to, but the shot had come from a long way away and without being able to locate the firing position accurately, there was little that could be done about it.

In the future I would be more careful about where I chose to sunbathe, but the shot was confirmation that the enemy did exist and in a funny sort of way it was quite exciting.

Up to that point life had been fairly peaceful at Hagaif, but now we began to get regular sniping attacks. They all came from the south where escape to the fastnesses of the Nahiz was easy, and they were mostly carried out in the late afternoon when the slanting sun was full in our eyes. We registered all the likely fire positions as mortar targets and we stepped up patrolling, but the enemy had the initiative and catching him out would not be easy. For some time I pondered the problem, then I hit upon the idea of sending out a small patrol before first light to lie up on a neighbouring hill close to one of the most popular firing points. For a few days nothing happened then one evening just before dark there was a solitary crack followed by a storm of fire from the patrol under Sergeant Shahbaz Khan.

There was no word from the patrol and no way of telling what they were doing, so I had to control my impatience until they arrived back in the position an hour or so later. Shahbaz Khan was full of himself, and assured me that they had followed up and found blood at the firing point. I was not totally convinced, so I told him to be ready to go out again with me in the early hours of the morning so that I could see for myself, and this we did. We arrived at the spot an hour or so before dawn, and we lay and shivered in the keen wind waiting for the sun to come up. When it was light enough to see we searched the position for traces of the enemy but there were none, and I remained sceptical of Shahbaz Khan's claims.

Every morning and evening we stood to, that is every soldier took up his allotted position with his weapon in his hand and his equipment on. It was a tedious routine and probably unnecessary as we lived permanently with our weapons close to hand, but it was an opportunity twice a day to get everyone into the right frame of mind, check the mortar tasks and test-fire weapons. It was also a good chance to get round and talk to the soldiers but it was bedevilled by the problem of prayer which I had not yet solved and which was a constant source of irritation to me. They had me over a barrel on that one, and they knew it.

Although it was bitterly cold, stand to in the morning brought a daily reward in the wonder of the dawn. I never tired of watching as the black sky alight with blazing stars gradually gave way to spreading shades of pearl, pink and orange and the coming of day brightened the horizon, silhouetting trees on the hills in sharp outline and resolving an unintelligible jumble of dark shapes and shadows into the familiar grey landscape of men, animals and buildings.

We had our usual quota of influential visitors at Hagaif, and one day we were visited by Sheik Baraik, the Wali (Governor) of Dhofar and close friend and adviser of the Sultan, accompanied by the brigade commander. Baraik was a cultured, polite man of great influence in the Sultanate and he had supported the coup which put the young Sultan on the throne in 1970. On that occasion he displayed considerable courage and he was the only person in the province as far as I could tell who had any control at all over the *firqa*. That was partly due to the fact that as the ruler of Dhofar he controlled the purse strings, but after a short time with him I realised that some of it was also due to his powerful and authoritative personality.

The local *firqa* decided to slaughter a cow and have a feast to honour their guest. The wretched beast was dragged up to the *firqa* picquet, tied by the legs and its throat cut. It kicked and struggled, raising a cloud of white dust in the bright air, but the tribesmen were hacking slices from its hindquarters even whilst it lived, and within a short time a reeking heap of meat and entrails lay on the ground ready for the pot. Whilst all this was going on Baraik and the Brigadier were touring the position chatting to tribespeople and soldiers and in a while they made their way up to the *firqa* picquet, where the feast had been prepared in a large *murcha* decorated for the occasion with carpets hung round the walls.

I sat well down in the pecking order as befitted my lowly status. Opposite me was a bright-eyed old man and on my right a young British soldier who had come up with the Brigadier to take photographs of the visit. The old man tucked into the steaming pile of grey stringy meat with gusto, cutting off chunks with a sharp pocket knife and chewing hungrily. Having witnessed the slaughter, I was not particularly hungry, and to judge by the way he was picking at the food, neither was the soldier. After a while the old man began to get into the best part of the meal and he selected a long greenish yellow strip of fat which he obviously considered to be one of the choicest cuts. Inevitably the Wali as the honoured guest was offered one of the biggest chunks, but he took it manfully and chewed away. As his eyes caught mine across the gloom, they rolled Heavenward in an eloquent gesture and at this point I began to look everywhere but in the old man's direction, for I guessed that I would be next on the list for his singular honour. I engaged my other neighbour in deep conversation, but the soldier inadvertently caught the old man's eye. In a trice he was given a particularly large, juicy morsel on the point of a knife, and the old boy watched intently, nodding his head in approval as the lad valiantly strove to get the disgusting mouthful down.

Later as we walked down to the helicopter together I apologised for not warning him and asked if he'd been offered any more choice bits. He had, but he'd coped very well, and he opened an ammunition pouch to show me the greasy lumps secreted there. Full marks for tact and ingenuity, I thought. At the helicopter there was much shaking of hands and many expressions of goodwill and we took off for the KJ position at a waterhole a few miles away on the Gatn where Hatim Ali and the recce platoon were temporarily based. The platoon held a rocky outcrop overlooking the blue green water deep in a rock cleft.

Although it was only a few miles from Hagaif it was a quiet place where the enemy never came for it was a long way into the dry moon country of the Gatn, and the platoon there had a quiet time. The only remarkable thing about my visit was a black and white spotted animal skin which a tribesman showed me. He used the Arabic word for lion in describing it to me, but it was obviously something else a lot smaller, perhaps halfway between a wildcat and a leopard in size. It was an example of the variety and richness of wildlife in Dhofar which sadly was harried mercilessly by the tribesmen who killed for the sake of killing.

On patrol later in the week we came across an unexploded bomb left over from the airstrikes which had accompanied the operation to put in Hagaif. It lay in the open, its tail fins ripped off by the force of its impact, and stencilled on its olive green flank was the legend 'For export only'. It had fallen close to a small cave in the shoulder of a low hill which, to judge by the fortifications at its entrance, had been an Adoo position and the presumed target of the bomb. Several others had been dropped nearby seemingly to little effect, and I should have drawn the obvious conclusion that bombing in such rocky terrain was only marginally effective, but it was only later, after a more immediate experience, that I did so. For the moment the bomb had to be disposed of and doing so would give me an excellent opportunity to teach the soldiers something about explosives. I marked its position on my map and decided to return next day with the means to demolish it.

Taking a satchel with fuse, detonators and plastic explosive I returned to the site with a small patrol led by Corporal Ibrahim Abdullah, a rakish, bearded rogue with a quick tongue, a tremendous sense of humour and a reputation for indulging in the risky business of courting and occasionally winning the favours of Jebel ladies. Leaving the patrol a few hundred yards away to keep a look out for us, we began work on the bomb. I showed Ibrahim how to check the safety fuse and measure out sufficient to allow us time for a dignified withdrawal to safety, and how to join the various components of the charge so as to achieve the desired effect. I demonstrated how to light the safety fuse and I impressed on him the importance of walking back to cover rather than running. When I had given everything a last check I told him, without looking up from my task, to light the fuse. There was no response for Ibrahim was already halfway back towards the spot in which I had decided we would shelter. He came back a trifle sheepishly when I called and after the fuse was lit we walked together to our shelter.

The measured time ran out, there was a pause of perhaps fifteen seconds or so and then a thunderous explosion. I looked quickly up from cover to see twin pillars of white smoke and brown dust shooting up into the sky. I snapped the scene with my camera, and dropped back again as clods of earth started thumping down. I began to think that perhaps we were a little too close for safety, and my feeling was confirmed when a large fragment of bomb casing swooped out of the sky with a demonic whistle and neatly decapitated a large tough-skinned bush between us.

I imagined myself where that bush had been, and this time it was my turn to grin sheepishly.

Towards the end of January we were relieved on Hagaif by a company of the Jebel Regiment. The Baluch were excited by the prospect of a move and there was a good deal of friendly ribbing and laughter as they packed the last of our stores. I was soon caught up in the general good spirits and although I had enjoyed myself at Hagaif I looked forward to a change of scenery and to seeing Harry Fecitt again. He had finished his leave and would be meeting us at Raven's Roost on our way across to Ashinhaib and White City.

The arrival of the company from the Jebel Regiment dampened my spirits immediately. Fresh from the debacle at Shershitti, the soldiers were sullen and silent and the two British officers seemed depressed. I showed them around the position as quickly as I could, gave them a brief outline of what had happened over the last month or so and left. Hagaif was not a lucky position. My predecessor there had been killed at Shershitti and of the British officers I handed over to, the second-in-command, Michael Shipley, was to be killed shortly afterwards when the helicopter he was in was shot down over the Wadi Nahiz near Hagaif, and the Company Commander, Patrick Shervington, was to find himself on the wrong end of a mutiny within a month of Shipley's death. On patrol to the south of Hagaif, he called down mortar fire which landed on the patrol's position causing fatal casualties. Rightly or wrongly he was blamed for the incident by his men, and when he got back to Hagaif he was threatened at gunpoint and forced to leave.

Chapter 5

A Dual Command

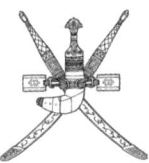

I met Harry at Raven's Roost and I greeted him cheerfully, ready to exchange gossip and get some news of home, but he was still getting over his leave and he was even more curt than usual so after a brief exchange of pleasantries I set off eastwards along the Gatn track, which had not long been open. For the first few weeks after it was opened the going was good, but as vehicles broke up the surface they ground it to a fine white powder which rose in huge clouds. In places it got so deep that Land Rovers would nose into it and heave solid waves along the bonnet and into the faces of the occupants. After an hour or so on the road we were indistinguishable one from another in our floury coating, and the Baluch looked quite bizarre with their dark eyes blazing out of death-white faces and their beards powdered as if for some fantastic piece of theatre.

Normally I didn't bother with the issue headcloth or *shimaag* and I went bareheaded, or later took to wearing the floppy headgear known in the British Army as a gobbin hat, but I had to admit that a *shimaag* came into its own on these journeys. Wound round the head with the trailing end covering the face up to the eyes, it gave a measure of protection from the heat and dust that nothing else could.

Although our four positions occupied a rough rectangle of the jebel not more than about twenty miles long by about ten deep, it took so long to get anywhere across the rutted tracks that Harry decided to base himself at Ashinhaib with Jelal's platoon and concentrate his attention there and on Medina al-San where Badil was now based. I would look after White City and Jibjat with Suleiman's and Mohammed's platoons respectively.

White City was a comic misnomer. Peoples in the East can be great litter-mongers, and the *Jebalis* were no exception. Old army positions on the Jebel were marked by piles of tin cans and from the air some parts of White City looked like gigantic rubbish tips. It was difficult to distinguish *firqa* dwellings from the mountains of rusting cans and other detritus surrounding them and months later when we were in Tawi Atair, some miles away across the hills, it was easy to pick out White City as the slanting afternoon sun glinted on waste metal. Exhortations to the *firqa* to organise a clean-up were quite futile, and in the end we all learned to live with it.

There had not been much of a chance to get to know the Firqa Khalid Walid during our previous short stay in White City, so we started slowly with a few short patrols. As we began to get used to working together, so we increased the range and duration of our activities all the while fostering a spirit of mutual trust and cooperation without which we could not operate effectively. A new SAS squadron had arrived in Dhofar and there was a larger detachment of them than before at White City under the command of an energetic and professional Guards officer named John Wyndham, but I knew they would not being staying long enough

Jebali girls at a watering hole north of Tawi Atair.

to have any real effect upon the local situation, and I therefore saw it as my job to rebuild the morale of the *firqa*. In this I was helped enormously by Salim Musalim, the *firqa* leader, and after an initial period of mutual wariness we became good friends. He was intelligent and unexpectedly broad-minded, partly because he had seen something of the outside world during service in the Trucial Oman Scouts. He had taken part in the rebellion against the old Sultan, but had changed sides after the 1970 coup. Like many *Jebalis*, he was not especially zealous in his faith, but unlike the majority, he respected his wife and even admitted to me one day that he helped around the house occasionally. His wife, who was extremely beautiful, was a strong and intelligent woman.

Jebali women did most of the heavy menial labour in the village and in their husbands' scale of things they came a long way down after his honour, his cattle and his sons, but despite their lowly status they took a much more active part in the affairs of the tribe than elsewhere in Arabia. They scorned the veil, stared boldly at any man and at times even raised their powerful voices to scold idle husbands.

Salim's wife was not exceptional in her beauty, but women on the Jebel aged rapidly and by twenty-five most would be showing the marks of the hard life they led. I remember visiting a village close to Tawi Atair and taking a cup of tea in a humble grass hut from the radiant mother of two small children whose lovely face and gentle manner moved me deeply and will stay in my memory always.

Jebali women were of course totally inaccessible to Westerners and usually even to the Baluch, although occasionally a Baluch would marry a local girl or even enjoy a secret relationship with one, but God help him if her menfolk discovered them. Ibrahim had a girlfriend in Tawi Atair and he never tired of hinting at the favours he had enjoyed in her house there, grinning lasciviously all the while, but he was lucky. The soldiers only went home for one month each year, and in the circumstances it was inevitable that there was some homosexuality amongst them. In common with most of the British officers I took the view that what they did amongst themselves was no concern of mine, but I did draw the line at officers and their orderlies walking around hand in hand and I took action on the one occasion when in my view it cut across rank and began to affect discipline. The problem concerned one of my platoon commanders and it was drawn to my attention by Charki whilst the officer was on leave.

It was alleged that the officer had taken the soldier out on driving lessons and after a while had tried to bully him into giving in to his advances. It was difficult to get at the whole story, for it was possible, though unlikely, that Charki was pursuing a vendetta against the officer, and in any case the soldier was reluctant to testify formally against his platoon commander knowing that the consequences could reach out beyond Oman and bring unpleasant repercussions in his home village. On the other hand I suspected from previous observation of him that the officer was not above suspicion on this particular score, and the next time I was in Arzat I mentioned it to the CO and suggested that in the absence of evidence that would stand up to scrutiny, perhaps the wisest thing would be to find a post outside the battalion for him. In his usual way Gordon-Taylor talked all round the problem without coming to a decision, and we compromised by sending the officer to another company. Not unnaturally he loudly protested his innocence when he got back from leave and the whole affair ended untidily and unsatisfactorily from everyone's point of view.

It was an object lesson in the clannishness which bedevilled attempts to raise the Baluch to positions of responsibility, for in all important matters in which officers and NCOS were expected to exercise impartial judgement, they were subject to considerable pressure to favour their own kinsmen and relatives, irrespective of merit. When I took command of the company in April of that year I decided at the outset that I would take personal control of two aspects of administration which I considered vital to the morale of the soldiers, namely pay and leave. It was a lot of extra work, and as time went on I grew increasingly impatient of administrative chores, but I knew that the soldiers had been cheated by officers and NCOS in both areas and I was determined that it would not happen whilst I was in command.

If the Baluch had many faults they also had many virtues, and for me service with them was very rewarding. They endured wretched conditions for months on end especially during the *Khareef*, and they had none of the motivation that we had to sustain them. We lived in gloomy, rat-infested hovels that leaked water incessantly so that none of our possessions were dry and we ate monotonous rations contaminated by vermin, but the soldiers' cheerful spirits never deserted them and they chattered endlessly amongst themselves through the dark wet evenings. They kept their weapons clean and bright and though such conditions would breed discontent in most troops I never heard a voice raised in anger even in the worst days of the monsoon.

Towards the end of an uneventful month at White City I had my first real fright since arriving in Dhofar and it had nothing to do with the Adoo.

Murchas were built of rocks which when shattered with a sledgehammer revealed a dazzling white inside shot with streaks of pink and orange, so that a new building presented a splendid target from some way off until it weathered to a nondescript grey and blended into the background. The rocks were gathered in and piled one on top of another to form walls three or four feet thick at the bottom tapering to a couple of feet at the top. Earth was packed in between the rocks and rough cedar beams laid across the top to form a low ceiling. Corrugated steel sheets ('chinko') were laid across the beams, and a layer of sandbags, rocks and earth to a depth of two feet or so completed the job. Built properly, the *murcha* was a fairly solid structure and it gave a degree of protection against small-arms fire and shrapnel, but it was vulnerable to rain and burrowing rats which undermined the walls, causing them to collapse without warning. In the dead of night my *murcha* did so. With a heart-stopping roar a large section of wall gave way, catapulting me from my bed and filling the air with a dense cloud of dust. Luckily that part of the ceiling which fell missed me which was just as well, for it could have killed me as surely as any bullet from an AK-47. I removed myself into the tent next door where I spent the remainder of the night listening to Mansoor snoring in the next compartment and rattling the plastic sheet which he used as a bedspread.

Next morning I surveyed the damage and decided that it was not worth repairing, and I began to make plans for a new structure. During that month I had inexplicably lost a number of small items, the most mysterious of which was my shaving brush. I had casually mentioned it to Mansoor, who had attributed the losses to rats, saying that they were especially partial to shaving brushes which they like to gnaw. I had heard quite a few of Mansoor's old wives' tales by this time, and I was inclined to dismiss this as just more of the same old nonsense, but when I began to look through the rubble, I had to concede that he was right, for there were a number of pencils and pens amongst the stones and there too was the stump of my shaving brush with every bristle nibbled off.

Salim and I were getting to know one another, and as time went by, we began to plan our next moves together, turning over the possibilities informally until a pattern emerged on which we could base a limited operation. Intelligence, which is essential to the ultimate success of any military undertaking, was not easy to come by, and I suspected that the *firqa* probably knew more than they were prepared to divulge. But like the Baluch, the *Jebalis* were inextricably bound up in a complex web of tribal loyalties which made nonsense of any attempt to impose a simplistic 'them and us' interpretation on the situation in Dhofar. Many of the *firqa* had sons, brothers or fathers amongst the Adoo, and they sometimes met in villages on neutral ground under informal truces. The issue of Government versus Liberation Front was in any case meaningless to many of the people in remoter villages, who rarely saw any evidence of Government influence in their daily lives and whose attention was wholly concentrated on the business of surviving. The tribe had been the focus of their loyalties since time immemorial so there was nothing on which to build any concept of nationhood, and ideology was irrelevant to them. In some ways they were more free than any other people I have come across, for they paid no taxes, filled in no forms, and went where and when they pleased. If they acknowledged any authority it was only acquiescence to superior force or in order to achieve some limited gain. Their cooperation was never anything but temporary, and would be withdrawn abruptly if it seemed advantageous even in the short term to do so.

This aspect of the *Jebali* character often caused great exasperation, especially amongst the less thoughtful of our brothers in arms in Dhofar, and quite a few people were inclined to dismiss them all as enemy sympathisers without stopping to think that they were judging the situation by standards that most *Jebalis* were unaware even existed. My view was simply that the fickleness of *Jebali* loyalties had to be accepted as a fact of life, and I worked on that basis, taking as my starting point the assumption that any careless talk around the *firqa* would find its way fairly quickly to the nearest Adoo gang, not because there were active traitors amongst us, but because the *Jebalis* were great gossipers, and military matters were the most interesting topic of gossip. The free-ranging nomadism of the tribesmen did the rest. A nice diplomatic problem thus presented itself, for if I was too parsimonious with information on my plans and thoughts, the *firqa* would become suspicious of my good faith and withhold cooperation. If on the other hand I took them completely into my confidence, every move we made would soon be common knowledge in the villages around.

No hard and fast rule ever evolved to cope with this dilemma and I tended to play each situation as it developed. This turned out to be a good way of operating as it showed the *firqa* that we were not entirely dependent on them, and thus curbed some of the more boisterous acts of indiscipline to which they were prone. Sometimes I would take them completely into my confidence, especially if there was a short time lapse between word and action and I could be fairly sure that the bush telegraph would not be fast enough to broadcast our plans to every single enemy soldier in the vicinity.

Salim and I met every day to talk informally on a wide range of subjects and for once I found my command of Arabic to be infuriatingly inadequate. Whilst Salim waited patiently I would flick feverishly through my dictionary to find the word I wanted, and though the process stilted our conversation somewhat, my Arabic improved in leaps and bounds. We got into the habit of meeting in the early afternoons, and sometimes we would talk through into the evening together. As time went on the conclusions I had reached from a morning spent pondering the situation would be mirrored by Salim's remarks later in the day, and I began to feel we were getting somewhere.

The *firqa* had a relaxed way of operating in the field, but it was a chilling sight to see men who until that moment had been shambling along laughing and chattering, suddenly unsling their weapons, spread out and generally become very businesslike indeed, for it was a sure sign that action was imminent. Seeing them, my breath would quicken and my heart pound as it always did at the prospect of a fight.

February 1975

Salim and I had discussed the village of Faiqaitha many times and we both decided that it was overdue a visit. It stood at the head of a small re-entrant running down to the Wadi Darbat to the south-east of White City, and there was a good track leading down into the fastness of that great valley. It seemed likely that the Adoo visited the village at night for food and gossip and returned to the Darbat early in the morning. We therefore decided to go down there before dawn with a platoon and some *firqa*, surround the village and wait and see.

Darbat is one of Dhofar's great valley systems and it has a unique geological formation, a dry waterfall of giant proportions almost a mile across at its lip and divided in two by a rugged outcrop rising a hundred feet above the floor of the wadi which long ago must have stood in the middle of a broad stream sliding over the falls and roaring down to the rocks 400 feet below. Further up, the valley floor narrows between its steep walls until it becomes choked in a tangle of trees and fallen rocks. At the great bend below Faiqaitha where it angles sharply away towards the east it is a jumbled mass of fissured rock and dense woods. At that point it is almost a kilometre from crest to crest and the lower ground makes an ideal hiding place for any number of men.

We moved out of White City at about ten o'clock at night and marched silently down the rock-strewn slopes towards the village, reaching it without incident just as dawn was lightening the sky above the hills on the far side of the Darbat. The huts lay in a small bowl with a gap at the eastern end where a re-entrant led off down into the main valley, and we quickly spread along the high ground and settled down to wait. Some of the *firqa* moved further down onto the crest overlooking the Darbat, and as it began to get light, I looked around to check that the platoon was in position. Slowly, the first cows began to wander out to pasture and a thin column of blue smoke rose straight up into the still morning air from one of the huts. Shadows of night lingered in the bowl, but details were becoming distinct and I hunched lower in the grass as an old man came out from a hut, stretched himself and stood looking around and taking in the new day.

Suddenly the radio crackled with excited *firqa* voices. Salim bent and listened intently, and amongst the babble I picked out the word 'Adoo'. He straightened. 'There are Adoo in a cave in the Darbat below us,' he announced, his eyes gleaming. I told him to show me and gathering up my small command group, we ran down the slope to a crest from which we could see into the main valley. Excitedly, Salim pointed out the base of a long grassy knoll rising from the valley floor and told me that the Adoo were in a cave there, but I could see nothing.

The cave was a long way from our positions and our arrival had already been announced by some of the *firqa* further down the slope who had fired off a few random shots in that direction. We could not hope to approach the enemy position undetected and in the thick bush and broken rock that covered the valley floor there was little chance of coming to grips with him now that he had been forewarned. On the other hand if we could get troops onto the high ground overlooking the caves fairly quickly it looked as though they might be able to cover escape routes from there by observation and fire, and with this in mind I called up Battalion HQ on the radio, made my report and explained the plan. To keep the enemy pinned in the cave I asked for an airstrike, completely ignoring the lesson I had drawn from the results of bombing around Hagaif.

After an impressively short interval my small Sarbe ground-to-air radio crackled with the voice of the leading BAC Strikemaster pilot whilst he was still below the horizon, and a moment later the two small planes appeared below us in the wadi. They stood off whilst we fired a smoke bomb to indicate the enemy's position then one after another they ran in over the target, bombing and strafing, and pulling up from the wadi to circle a couple of hundred feet above us.

There was a lot of smoke and noise and as the planes withdrew a short distance to give top cover, a characteristic 'wock-wock-wock' heralded the arrival of helicopters with a couple of platoons of B Company commanded by David Bills. As they landed on the flat grassy top of the hill they were immediately engaged by another group of Adoo at the top end of the LZ [landing zone] who had been drawn as if by a magnet to the sound of fighting. The chaos of battle closed in and I could only watch helplessly as the Adoo skilfully pulled back up the hill, drawing B Company away from their blocking position despite my frantic messages on the radio. Harry Fecitt arrived from Ashinhaib to take command of the battle, bringing more platoons with him, and as the fighting moved further and further away across the hills I could hear Gordon-Taylor at Arzat exhorting us all to 'Hold the contact'. This particular order was a great favourite of his but I never did understand what he meant by it, for if the Adoo had an open exit they were able to break off contact and disappear into the countryside whenever they chose.

By late afternoon it was clear that the Adoo had slipped out of our grasp and despite the CO's determination that we should press on, we decided that nothing would be gained by doing so and we called up the helicopters to lift us back to our various bases. Shortly before we moved out I saw a small procession carrying a burden of some sort across an open patch of grassland below us in the direction of Faiqaitha, and I asked Salim who they were. I was stunned when he told me in a matter of fact sort of way that they were people from the village and they were bringing up the body of a woman who had been killed by a stray bomb splinter early in the day. Guilt overwhelmed me for it had been my decision to order the strike, and I had given little thought to anyone else who might have been in the area. I had no qualms about killing Adoo, but the death of an innocent non-combatant and a woman at that filled me with remorse, and I was even more appalled when Salim added that the woman's brother was on his way up to our position and wanted to speak to me. What in God's name was I going to say to him?

Desperately I began to compose some phrases of regret in Arabic, and when he arrived I mumbled them at him in my shame. He listened patiently, nodding his head, then broached the main reason for his visit to me. He had heard that we were going back to White City by chopper, so could he please have a lift with us?

The day had taught me a number of valuable lessons. The most striking one was that the Adoo would 'march to the sound of the guns' and when they arrived they showed themselves to be masters of low-level tactics. It had also been brought home to me forcibly that we should carry sufficient water and food for twenty-four hours every time we went out regardless of how long we thought we might be away, for at the end of that day we were very thirsty and hungry indeed, having come out equipped only for a short patrol. The day's action had also demonstrated once again the relative ineffectiveness of bombing as a method of dealing with an enemy in broken ground, and I was to be much more sparing of air power in future engagements, using it only to get myself out of a tight spot when all else had failed. Not the least of the day's surprises was the attitude of the dead woman's brother which was confirmation if any was needed of the *Jebalis'* callous attitude to their women.

A few weeks after the fight at the Darbat it was decided that KJ, reinforced by BATT and some *firqa* from Ashinhaib, would mount a sweep in a large wadi complex to the south-west of Ashinhaib. Harry and I were summoned to Arzat and from there we made our way up to Raven's Roost where the BATT and *firqa* components of our force were assembling. The formal briefing took place in a large marquee which had been brought all the way from Arzat and erected for the purpose and we crowded in. Besides the officers from KJ it seemed that every member of the *firqa* and most of the BATT who were going to be involved had come along to hear the briefing for themselves, so we were a good crowd and it was a tight squeeze. The briefing was long and rambling and I was left with the impression that the operation would be rather informal and we should play it by ear. In outline the plan was that I would move out overnight from Ashinhaib with a platoon, some BATT and some *firqa*, and arrive before dawn on the high ground overlooking the largest of the wadis that we were to sweep. The main body of troops would move down from Zeek a little later and do the hard work whilst we watched the wadi from above.

I drove back along the Gatn to Ashinhaib, briefed Jelal and went down to the BATT hut. The three troopers there seemed unenthusiastic about the idea of being briefed by me and they submitted to the process with bad grace, but they were better than the local *firqa* who dismissed the battalion plan outright and said we should go to another place entirely. I could see that it was going to be a difficult evening, but I was quite firm with them, saying that I had no power to change the plan and that if they didn't like it they would have to lump it. I said that we would assemble at midnight at the southern entrance to the wire, and left to make myself a quick meal and a welcome cup of tea.

A few minutes before midnight Jelal's men began to gather silently in the darkness, and after a quick whispered check, we moved to the perimeter wire. The BATT troopers were already at the rendezvous and they told me that the *firqa* would be along shortly. We waited for a while and just as I was about go without them, the *firqa* joined us and we set off in the moonless night.

At first our route took us across easy, gently undulating ground and we made good progress, but as the night wore on we began to drop down towards the headwaters of wadis running south from the Gatn, and as we crossed these rocky channels one after another the going became harder. At length the *firqa* grew bored with walking and they began to assert more and more insistently that the next wadi was the one we wanted. We had not yet received the detailed 1:50,000 maps that were to transform the business of navigating in Dhofar, and I was not 100 per cent certain of our position. But I knew that we had further to go, and once again the *firqa* were told that they could come or stay as they chose, it was all the same to me. They sat down in a huff and we left them behind in the darkness.

As dawn approached we came to the last wadi before the hill we were to occupy. The bottom of the wadi was invisible in the gloom, but it was deep and crossing it would be hard work. The senior BATT trooper chose this moment to assert that in his view we had reached the appointed place and we stopped for yet another whispered conference whilst I convinced him that we had not. We dropped down the steep side of the wadi, stumbling in the darkness, and clambered out the other side, arriving on the picquet just as dawn was breaking. I had been worried that perhaps I was mistaken, so it was a relief when daylight revealed that we were in the right place after all. Across the hills we saw the *firqa* shambling sullenly in our direction, and they joined us later in the morning.

We settled down to wait for the arrival of the force from Zeek, and the BATT troopers set up their GPMG and a powerful telescope with which they began to scrutinise the wadi sides and bottom. At about nine o'clock I was talking with Jelal some way from the BATT position when without warning, the GPMG began firing. I ran down the short distance to the gun position, and dropped to the ground beside the gunner. 'What's going on?' 'Adoo, boss. About a thousand metres down the wadi.'

I grabbed the telescope and swept the valley at the point he had indicated. The thinly wooded slope leaped into focus and I saw a lean old man striding away from us through the trees, a knobkerry slung on one shoulder. As bullets from the gun cracked over his head he turned and looked disdainfully back up the valley towards us, scorning to run. 'OK knock it off, It's just an old man.' I said. 'Free fire zone, boss. They're all Adoo down there.' 'You've been reading too many books about Vietnam',

I retorted angrily, 'Now I said stop firing and I mean it.' The gun stopped, and an awkward silence fell. The troopers were ashamed of themselves, and I let them stew.

The rest of the day was uneventful, so much so that I told Jelal to wake me if anything interesting happened, and dozed for an hour or two in the hot sun. Early in the afternoon Gordon-Taylor evidently decided that we had done all that could be usefully done, and he gave orders for us to begin pulling back. The route led across open country sloping gently up towards the Gatn, and the withdrawing troops made quite an impressive sight as they strung themselves out across a mile or two of Jebel in platoons and companies. It was unlikely that the Adoo would take on such a large group in the open, but they might have tried a long shot or two, and with that possibility in mind, I picqueted the high ground overlooking the withdrawal route, using the three platoons of C Company which I had gathered up and now had under command. As a result we arrived on the road somewhat later than everyone else.

The Wadi Ethon and its waterhole a few miles south of White City had begun to engage my interest and attention as it lay on one of the routes from Darbat to the west, and when the BATT team at White City indicated that they wanted to do an ambush there, I said that I would like to go with them and take a platoon along. We agreed that BATT would mount close watch over the waterhole itself whilst we picqueted the high ground. I would have preferred to do the operation with just a few *firqa*, and I disliked the secondary role that I was obliged to accept, but they thought of it first so we had no choice in the matter.

The day before we were due to go out I was taking stock of the various dumps of ammunition around White City and was delighted to find a great pile of metal boxes containing 60-mm mortar rounds of apparently Iranian manufacture. The boxes looked a little the worse for wear on the outside, but the rounds themselves seemed to be in good condition and as we were short of this particular calibre of ammunition it was a lucky find, and I gave orders that some should be taken on the operation next day.

It was only the second time that I had been out with BATT, and whilst I was impressed with the formidable array of equipment they took, I was not so taken by the noise they made as they clumped across the hillside burdened like donkeys, tripping and crashing to the ground every now and again. A few minutes after we reached the lip of the wadi the silence of the night was broken by the sharp chinking of a pick on rock and when I crept over to investigate I found a trooper trying to dig in the hard ground. When I taxed him with the noise he was making, he informed me in no uncertain terms that he was not going to be without cover when the sun came up. It was a reasonable point of view, but the noise he was making could easily negate the whole purpose of our being there, which was to catch the Adoo by surprise. After a short discussion along this line he grudgingly conceded my point and stopped work.

A small group of BATT and *firqa* had gone down deeper into the wadi to watch the waterhole more closely, and shortly after dawn they came up on the radio and asked for mortar fire on the hillside opposite where they said they could see a single Adoo soldier moving. From our position we could see neither the waterhole nor the soldier, but we obligingly opened fire with our hand-held 60-mm mortar in the direction indicated.

There was a pause followed by a bang far down in the wadi. The radio came to life with a squawk of protest from the BATT team below asking us stop bombing them and in alarm I checked the charges on the round which was about to be fired. The mortar-man fired again, and there was another bang in the wadi, closer this time, and an even more indignant protest accompanied by some colourful language. I couldn't see what was wrong. The soldier was reliable, and I had seen him achieve a near miss in practice at much longer ranges than this. I pointed out a large solitary green tree about a thousand yards away on the other side of the wadi and told him to try again. He pulled the short lanyard, the mortar kicked and the round rose into the air in an erratic corkscrew, feeble orange flames flaring out at a variety of angles from its tail. Clearly it was not going far and we beat it into cover by a narrow margin as it thudded to earth twenty yards in front of our sangar.

That was the end of fire support for the day, and shortly afterwards the BATT and *firqa* group came up from the wadi and we prepared to move out. Just as we were about to do so, a storm of firing broke out from a short distance away where the *firqa* had been gathering. Thinking that we had a contact after all I galloped across only to see them firing wildly into the air with their weapons on automatic. When I asked what the hell they thought they were doing, they grinned sheepishly like naughty schoolboys caught out in some foolish prank and said '*tamreen*' (training). Considering that they had been pestering me mercilessly for ammunition only a day or two before, I thought it a bit steep and said so. Later one of the BATT troopers told me that it was normal practice for the *firqa* to fire off their ammunition at the end of an operation to save the trouble of carrying it home.

The day had dawned still and crystal clear but we had not been long on the march back when the wind began to blow out of the north. In a short space of time it increased almost to gale force, blowing a mixture of Jebel dust and powdered cattle manure into our faces and obliging us to bend our heads into it to make any progress. When we reached White City and looked down into the depression where most of our tents were pitched a sorry sight met our eyes. Much of the mildewed canvas had given up the uneven struggle at an early stage, and was now streaming in tatters from guy ropes and tent poles like so many Tibetan prayer flags, and other tents had simply blown away or collapsed. When I arrived at the marquee which I was using whilst my *murcha* was being rebuilt I found Mansoor in a very sour mood indeed. He had laboriously decorated a low earth wall around the inside of the tent with beer cans which I had emptied over the last few months, and his handiwork lay in ruins. I was hungry and tired and perhaps I should have given his little personal tragedy more sympathy, but I didn't, and Mansoor's resentment increased still further.

The wind blew for two more days by the end of which everyone had lost their sense of humour.

After the debacle on the Wadi Ethon with our Iranian mortar ammunition I decided to do a thorough survey of everything we had and get rid of all the unserviceable stuff. This exercise took me longer than expected and I turned up all kinds of things from a thousand rounds of 81-mm mortar ammunition to a batch of Claymore mines. Much had been ruined by storage in *murchas* which flooded during the *Khareef*, but some was simply third-rate stuff which had never been any good. I decided to take a few boxes of the 60-mm mortar bombs up to a deserted part of the Gatn and blow them up. I found a low cave well off the beaten track and stacked the bombs at the back of it, reasoning that the low roof would concentrate the force of the blast onto them, and set charges of plastic explosive around the cache. I lit the fuse and withdrew a short distance. There was a muffled thump and a cloud of dust, and when I went back to the front of the cave to see what had happened I saw bent and twisted mortar bombs scattered in the dust around the cave mouth. None had actually been destroyed and it was obvious that expert help would be needed. In the end KJ called in an ammunition technical warrant officer from Muscat who arranged for my lethal detritus to be lifted out by air and dropped from the back of a Skyvan out over the Indian Ocean.

March 1975

At about this time Keith Brett, the Battalion Second-in-Command, left KJ for more congenial pastures in Northern Oman and his place was taken by a seconded officer newly arrived from the UK. Douglas McCully of the Queen's Regiment was a breath of fresh air in KJ, and he brought a cheery good humour and common-sense approach to the Battalion that had been sadly lacking up to that point. A graduate of the Indian Staff College, Douglas liked to play the pukka sahib and he possessed an elegantly ironic wit which was often lost on the grosser minds in our midst. He sported a flowing Viking moustache, and his mane of blond hair was considerably longer than the crewcuts favoured by the mercenary fraternity. He quickly cultivated an all-over tan which he took some trouble to maintain through his tour, and he loved gossip which he would gleefully retail to anyone who cared to listen. More important from my point of view, he took his job seriously and he was to prove a valuable ally at court.

Just after Douglas' arrival in KJ the long sequence of comparatively fruitless operations was interrupted by a spectacular ambush success in our company area. Medina al-San had suffered a number of stand-off attacks by mortar and small-arms fire and Harry Fecitt had sent out ambushes and patrols to areas the enemy was thought to be using. In particular he watched the perimeter of the new airstrip closely each night to prevent the Adoo from mining it. Then he began to get reports of Adoo activity around a waterhole about a thousand metres to the east of the position and he decided to mount an ambush there, using Mohammed Salim's platoon. At the ambush he lined the track leading to the waterhole with Claymore mines, gathered the firing cables into his position, spread the Baluch up the hillside behind him to give him support and settled down to wait.

Shortly before midnight Harry had had enough of lying on the stony ground in what was beginning to look like another abortive ambush and was about to call it off when suddenly he saw a single file of shadowy figures coming silently out of the darkness towards the waterhole. After so many long, profitless nights spent in ambush, he had difficulty believing the evidence of his own eyes and, in his graphic phrase, 'I almost fuckin' shat myself.' As the Adoo patrol walked into the killing tone Harry squeezed the triggers of the Claymores, there was a thunderous roar in the confined space of the steep wadi, and hundreds of ball bearings scythed into the enemy patrol at point-blank range. The Baluch immediately opened up into the killing zone with a hail of small-arms fire, end when the firing died away, it was found that four of the six men in the Adoo patrol had been killed. One, a young lad barely old enough to carry a gun, had been wounded and was captured, and the sixth member of the group escaped. Later Harry voiced the view that for number six the war probably ended when the Claymores spat death at his comrades so suddenly, and it took no great effort of imagination to see what he meant.

It was a spectacular success and it was followed by an almost equally spectacular expenditure of mortar ammunition as Harry spent the rest of the night bombarding all possible exits from the wadi in an attempt to prevent number six escaping from the valley of death that he had created. He sent a message by radio to Battalion Headquarters to the effect that he had Adoo trapped in the wadi and needed a resupply of mortar ammunition, which unfortunately was corrupted in transmission to give the impression that it was Harry who was trapped by the Adoo. Staff officers at Brigade Headquarters were dragged from their beds to organise helicopters to lift in the extra ammunition, and at Arzat criticism of Harry's action mounted. His bluff cynicism and direct manner had infuriated Gordon-Taylor on many occasions, and being a man of black and white judgements, the CO was unable to assess Harry's military ability in isolation from his admittedly abrasive personal characteristics. He disliked him and therefore considered that he must also be incompetent, and now it looked as though his view was being vindicated. It seems that little concern for Harry's personal safety or indeed for that of his men was shown that night at Arzat, and in the end Harry received little credit for what was a resounding success by any standards.

The affair did nothing to reconcile Harry and the CO and until the time that Harry left KJ they were unable to speak of one another without rancour. Shortly after the ambush Harry summoned me to Ashinhaib and announced that he had had enough of Dhofar in general and Gordon-Taylor in particular and that he was going to apply for a post in the Dubai Defence Force. He advised me to move quickly if I wanted to be sure of succeeding him in command of the Company as the CO was prejudiced against seconded officers and would install a mercenary officer instead of me if I did nothing. I needed no second bidding for I remembered only too well almost the first words I heard the CO utter on the subject but there were other jobs that had to be done before I could tackle him.

Early in March the decision had been taken to drive a vehicle track down from Ashinhaib to Medina al-San finally linking all four of our positions, and we had the long and manpower-consuming task of protecting the road party whilst it worked. The construction team supplied by Taylor Woodrow consisted of a group of Pakistani labourers led by Mike Martin, a small red-haired Geordie with a great bush of a beard who strode heedlessly round the Jebel in shorts, sandals, dark glasses and a red and white Palestinian *shimaag* wound round his head. Mike was inordinately proud of his headgear and he stood out sharply against the dun hillside making an excellent target, but though I advised him many times to adopt a less conspicuous dark green Army *shimaag* he never did. He seemed oblivious to the risks which deterred lesser mortals, and he was never happier than when he was roughing it on the hill with his phlegmatic Pakistani bulldozer driver. Like many expatriates in Oman at that time Mike was a man of varied but mostly unofficial skills, and he had a chequered history. Ex-Royal Marine, ex-sailor, ex-marine engineer, Mike enjoyed more freedom and responsibility in Dhofar than he could ever hope for in Britain and in common with so many in his situation, his exile offered refuge of a sort from a crumbling personal life at home. He was an amusing and hospitable companion with a prodigious capacity for alcohol, and when I was working with him on the road I often enjoyed an excellent curry cooked by his Pakistanis.

With an assured sweep of his arm Mike would indicate the next stage of construction, and he spoke with such authority on the subject that it was some time before I realised that the only engineering or surveying qualifications that he possessed were that he was there and had done it before, and in our unsophisticated world they sufficed. He had a simple procedure: plot a rough track on the map, recce it from the air if possible, discuss it with the commander on the ground and walk the route, settling the exact line a kilometre or two at a time. These stretches would be picqueted whilst the bulldozer ground back and forth, filling in the worst holes and clearing obstacles, usually large boulders or jagged reefs of rock sticking up through the topsoil. The result was a rough road, smooth enough for the first few days or so, which quickly degenerated into a rutted, potholed track suitable only for Land Rovers and Bedford trucks but a great advance on what had existed before.

13 March 1975

On 13 March we drove across the last few yards of scrub to link up with the track out of Ashinhaib to White City and at the end of the day, Mike and I returned there to celebrate both the completion of the track and my win in a lottery which would bring me a seat back to England on one of the Sultan's BAC 1-11s returning to Hurne airport near Bournemouth for maintenance. Although strictly speaking I was not yet entitled to any leave, winners of these lotteries were indulged and allowed extra time off so that they could take advantage of the win. We ate an excellent dinner prepared by Mansoor and drank so much beer that later in the night I was heartily sick outside in the dust.

14 March 1975

The next day I went down to Arzat with a sore head to tackle the CO. From the point of view of seniority, knowledge of the Company and familiarity with the area, I was the best qualified officer in the Regiment to command C Company and we both knew it, but Gordon-Taylor had set his face against having me or any other seconded officer as a company commander and he hummed and hawed and twisted this way and that in an effort to avoid committing himself. But I had gone to Arzat determined to get my way and I stuck to my guns, reiterating the same arguments relentlessly until he gave in and grudgingly conceded that I would command the Company when Harry left.

I was very excited by the prospect of going home, and it was a joy to telephone Carol from the Cable & Wireless office in Muttrah and hear her voice so much more clearly than on the crackling wires from Salalah. It was correspondingly disappointing when after three days of frustrating delays, the flight home was finally cancelled, but on the plane back to Dhofar I consoled myself with the thought that I had secured command of the Company and thinking how short a time it was before my leave was due anyway, I put the disappointment behind me. On arrival I learned that the Firqa Khalid Walid at White City had clashed with a small Adoo patrol a few miles south of the base, killing two of their number. The FKW North leader had been wounded in the fight and now lay in the Field Surgical Team (FST) hospital at RAF Salalah. Yarpy Wardle had surprised everyone by rushing up to White City by helicopter and hastily organising a patrol of Baluch with which he had allegedly gone out to succour the *firqa*. Gordon-Taylor's loud praise of this heroic act was in marked contrast to his reaction to Harry's recent success.

Whilst I was away the Adoo had waylaid a truck with four unarmed Pakistani labourers on the Gatn road between Zeek and Ashinhaib and murdered them in cold blood. Harry had arrived on the scene first and he described to me how one of the unfortunate men had attempted to escape by running into the low brushwood that bordered the track, but the Adoo had followed his blood trail and ruthlessly finished him off when they caught up with him. Harry was very depressed by it all, and was counting the days until his departure from Dhofar.

My interest in the Wadi Ethon was growing daily and it seemed likely to me that the Adoo used the thickly wooded valley floor as a covered route, crossing over the narrow strip of high ground at its headwaters into the Darbat which ran at a right angle to it. If an operation could be mounted to seal off the eastern end and cover the high ground on either side of the wadi a dragnet moving up the floor of the valley from west to east should flush out any enemy. I had already persuaded Harry that we should do an operation there, and not long after Douglas arrived I discussed the subject with him and sketched out the way I thought it should be done. He agreed with my views and said he would put it to the CO.

Surprise was vital, because in that rough country the Adoo could slip through the tightest cordon, especially in the dark, and our only chance of success lay in driving them onto positions manned without their knowledge. That meant we had to go in on foot and by night, but as it turned out the plan took an entirely different shape to that which I had envisaged. The centre of gravity of the operation was moved far down the wadi to the west, and it looked as though it was going to be another old-style picquet and search operation. The revised scheme envisaged moving most of the picqueting force into position by helicopter, thus effectively signalling all our positions to the Adoo before the operation even started. Battalion headquarters was to be sited on a high point on the Jebel Aram overlooking the Wadi Ethon from its south side, and C Company was to concentrate at White City and march out overnight to occupy the high ground opposite. A company of Frontier Force would be moved up to look after our four bases whilst we were away. I went down to Arzat to find out why there had been such a drastic alteration to the plan, but when I asked him Douglas shrugged his shoulders and said that was the way the CO wanted it.

The military machine began to grind ponderously into action. The replacement company of Frontier Force rolled out along the Gatn road twenty-four hours before the operation was due to start, raising vast quantities of dust and a great deal of speculation amongst the tribespeople as to the reason for all this unwonted activity, and Harry and I gathered in our scattered platoons leaving skeleton garrisons to guard the other three bases. My task was to take Salim Musalim and a detachment of the Firqa Khalid Walid together with a platoon of C Company down one of the long tributary wadis of the Ethon which started not far from White

City, and block it against any enemy attempting to get out of the area once the operation got under way.

We marched out in the early hours of Sunday morning and by daylight we were ensconced in a rocky outcrop overlooking the top end of our wadi. Harry had left shortly after us and up to that point I had no contact with him, but as the spreading light of day illuminated the rolling expanse of grass and rock below us I swept the ground to the south with my binoculars and picked up a column of tiny, ant-like figures strung out and hurrying towards the prominent hill above the Ethon which Harry had chosen as his headquarters for the operation. He was engaged in the time-honoured SAF tradition of 'adjusting his position' by the light of day, and I chaffed him for it on the radio.

We climbed down an almost vertical slope into the wadi and for the first couple of hours the going was easy. By mid-morning however the sun was well up and the temperature in the airless chasm was rising rapidly towards 100 °F. The path which up to then had been smooth and wide now narrowed and ended abruptly in a rock cliff some thirty feet high. The only way round it was to move up the sheer sides of the wadi, an exhausting climb of 500 feet or so in the growing heat, to a narrow goat track which followed the side of the wadi, dropping down to its floor some way beyond the cliff. Once we found a way down we had to force our way through tangled thickets and fallen rock, and our progress slowed to a crawl. It was late afternoon before we reached another low cliff overlooking the Ethon waterhole a short distance from the junction with the main wadi, and we were all exhausted. A thousand feet or so above us Harry sat with his platoon on the picquet, and I reported to him by radio that we were in position and intended to halt there for the night. No-one had any water left, and I divided my little force into two so that they could take it in turns to visit the waterhole and drink.

In the harsh, crackling heat of the wadi bottom the waterhole seemed a paradise. The water sprang cool and clear from a small cave at the foot of the cliff where we had made our base and filled a couple of pools which had been constructed to provide separate drinking facilities for people and livestock. Cool green trees hung over the surface dappling its face with their reflections, and azure kingfishers and small birds of a vivid scarlet plumage flew in and out of their branches. There were fish in the pools and I wondered how they avoided being sucked up when the cows and camels came to drink. A few of us stripped and immersed our sore, sweaty bodies in the cool water, drinking and bathing at the same time, but the *firqa* scorned such frivolity, and sat around chattering. Cattle wandered in to drink, raising a low cloud of white dust from the flat trampled ground beneath the thorn trees.

For all their beauty, waterholes were treated with caution by both sides for they were natural meeting places and though the Adoo usually shunned them and sent civilian sympathisers down to collect water if they knew that SAF was in the area, there was always a chance of an accidental meeting if one side or the other arrived at the waterhole undetected. I therefore gave orders to set a watch and ring the water with Claymore mines in case unexpected visitors arrived during the night.

After we had drunk and filled our water bottles we made our way back to the cliff top and cooked the evening meal. Habib Ullah produced an unsavoury mess of heavily spiced mutton stew which I refused, and after checking the arrangements for the night I settled down to doze fitfully on the hard ground. I had given orders that the soldiers were not to take off their boots at night on operations, and at some time in the dead hours of the very early morning I told my signaller, Saleh Mohammed, to put his boots back on. The Baluch did not normally smell, but it had been a long hard day, and I knew by the rich aroma wafting across to me on the night air that he had taken off his boots the better to relax. Saleh, who was a prodigious sleeper even in the most nerve-racking situations, was aggrieved and not a little surprised that I should have detected his offence in the blackness under the trees.

Despite my weariness I hardly slept and several times in the night I went round checking the sentries, for by now I knew the Baluch would sleep if the Devil himself were prowling round and the *firqa* would certainly be taking their ease. We were up before the day, and as the sun rose over the rim of the wadi we moved out to begin searching. The method we adopted was to move slowly and systematically with a strong group on the wadi floor supporting smaller groups traversing the wadi sides searching the thousands of possible hiding places. There were innumerable small caves with soft sandy floors and a healthy snake population which caused most of the excitement over the next couple of days as we flogged back and forth. We were now well into spring, and on the hilltops the warm sun combined with a cool Jebel breeze made the task of picqueting a light one. But in the wadi bottoms that same sun was focussed onto us as if with a burning glass and we gasped under its hammer blows. By the middle of the second day I was weak from dehydration and lack of food, and every now and again, struggling along the steep ground from one cave to the next, I had to pause to let waves of nausea and dizziness pass. Search parties had reduced their equipment to the minimum of rifle, ammunition and one bottle of water, but the effort of climbing the sheer sides of the wadi became a grinding toil from which there seemed to be no escape.

At the end of the first day's search we made our way back to the waterhole and prepared the evening meal. I had eaten nothing for twenty-four hours so when another mess tin of warm tinned mutton laced with unground seeds of curry spice was thrust under my nose I forced a few spoonfuls down. My stomach began to protest immediately and within a few minutes I was retching painfully.

Harry kept us all amused during the early hours of the evening by coordinating an artillery and mortar shoot onto the western slopes of the wadi at nothing in particular and when he had finished playing we turned in for the night. I slept no better on the second night than I had on the first, and by the third morning of the operation I was beginning to feel distinctly jaded. My spirits were not raised by a rumour that a group of Adoo had slipped out of the wadi during the night past that part of the cordon manned by D Company. Even being able to say 'I told you so' did nothing to cheer me up.

The third day passed in much the same way and when we gathered in the evening by the waterhole all we had to show for three days of unremitting labour was a Soviet RPG-7 rocket launcher, some mouldering cases of medicines and a few old sacks of grain sent with love from the Peoples' Republic of China.

During the night the Shimaal began to blow and as dawn was breaking Harry greeted me with the cheerful news that we would not after all be lifted back to White City straight from the wadi floor opposite our waterhole. Because of the wind we would have to get onto the picquet opposite him, a climb of a thousand feet or more. We hauled ourselves to our feet and began the long climb, grumbling mightily in the cold, dusty gale plucking at us on the steep hillside.

We were greeted at White City by the news that a helicopter had come under fire as it was lifting off from one of the picquet positions on the Jebel Aram. First reports were confused, but a couple of hours later the details emerged. The Adoo watched helicopters taking out components of the force and concluded correctly that the operation was coming to an end. They selected their target with care, choosing a position surrounded by steep slopes and thick trees impossible to assist quickly and one of the last to be evacuated, so there were few other troops in the area. As the chopper rose across the steep sides of the wadi, a burst of AK-47 fire ripped up through its floor, wounding one of the pilots and fatally injuring the Omani loadmaster in the back. The other pilot immediately radioed for help and flew the damaged aircraft down the wadi and on to Arzat where it was met by another which had flown there on hearing of the contact. The wounded pilot was lifted out to the FST but in the rush no-one checked the back where the loadmaster lay dying of his wounds. By the time he was discovered and taken to the FST it was too late and not surprisingly the tragedy caused some bad feeling.

The gunners were not leaving White City until the next morning so despite Mansoor's undisguised annoyance at the unwonted interruption to his domestic routine, we entertained them to dinner. In typical SAF fashion the tension and weariness of the last few days was released in gales of wild laughter as we downed copious quantities of beer and regaled one another with anecdotes of the operation. To the casual observer we might have seemed callous in view of the mornings' events, but we were not; we grieved for every loss but we had our own lives to lead as well.

The evening's merriment palled somewhat when I went out to relieve myself in my private and carefully guarded loo, and discovered that most of the company that was in White City whilst we were away had found my secret place. They left their calling cards all over it.

Shortly before the Company moved out of the positions we had been occupying since December, a Land Rover pulled up outside my tin shack in White City with our latest arrival in Dhofar. A tall, slightly stooped officer with a shock of red hair climbed out and introduced himself. John Moody came out on secondment from the Queen's Royal Irish Hussars and like many cavalry officers had to be content with the role of an infantryman because of the limited number of jobs in the armoured car regiment. Now he was to spend a couple of days with us to get the feel of life on the Jebel before taking his place in one of the rifle companies. We had barely introduced ourselves when Saleh came up and announced that Harry wanted me on the radio. He had been told that an Adoo patrol was going to visit a waterhole near Ashinhaib that evening, he was going to take a patrol out to set an ambush and I was to bring the White City platoon down to provide a back-up. It was already late afternoon, so there was no time to spare. I quickly briefed the platoon commander, we piled into a Land Rover and a couple of trucks and bounced out of White City a few minutes later.

We met Harry on the track a mile or so east of Ashinhaib, got out of the trucks and followed him southwards through the head-high scrub as the sun was setting in a washed-out pale blue sky. We stopped after a mile or so whilst Harry went on down into the wadi below us. My platoon spread itself round in a defensive position and John and I settled down to wait. We talked about this and that in a low whisper and shortly the discovery that his parents lived only a mile or two from our house in Gloucestershire forged an immediate link between us. The night drew on and towards midnight Harry came back and announced that he was calling off the ambush.

At the end of March trucks arrived at our positions to move us all back to Arzat and we pulled out of White City for the last time. The drive through Ashinhaib and Medina al-San was long and tedious, and when we arrived at Ayn Arzat after a hair-raising ride down the precipitous track from Medina al-San I had to restrain my impatience whilst the soldiers stopped to pray alongside the *falaj*, which of course provided ample water for the prescribed ritual cleansing. We drove into Arzat shortly before dusk to be greeted by Harry at the gate. I climbed out and he shook me by the hand, grinning broadly. 'Congratulations, Sunray Callsign 3' he said. I was the new Company Commander of C Company of the Southern Regiment and it felt very good.

Chapter 6

Miscellany

When a company moved onto the hill for any length of time it took with it a small band of camp followers consisting of a barber, some civilian cooks and a steward to look after the officers. Just before he left for his Christmas leave in England Harry told me that he had arranged for Mansoor to go up to White City. 'He's a bloody old woman,' he said, 'but he hates working with the other members of the mess staff in Arzat, and he's a good cook.'

I only spent a few days in White City before going off to Medina al-San and then Hagaif, so it was a couple of months before I enjoyed the uninterrupted blessings of Mansoor's company, and I realised how accurate Harry's description of him was. Mansoor and I fought a year-long battle over the domestic arrangements in each part of the Jebel where we found ourselves. The nub of the problem was that Mansoor's horizons were as small as the little world he inhabited and he steadfastly refused to concede that I might be justified in asking for food and drink at times other than those laid down in an immutable daily schedule. When I arrived back in mid-morning from an all-night ambush, weary, prickly eyed and thirsty, he would produce a meal or a beer only under protest and sulk for the rest of the day. He invariably dressed in Army olive drab fatigues with his shirt tails hanging out, and I never saw him without his own peculiar style of gobbin hat. He had a mournful face and rarely smiled, which given his circumstances and the fact that he lived in constant terror of sudden death on the Jebel, was not surprising.

He had worked for a while in London where he insisted that he had been a waiter at the Dorchester, but I thought that it was more likely to have been a Lyon's Corner House, for his demeanour was not that which one immediately associates with the worldly denizens of that august establishment. Although he had seen something of the world and could speak English and one or two other languages quite well, he was a simple man with a childlike naivety which could be quite astonishing at times. He lived a very lonely life – being Pakistani the Baluch would have little to do with him. He despised them as illiterate country peasants whilst they regarded him as a womanish menial, and made him the constant butt of their robust ruderies. As a result I was the only person that he had much to do with, and he would talk to me endlessly, especially in the evenings when I sat down to eat my dinner. I usually let the harmless chatter flow over my head, grunting from time to time to assure him that I was still listening, but there were times when the sheer absurdity or hilarity of what he was saying broke through into my consciousness, and I would put down my knife and fork and give him my full attention. He loved to reminisce about his time in London and one evening he was telling me about a low drinking haunt that he occasionally visited somewhere in the southern suburbs. He described in graphic detail how a quarrel started between a very large Irishman and an equally large West Indian and developed into a free-for-all.

'So what did you do Mansoor?' I asked.

'Well sir, I was very afraid,' he replied in his precise, sing-song accent, 'so I ran into the ladies' lavatory and hid myself.'

I almost fell off my chair laughing, but poor Mansoor could see no joke at all and was most offended by my rude mirth.

In the evenings I would often wander round the position at dinner time and natter with my soldiers as they squatted on the ground in small, companionable groups reaching into a common dish of rice or chapatis and when I returned to get my own food Mansoor would chide me for demeaning myself by eating with 'those people'. After the third such rebuke I cruelly told him that their cooking was better than his which was both inaccurate and unjust, but I was goaded into anger by his contempt for the Baluch. In fact he was a most resourceful cook, and achieved wonders with the indifferent rations that I gave him and he guarded my pantry zealously, a somewhat unnecessary duty as no self-respecting Muslim would dream of taking food from the tainted store of an infidel.

Mansoor whiled away the long hours of his day in all sorts of ways. In White City he carefully hoarded all my empty beer cans and used them to decorate the low earth walls which he built around the inside of my tent to keep out the cold Jebel wind at night and he was most upset when the Shimaal blew and scattered them. Each can had a modest pinup girl on the back but despite my teasing, Mansoor kept them firmly turned to the tent wall so that only the manufacturer's labels were visible. When we arrived in Tawi Atair he planted some of the spice seeds that were issued to the soldiers but his garden fared no better than his beer cans, for as soon as the first green shoots appeared goats ate them. He knew I was interested in photography and one night in White City he produced a cheap, battered flashgun which he asked if I could repair, 'because you see sir, if you can repair it for me then I can buy a camera to go with it'. I was nonplussed by the bizarre ordering of his priorities, but I was feeling charitable that evening and I let him down gently by explaining that usually when that sort of thing went wrong it was necessary to buy a new one, and I offered to advise him when he finally made up his mind that he wanted a camera.

Mansoor looked after me well, but one day at Tawi Atair he overreached himself. It was late in the morning, I had been out all night pounding the Jebel and I wanted a beer. When I asked him for one he informed me that the bar was not open, whereupon I told him to pack his gear and get on the next plane out. It was a mistake and I never ate as well again, but pride would not allow me to admit it. Lalu the cook was one of the Company characters. He was as thin as a rake and his large brown eyes glittered with half suppressed madness above a thin beak of a nose. Like Mansoor he invariably dressed in olive green fatigues with the shirt tail hanging out and a cheap pair of plastic sandals (or 'chupplies' as the Pakistanis called them) on his feet, but he sometimes sported a red kerchief tied jauntily round his head which gave him a faintly piratical air. Every now and again he would cackle wildly in his cracked high voice at something that amused him and his greeting to me never varied. 'Hello, sahib,' he would shout, shrieking with laughter at some private thought which my presence always seemed to provoke. He worked at great speed and could produce hundreds of chapattis in a single afternoon but when I tried to copy the apparently effortless way in which he turned out all those identical flat cakes of dough, I finished with a sticky mess up to my elbows whilst Lalu howled with maniacal laughter.

Army rations were monotonous but adequate. The staples were rice and flour, and there was always tinned meat and fish and an endless supply of tomato puree in small tins which the soldiers used in curry. There was tea and condensed milk in tubes from West Germany and the Baluch would use these to make tea so thick and sweet that like cocoa a skin formed on it as it cooled. 'Genuine Scotch Shortbread' from 'The English Biscuit Factory, Cantonment Road, Poona' was also issued sparingly, and loved dearly by the soldiers who enjoyed anything sweet.

When the weather was good goats were supplied, live if possible, for meat quickly spoiled in the heat of summer, but when the rain and mist of the *Khareef* made air and road resupply impossible, we lived on tinned rations which after a month or so became very tedious. I was not entitled to soldiers' rations and I made do with a mixture of British Army tinned food which I obtained from BATT and the Royal Engineer Squadron in exchange for beer, supplemented with tinned or fresh food from the market in Salalah. At Tawi Atair we were also issued with raffia baskets of dates for the three donkeys which were kept there, but although the dates were perfectly edible they were such dreary fare that not even the sweet-toothed Baluch would bother with them.

Most of the ration stores on the Jebel were primitive affairs of corrugated sheeting with flat roofs and earth floors. They quickly became infested with rats which contaminated flour and rice and filled the place with a choking, musty smell. In badly supervised bases food would be taken from the front of the store leaving old supplies to moulder at the back and the heat in summer swelled and burst cans of food creating an indescribable mess.

Badgers could not resist the tubes of sugary condensed milk and when I had a purge on the food store shortly after taking over at White City, I found they had drilled neat holes in the bottom of dozens of tubes and sucked out the contents, leaving them perfectly rounded and only their lightness to betray the theft. One night there was a great commotion from the store where the soldiers had found a badger and being unwilling to see it tormented to death as it certainly would have been, I put on a heavy pair of wiring gloves and went in to see if I could evict it peacefully. After a lot of scrabbling about in dusty recesses at the back of the store I eventually cornered it. It was a large beast and as I reached out to lift it, it reared and snarled at me so fiercely that I recoiled instinctively. After a couple more tries I decided that it was not worth the trouble and we left the door open for it to depart in its own time. The next day we dug a trench round the store and filled it with large stones in an effort to keep out the badgers, but they rolled the stones aside without apparent effort.

Mines large and small were a constant threat to life and limb. A day or so before I left England Mike Rose, one of the KJ company commanders, had stepped on an anti-personnel mine outside Simba, losing a leg and almost dying before he reached the FST. Casualties of this sort were not uncommon, and when I visited the FST on my return from Northern Oman in March one of our soldiers had just been admitted after losing both legs to a mine near White City. It was standard practice that we never went into old sangars because the Adoo had a nasty habit of mining them, but the corporal had grown complacent and despite all his training did just that. But when I saw him in hospital no more than a couple of days after the incident he was sat up in a wheelchair, laughing and joking with his friends in a remarkable display of fortitude, especially when it is remembered that up to then a crippling wound had meant discharge and a life of beggary back in Baluchistan. The corporal was lucky, if that is the word to use, for John Gordon-Taylor had been at work on behalf of our soldiers, and he was sent to England to be fitted with new legs and rehabilitated at the Sultan's expense. When I next saw him in London he was transmuted into a sophisticated man about town in a three-piece pinstripe suit and he was discussing the latest West End show in faultless English.

The Adoo were also in the habit of mining roads and tracks, and four times vehicles detonated anti-tank mines in areas for which I was responsible. The mines they used were powerful Soviet TMNs and although the results could be horrific if a small vehicle such as a Land Rover caught the blast, some occupants of larger vehicles had lucky escapes. The first such incident I encountered was the mining of a water bowser on its way from White City to Jibjat, but although the mine removed a rear wheel from the heavily laden truck and dug a large crater in the ground, the driver escaped with no more than a bad case of ringing in the ears. The second incident, which took place close to the archaeological site at Sumharam, resulted in the death of the Government archaeologist and serious injury to others in the vehicle. The third attack involved me directly and it occurred just outside Taqah on the Mirbat road. I had overtaken an Aveling Barford heavy recovery vehicle belonging to the Royal Engineers on the way out of the town, and was halfway up towards the Darbat picquet when I heard the unmistakeable thump of a mine detonating. I looked back and in the distance I saw the Barford stopped and a large pall of brown smoke rising from it. We turned the Land Rover and raced back down the hill, bracing ourselves for nameless horrors, to find the young Sapper driver sitting gloomily by the side of the road, surveying an empty socket where the front wheel had been. The fact that we had been over the same stretch of narrow track a few minutes before in a much more vulnerable vehicle gave me a few moments of quiet thought.

The Adoo sometimes combined a mine with a small-arms attack, and I was subjected to a variation on this theme a few months later in my fourth mining incident. On another occasion a convoy of B Company took casualties on a steeply winding track when the rear wheel of one truck detonated a mine, hurling shrapnel and rock splinters across the narrow wadi and killing and injuring men travelling in another vehicle following behind. It was not easy to be philosophical about mines, nor did many people joke about them as they did about other aspects of the war. Mines had a nasty way of thoroughly mangling people without always killing them, and we all had friends who had been crippled that way. Some people never came to terms with the threat, and at least one officer was known to walk carefully in vehicle tracks even just outside the wire at Arzat, which turned out to be a sensible precaution when, in mid-1976, a truck full of Pakistani labourers hit a mine near Mamura, not a quarter of a mile from the barracks. The Adoo chose a spot where vehicles turning onto the Mamura road cut the corner and drove off the tarmac onto the sand; the position of the mine demonstrated an unnerving eye for detail and an original turn of thought. I never became as fatalistic as some people about mines and although there was little one could do to guard against the possibility of being blown into small pieces I always took a keen interest in the track ahead and scanned it for any sign that the surface had been disturbed. A full sweep every time a track was used was just not practical.

We all grew very fond of our 81-mm mortars. I spent many hours training my team until they were as good as any in the Province and I took care to practise my officers and NCOS in the gentle art of mortar fire control. Each company on the Jebel had a section of two and their accuracy, high trajectory and rapid rate of fire made them amongst the most effective weapons at our disposal. Sergeant Imam Din was in charge of my section and he took his job very seriously. It was standard practice to register any likely targets on arrival in a new area by shooting onto them, correcting the fall of shot and noting the elevation and direction of each task. If a particular target had to be engaged quickly, all that was necessary was to set the values for that target on the mortar dial sight, line up with an aiming post and fire. Registered targets could also be used as reference points and it was much easier for the mortars to make an adjustment from one of them than to engage a completely new target from scratch. The main aim of training, which was a continuous process, was to improve the speed and accuracy of response. Twenty-five metres was normally the smallest adjustment available, but by sharpening our pencils we managed to halve that, so that with a little practice we were able to drop bombs into the mouths of caves.

It was important to locate the mortar baseplates accurately on the map otherwise target coordinates were useless and whenever possible we would fix them by means of three bearings plotted on the map from known features. Imam Din was a good mortar man, but ignorant of this method so one day in Tawi Atair after we had moved the mortars I demonstrated the technique to him, plotting the lines on the map and ending with a triumphant 'So you see. Imam, if you plot the three back bearings, where the lines cross is where you have got to be.' *'Inshallah, Sahib,'* he said, 'If God wills it.'

Mortar fire control was not easy in Dhofar because steep hills and deep wadis made the fall of shot difficult to spot, so good teamwork between the controller who could actually see the target, the plotter who did the sums and the mortar teams who fed the tubes was essential. They had to work together until they knew almost instinctively what each was trying to achieve, and company commanders ignored this aspect of training at their peril. I remember listening on the radio to a company commander trying to adjust the fire of his mortars during a contact on the Jebel ash Shawr south of Tawi Atair. He gave the map coordinates of the target and ordered a ranging shot which fell into a deep wadi out of his vision. In an attempt to bring the next round into sight he ordered an adjustment which he thought would put it onto a hillside in front of him, but it merely resulted in another echoing bang somewhere in the same wadi. In desperation he ordered a massive adjustment which resulted in the third round falling in a completely unexpected place and lacking confidence in his man on the mortar line, he abandoned the effort with a despairing 'Oh, forget it, stop firing.'

Under Harry's tutelage I learned to use our mortars to the full, and we worked out a number of variations to cope with the particular problems we faced. We broke mortars down into man-packable loads and carried them into action on our backs, thus extending their radius of action. One night we even conned the *firqa* at White City into carrying a couple of bombs each, but one taste of the unaccustomed labour was enough to deter them from agreeing to anything so foolish again. We used white phosphorous bombs to register targets.

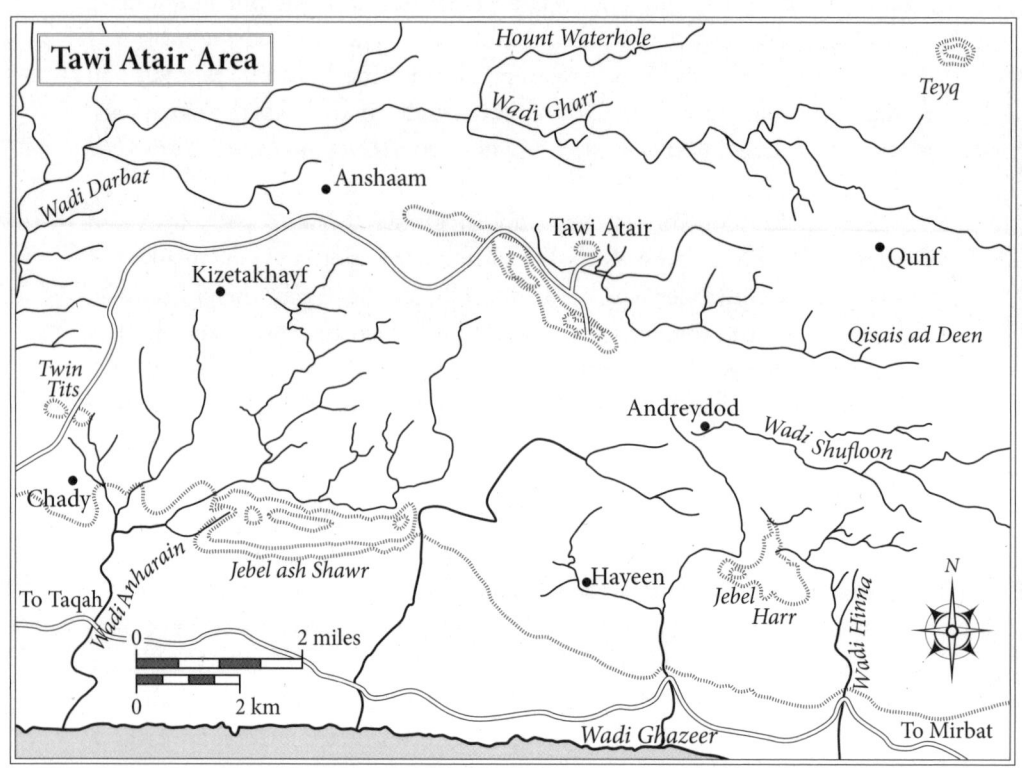

Chapter 7

The Darbat Picquet

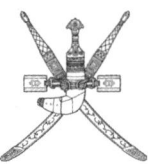

We were ordered to move to Tawi Atair and take over from B Company and in late March I flew across from White City to visit Geoff Ritson and David Bills and be briefed on the area. David was his usual avuncular self and when I asked him if there had been much activity in the area he waved a hand dismissively and said with a chuckle, 'No, none at all dear boy. We keep patrolling and move 'em along. That's the secret y'know, just keep 'em moving along.' It was typical of David's carefree attitude that he should treat the war like a neighbourhood bobby discussing the local villains.

David and Geoff lived in a fortress-like *murcha* about forty feet long by twenty wide built the year before by a Baluch company commander in Frontier Force. It stood about eight feet high and inside were two small rooms divided by a tiny entrance hall. The walls were a mixture of sandbags, stone and packed earth up to four feet thick in places and it was rumoured that a year's allocation of sandbags had been used in its construction. It was ventilated by narrow air shafts at head height which let in very little light so that even at midday it was dark and gloomy inside. A thick covering of sandbags and rock completed the building, which looked as though it would withstand a direct hit from a shell. Looking inside I noticed that they both had nets slung over their beds and I asked if mosquitoes were a problem. 'Oh no,' said David with another chuckle. 'We started using those when a rat fell on Geoff's face one night and bit him.' I shuddered.

The most striking feature at Tawi Atair was a great natural shaft in the rock from which a constant supply of good water was drawn. Situated in a hollow at the junction of a couple of small wadis, it was 200 feet across at its lip and perhaps 400 feet deep, a comparatively easy scramble down fallen rock and tangled vegetation for the first half of the way, but a sheer

Mobility at Tawi Atair. C Company had one Land Rover to resupply its various positions and ferry kit around.

drop the rest to an uneven, boulder-strewn floor. At one corner it was just possible to see the mouth of a cave but there was no hint of the deep underground lakes that lay within.

The company occupied the main ridge overlooking Tawi Atair from the south with a platoon on a smaller feature about a kilometre away to the north. There was a store and a small clinic near the well where the *firqa* were ensconced and the rest of the population lived in little groups of huts dotted around the position. At the wellhead cattle troughs and water tanks had been installed and water was raised by electric pumps through pipes dangling down the sheer sides of the shaft. On the other side of the main ridge from the well was a short dirt airstrip marked by a wrecked Caribou at one end and a derelict Skyvan at the other, mute testimony to the difficulty of approaching and landing at Tawi. Pilots relied on the slope at its eastern end to slow them on landing and give them a boost taking off and they always landed the same way regardless of wind direction.

When I arrived at Tawi there was no track out although one was promised and construction was due to begin shortly. A Land Rover and a small bulldozer had been airlifted in early on, but the dozer was now derelict and the Land Rover was on its last legs, beaten into a wreck by the rock-strewn tracks joining various parts of the settlement. Its sides hung over the back wheels and bounced up and down as the vehicle jolted its way round, and the day we finally pushed the track into Tawi they fell off altogether, leaving just the bonnet, driving compartment, transmission and axles.

Tawi occupied a good central position with the Wadi Darbat system to the west and north and the wooded peaks of Qisais ad Deen and the deep bowl of Tayq to the east. South-east lay the sprawling, meandering headwaters of the Wadi Shuffloon extending as far as the scarp above Mirbat, and to the south rolling downland stretched to twin clefts in the coastal hills where the Ghazeer and the Hinna cut through and plunged steeply to the coastal plain. To the south-west, folds of hills fell away in tiers mile after mile to the scarp by the Darbat Falls and, on a clear winter morning with the red sun low in the east, individual buildings could be distinguished fifty miles away in Salalah. The company commander at Tawi was responsible for perhaps 400 square miles of country, but no real limit had been set on his fiefdom to the east. It was a land of awesome grandeur and spectacular beauty and I fell in love with it at once and for ever.

Underfoot the going varied from gently undulating pastures to stony, ankle-breaking wasteland where the rocks were set so close together on the unyielding ground that it was impossible to put a foot evenly between them. There were sheer slopes that would make the fittest man gasp for breath, and narrow, steep-sided wadis choked with vegetation so tangled that movement across or along them was all but impossible. There were dry, yellow tracts along the Gatn without so much as a blade of grass or a leaf, and there were verdant waterholes hung with willow and edged with lush reeds and grasses. The enormous blue vault of the sky arched over boundless vistas and on patrol I would often make an excuse to stop and gaze, lost in contemplation of them.

It was an area of rich grassland jealously guarded by the al-Amri tribe who grazed large herds of cattle, goats and camels, bringing them into Tawi to water each day at the well. In spite of the richness of their tribal lands the al-Amri were a notoriously awkward and truculent people and it took me a long time and a good deal of patience before I gained any degree of trust amongst them. My difficulties were compounded by the fact that the local *firqa*, who took the tribal name, were dominated by outsiders, and this caused much grief before it was resolved.

Taylor Woodrow had been asked to drive a track through to Tawi, starting on the coast near Taqah, and by early April they had established a base camp just outside the town and were making a start on the approach to the bottom of the scarp east of the Darbat Falls. The Adoo were still active in and around the Darbat, as I had discovered during my time at White City, and it was therefore decided that the Tawi Atair company would be responsible for manning a strong picquet of two platoons above the Falls, which would also patrol the area and protect the road-building party. Driving the road up the steep scarp would be a long job and it was estimated that the picquet would need to remain in place for at least a couple of months. It seemed a likely trouble spot so I decided to go there for the first few weeks with half the company and send John Moody, who by this time had been appointed second-in-command, with the other half to Tawi. John was to take over first from David Bills at Tawi Atair and I was to go straight to the picquet a day or two later and take over from Geoff Ritson. I drove up a couple of days beforehand to talk to him and see the position for myself.

The picquet occupied a ring of small knolls overlooking the Falls and sangars were sited so as to cover the approaches to the position and afford observation over the Darbat. To the north and about 2,000 yards away there was a pair of low hills which inevitably became known as Twin Tits, and to the east the open ground led down to steep wooded valleys dividing it from the Jebel ash Shawr. To the south the scarp fell away steeply towards the coastal plain, its slopes also thickly covered in grey trees and criss-crossed with cattle tracks leading down into the wadi.

It was now getting very hot by day, and on the picquet there was little shelter from the sun. In the open sangars soldiers broiled like sausages in a frying pan, and I decided straight away that we would bring some tents and put them up in the dead ground in the middle of the position. The sangars could be manned on a sentry basis by day and quickly occupied in the event of trouble. I spent most of the morning with Geoff and drove back to Arzat to enjoy the last few days of comparative civilisation.

We did not think that the Adoo would sit idly by whilst we went ahead with a road which was bound to circumscribe their activity still further, and they could hardly be expected to ignore the challenge which a strong picquet looking down into the very heart of the Darbat represented. They were slow to react at first, but as the days went by incidents began to build up and for a while the Darbat picquet became the main trouble spot in Dhofar, temporarily eclipsing even beleaguered Simba on the border. The day before we were due to relieve him Geoff bumped an

Adoo patrol on the scarp below the picquet. Both leaders fired, Geoff was hit in the leg and brought down and the Adoo fled. Back at Arzat the news was received with dismay, not least by me, and I remember the palms of my hands suddenly going sticky as I heard what had happened. The Quartermaster, a sour Scot, remarked lugubriously that he had done the sums and he reckoned that British officers serving on the Jebel had taken 30 per cent casualties since Christmas. No doubt he reached the figure by means of some fairly selective calculations, for Geoff was only the eleventh casualty in that category so far, but the thought hardly cheered me up and I wondered if I would be next for the chop. People did seem to be dropping all around.

I went to see Geoff that afternoon at the FST and tried to get an account of what had happened but he was dozy from the morphine and probably still in shock, so I stayed with him for a while making small talk and then left.

13 April 1975

I decided to reinforce the picquet with my section of mortars and, after giving orders for them to join me there without delay, I went next day to the Darbat and took over from David Bills who had come down from Tawi after Geoff had been hit. David was totally unruffled by what had happened and set off down the hill with a cheery wave. It was the day before my thirty-third birthday.

We received a salvo of small-arms fire on the first afternoon from the area of Twin Tits, and it was provoked by a tent which had foolishly been erected just on the edge of the dead ground. We established the routine of stand-to each morning and evening and it was as well that we did so for the Adoo began to snipe at us with obliging regularity at those times and we were usually well prepared to respond. We quickly registered all likely enemy firing positions, approach and escape routes with the mortars and at stand to I practised the officers and NCOs in controlling them. It was also a valuable map-reading exercise as one by one we fixed all the prominent peaks and wadis around and I remember one evening arriving at a sangar where Ibrahim and his section were on duty. I jumped into the sangar, told Ibrahim that we were going to play with the mortars and asked him to get his map out. Reaching into his shirt he pulled out an enormous roll that seemed to go on and on like a conjuring trick until he had all the maps covering the entire province of Dhofar laid out in the dust, stuck together as one sheet. Before that evening I thought he was a thickset man, but now I saw that he was quite thin.

I assumed that the Adoo would be observing our mortar practice and would not be so foolish as to choose one of our registered targets as a firing point, but one night they did just that. I was making my way across dead ground to visit the northern positions when a storm of firing broke out from that direction. I broke into a run and scrambled up a short slope until I was just below the crest and paused for a second. Between me and the sangar under fire lay 200 yards of open ground and there was an awful lot of shooting going on out there. It flashed across my mind that if I hesitated any longer I would never move, so I counted to three, jumped to my feet and flung myself down the slope, jinking madly and leaping over the wall of the sangar to land in a tangle of arms and legs amongst its occupants. Despite the fact that one of them had been slightly wounded and was bleeding profusely from a nick in his earlobe, the soldiers were much amused by my undignified arrival, and quickly pointed out the Adoo position. I checked on the map and saw to my astonishment that it was right under one of the black crosses of a fire mission. I knew Imam Din would be standing by on the mortar line and I ordered ten rounds rapid on the target.

Behind us the mortars began to thump and after a short pause the first rounds began to land, right on target. I was delighted and gleefully ordered another ten for good measure, then tried to work out which way the enemy would run. He would be moving or dead by now, and I began to adjust the mortars to follow a supposed withdrawal route down a small side wadi behind the firing position into the Darbat itself. By the fourth salvo, his predicted track put him in a position which meant that the mortars were shooting over our heads down into the main wadi, and I ordered a final ten rounds to finish off. It was almost completely dark as the mortars began to thump again behind us, and the first round crashed into the wadi below. The next came whistling down at us out of the darkness, and we flattened ourselves on the ground as it exploded ten yards away from the sangar. With eight rounds still in the air, the next minute or so was a nightmare in which we waited helplessly to die, but as we held our collective breath, the remaining rounds dutifully dropped into the wadi. I was furious with Imam and lost no time in getting back to the mortar line to tell him so. In the excitement a mortar-man had taken off one tail-fin charge ring too many from a bomb, reducing its range by a thousand metres, which just happened to be exactly the distance from our sangar to the target.

Early the next morning I led a patrol out to see if there were any clues as to what had happened, but though we climbed down the steep wadi into the Darbat itself, we could find no trace of the enemy. I was disappointed but not surprised. As soon as the mortars started the Adoo would have taken off if he had any sense, but I liked to think that the surprise and accuracy of our response at least gave him a fright, because for the next few days things were a little quieter.

We had been further reinforced by the arrival of three Saladin armoured cars under the command of an imperturbable Staff Sergeant by the name of 'Whimpy' Waite. He was an experienced Dhofar hand on his second tour and loving every minute of it, and he was a valuable subordinate to whom I could entrust independent tasks. He was also a pleasant companion, and it was good to have someone of my own race to gossip with in the evenings. Shortly after he arrived I decided that we would use a couple of his cars to scout a route across to Tawi Atair, and taking my signaller Saleh Mohammed and a couple of other soldiers we set off across the rocky terrain. We climbed Twin Tits cautiously and crossed rising ground, passing small circular fields where the stones had been cleared for planting. We skirted the heads of side wadis, following the general line of the Darbat north until we came to the great bend as it turns eastwards, where we stopped to look out over the tumbled, broken ground towards Faiqaitha where we fought the futile engagement in February.

As we turned eastwards the ground dropped gently towards a small group of huts called Anshaam, huddled on the edge of the wadi and apparently deserted. On the other side of the huts were several quite large circular fields surrounded by walls about four feet high and on our side, a pan of black rock stretching away to the lip of the wadi, its surface pitted, razor edged and quite impassable even to Whimpy's six-wheeled monsters with their huge thick tyres. The easiest route lay between two of the walled fields and as we twisted through the narrow gap I remember thinking what good opportunities for ambush the area offered. It was a prophetic thought.

The last stage of the journey into Tawi was quite difficult and the cars took a long time to get over some of the rock ledges barring the shortest route into the position as they stepped up and down, their suspension stretched almost to the limit to cope with the uneven surface. Later, when the final route was decided on we were forced to make a detour round the northern end of the western picquet, as the rocks on its south side proved to be beyond ordinary wheeled traffic.

John was expecting us and it was good to see him again. Even Mansoor looked pleased to see us and he produced an excellent lunch.

We drank some wine and chatted in the warm sun but at about two o'clock I regretfully told John that we would have to go. We mounted up, easing our bruised buttocks back onto the engine plates and set off in good spirits. Knowing the way, we made better speed, but as we approached Anshaam, I had a sudden premonition that we were heading for trouble and I hauled myself up to speak to Whimpy. He was wearing headphones and was preoccupied with the business of commanding his car and it took a moment to get his attention, but as I did so, I saw a young lad run across the open space between the huts and I gestured towards him, yelling at Whimpy to watch out. A second later a fusillade of shots cracked over our heads from the other side of the rock patch, followed by a thunderous bang and a cloud of dust as a Soviet RPG rocket whizzed over us and exploded a few yards away. I slid down to a sitting position, thumbing off the catch of my FN and loosing off a magazine in short order at the firing point and as I was changing magazines the main armament swung round and let fly next to my ear. The world went silent for a second and then my head began to ring. Not wishing to wait around until the next rocket brewed up a car, we scrambled off the Saladins, spread out along our side of the rocks and began a vigorous fire. The cars sensibly carried on along the track distancing themselves from the RPG gunner and after a few moments the enemy fire stopped. With only four men there was little I could do by way of a follow-up so we got up and trotted after the cars.

Once again the enemy had shown ingenuity in marking our passage and selecting the one place where there was not only an excellent escape route into the wadi, but also a natural barrier that would effectively prevent armoured cars from attacking the ambush position. After we had recovered from our excitement Whimpy and I drove home in thoughtful silence. Winston Churchill wrote that there is nothing so exhilarating as being shot at without result, and back at the picquet, sitting on a rock with a mug of tea in my hand, it was a point of view which I could understand but not entirely endorse. Later we learned that one of the enemy involved in the ambush had been shot in the arm and leg and with all that ordnance flying about the news hardly came as a surprise. I had fired off the first shots in reply so I awarded myself a credit for the blooding.

The Gunner battery at Taqah lived in a splendid *Beau Geste*-style fort on a slight rise overlooking the town and I regularly sent down parties of soldiers to get a wash and a break from the heat and discomfort of life on the picquet. The officers had taken over the upper storeys of the tower and the seaward-facing windows caught the breeze which together with thick stone walls ensured that the building was always deliciously cool even on the hottest days. There were breathtaking views along the coast and across the green palm plantation at the edge of town and only a sense of duty kept me from going there more than twice a week. The gun-lines occupied a flat, arid square of ground on the other side of town with a washdown next to the tented cookhouse which consisted of a couple of large plastic drums (burmails) of water and a flat piece of rock to stand on. Arabs and Baluch are notoriously prudish about nakedness, but on my first visit I ignored the incredulous stares of the cooks, stripped in the hot sun and washed off the caked sweat and dust of three days, revelling in the feeling of being clean for a change. After a couple of visits the cooks got used to this odd habit of mine.

After one such visit we drove back up to the picquet and arrived in the midst of a scene of frenetic activity. The mortars were banging away and sporadic automatic fire was still coming from sangars on the west side of the position. I hurried over to Company HQ to be told that the enemy had mounted a stand-off small-arms attack on the picquet and mortared the Taylor Woodrow camp outside Taqah, whilst we ground our way up the hill through it all in blissful ignorance. There were no casualties, but there were a lot of frightened Pakistanis who for a few hours refused to have anything more to do with the Tawi Atair road. When they were told that flights home were being booked for them, they hurriedly changed their minds and work on the road resumed without further ado. Being an immigrant labourer anywhere in the Middle East was no fun, but the Pakistani labourers in Dhofar at that time bore an especially heavy cross, and I felt sorry for them.

Towards the end of April John brought the other two platoons down to the picquet and a day or two later, reinforced by D Company, we launched another great KJ operation to sort out the Adoo, as we liked to put it, in the Darbat. Once again it was impossible to camouflage our preparations as a host of extra people and equipment arrived on the picquet the night before we were due to start. John Gordon-Taylor had gone on holiday leaving Douglas McCully in charge and Douglas was a man who liked doing things in style. Late in the afternoon I was astounded to see Officers' Mess staff in their whites unloading tables, chairs, glasses and bottles and all the paraphernalia of a Mess outing from a truck which had just arrived. It offended my military instincts deeply, but Douglas meant well and I could hardly skulk like Achilles in his tent, so I dined in more style that night than for the previous two or three weeks. Douglas had already shown himself a generous and thoughtful man by looking up the date of my birthday and arriving below the picquet early on the day with a bottle of champagne for me. I was touched by the gesture and, though I sometimes disagreed with his methods, I could not fault his style.

The next day was a considerable trial for it was now very hot, especially lower down in the wadi. D Company trudged up and down the spurs and valleys across the Darbat whilst John and I did the same on our side. I was fairly fit but by late afternoon I was feeling very weary indeed. That night we were tasked to go down into the Darbat and occupy the picquet which bisected the Falls in order to deny it to the Adoo so that operations in the wadi could continue without hindrance the next day. We scrambled down a steep wooded slope for the umpteenth time, stirring up clouds of choking red dust, and plodded across derelict fields which even at that late hour simmered in the baking, airless heat. From time to time I had to stop to fight off waves of dizziness and nausea, and it was a blessed relief when we eventually scrambled to the top of the picquet and could rest for a while. It was a quiet night, but the stony ground offered no comfort and I hardly slept despite my fatigue. Next morning we climbed out of the wadi and started again, but in the middle of the afternoon Douglas decided that the Adoo were not going to respond and the operation was brought to an end without so much as a shot being fired.

29 April 1975

A few days later the two halves of the company changed over and I went up to Tawi Atair. Much as I was looking forward to going home on leave, the *Khareef* was approaching and there was work to do in preparation for it. One glance into the ration store was enough to convince me that the first priority was a sort out there and I gave orders to start on it right away. Ration stores were always a problem on the Jebel and the one at Tawi was older and in a worse state than most. In typical lackadaisical Baluch fashion the rations nearest the door had been turned over regularly because it was less effort to get at them, whilst those at the back provided a musty, mouldering home to every gnawing, champing, scurrying pest imaginable. Rotting, mildewed and infested, the store would have given a sanitary inspector in England a heart attack but in Dhofar it was a normal part of life.

I told Hajji Bilal to get the store cleared out completely so that we could take stock and start again and went off to attend to some other matter. In the hot morning sun the Baluch worked away hauling out sacks and cartons in ever increasing clouds of pungent dust. The pile of contaminated food grew higher – stained rice, gnawed and rotten tubes of sticky brown condensed milk, mildewed and crushed biscuits and tins of meat and fish swollen with the gaseous decay of their contents. At about nine we were due to stop for breakfast and I was just about to sit down to mine when the soldiers began shouting excitedly and rushing about as they always did when they had some wretched animal trapped. Hajji Bilal came running up to summon me to see the catch and reluctantly I followed him to the store. He lifted the lid of a pristine new plastic dustbin issued for the storage of rice and flour to reveal a mass of rats and mice of all sizes struggling to get out and I turned hurriedly away, trying not to shudder at the sight and fell everyone out to breakfast which, no doubt, they heartily enjoyed. For myself, the thought of what I had seen took the edge off my appetite and I wondered how on earth we were going to dispose of them. Wild mental pictures of machine gunning the dustbin or even perhaps setting off a Claymore mine next to it rose in my imagination, and I giggled hysterically at the thought. I had in fact almost decided on the latter course of action when I went back to the store about half an hour later, but the sun delivered me of the nightmare. Hajji had put a plank of wood over the bin to prevent a mass escape whilst he was away at breakfast and in a sort of rodent Black Hole of Calcutta the rats and mice had perished of suffocation. I felt a momentary twinge of guilt over the animals' suffering, quelled it, and told Hajji to get rid of the Satanic burden. I have no doubt that despite my instructions the bin found honourable employment again as a food container.

With little idea of what to expect from the *Khareef* I made what arrangements I could and in the middle of May departed joyfully on my first leave.

Leave was an anticlimax, as it almost always is in such circumstances. In the imagination it builds up into an impossible month of unalloyed bliss and contentment which is never fulfilled. In our dreams our wives or girlfriends waited us with open arms and never a word of complaint about the bleak months of loneliness, the children behaved like angels and suspended their normal patterns of bloody-minded behaviour just for us, it never rained and every pint of English ale was nectar. In reality the tensions which built up over long months of separation began to corrode the atmosphere almost as soon as the first ecstatic greetings were over, and the let-down when it came was all the harder to bear for its unexpectedness. Not until my last leave from Dhofar was I able to discipline myself and not think about it too much in advance. I therefore went home without inflated expectations and as a result it was a good deal more tranquil and satisfying than the others had been.

There was a lot of work to be done on that first leave, and the weather was glorious from start to finish. Deeply tanned from months of Arabian sun, I worked twelve hours a day in nothing more than a ragged pair of cut-off SAF shorts and turned-down wellingtons, demolishing useless old structures in the garden, clearing tons of builders' rubble which had been buried under a few inches of topsoil, concreting pathways and generally tidying up. I quickly got to know the neighbours, who had moved in after I left for Oman the previous November, and earned the dubious accolade of 'Army? More like bloody Dad's Army if you ask me!' from discussion with the landlord of the local pub after he had seen me a few times in the village, with my long hair bleached by the sun and grubby from toil. The days flashed by and suddenly we were counting off the last few and the prospect of parting again loomed larger and larger like a storm-cloud threatening a bright summer afternoon. Our last day together came and went and then we were going through the melancholy ritual of goodbyes at the airport. I embraced Carol and the boys, walked through the gate, numb with misery, and sat down to await departure time. Most of the rest of the passengers on that flight must have been feeling much the same way and the stewardesses of Gulf Air, with an unspoken understanding rare in airlines for all their advertising jingles, instinctively knew the answer. They plied us with alcohol until we slumped in a daze, our pain anaesthetised for a few hours.

Chapter 8

Tawi Atair: June–August 1975

As usual the plane was invaded at Bahrain by a horde of Arabs making their way down the Gulf, but the wine had flowed freely the previous evening and despite the noise most of us slept on. Over the Batinah Coast a nasty brown smog filtered the fierce summer sun so that it glinted pale greyish yellow on the tin roofs of the hangars at Seeb.

It was good to get back to Dhofar and KJ. I arrived at the Mess just before lunch and Dinn, our Goanese steward, greeted me with a special brandy and sour, handing it across the bar with one of his quiet smiles. The skies were now heavily overcast with the approaching monsoon and there was no relief from the heat and humidity by day or night, but even so it was cooler than Northern Oman. I could not afford to wait around in Arzat for long because the weather was closing in and any day communications with the hill positions might be cut. Once it started raining, the dirt tracks would become impassable and there would be no more flights into Tawi Atair. Wheeled vehicles would only be able to get as far as the Darbat Falls under those conditions and from there it was a long walk. The next resupply might be several weeks hence and I did not want to carry home comforts all the way to Tawi Atair on my back.

Shortly after I returned Gordon-Taylor told me that he had transferred John Moody to B Company and replaced him as my second-in-command with a large, aggressive Australian mercenary by the name of Peter Harris. Harris had served with the Australian Army in Vietnam and not long after arriving he let us know in no uncertain terms that in comparison with South East Asia, he considered the Dhofar war to be a piddling sideshow. He had a point, but it was our war and we were secretly rather proud of our part in it. I patiently explained several times to him that if we died, it made no difference whether we were killed by the Vietcong or the Adoo, but I might as well have saved my breath. Harris affected all kinds of exotic gear, from mine-proofed US Army boots to a mixture of leather and canvas web equipment and he was quickly dubbed Vietnam Pete by the rest of us. I was relieved to hear that he was not to be my 2iC for long because I suspected that he and I would have difficulty in working together. In the event he was transferred to another job in the Battalion after a few weeks with C Company.

The arbitrary changes that Gordon-Taylor had made were irritating, but I counted myself lucky that he had not given the company to someone else in my absence, which he was perfectly capable of doing. He had an alarming tendency to act on the last suggestion made to him, particularly if it came from one of his mercenary cronies and my absence in England was a good opportunity to rearrange matters and put in a company commander more attuned to his way of thinking. I was relieved and not a little surprised that he did not take it.

19 June 1975

Giving Harris the job of supervising the platoon that had been left in Mirbat, I joined a convoy up to Tawi Atair and arrived just as the first rain of the *Khareef* began to fall. Within a few hours we were effectively cut off from the world.

I was unprepared for the devastation that one month of neglect had wrought in the living quarters and more importantly, in the kitchen. A few scraps of food mouldered in the kerosene fridge which was silent and warm and cockroaches scuttled over the floor of the little shack, which had clearly not been used or cleaned for weeks. The tinned food I had carefully collected and stored for the *Khareef* had all gone, eaten by casual visitors, and there was no sign of Mansoor. I was not entitled to share the soldiers' food and I had already decided that I would be independent as long as possible during the wet season. The chances of achieving that depended upon efficient domestic arrangements and the sight of the kitchen was not encouraging. I dropped my kit in one of the two small cubbyholes that served as bedrooms and took a closer look around. Whilst I had been away the soldiers had been hard at work waterproofing *murchas* by spreading large, expensive sheets of heavy-duty black plastic over them which they weighted down with sharp edged stones, thereby puncturing them in a number of places and rendering them quite useless. For a moment I was seized with black rage at their stupidity then I breathed deeply, collected myself and called Ahmed Dur Mohammed, the acting sergeant major, to accompany me on a tour of the position.

It was soon clear that I had made a major mistake in going off on leave just before the *Khareef*. In the absence of a British officer almost nothing had been done to prepare for the wet weather although the Baluch officers and NCOs knew better than we did what to expect. The stockpile of rice, flour, tinned goods and ammunition which had been flown in to last us through the next two months or so lay in the open where it had been dropped and no attempt had been made to get it under cover. The black plastic which could have made us snug and watertight had almost all been ruined by careless handling and despite my orders, no new building had taken place. Before I went back to England I managed to scrounge a small stock of building materials with which to concrete the floors of the ration huts and it had been delivered whilst I was away, but nothing had been done, and now we would have to work fast before the rain turned the bags of cement into just another rock on the hillside.

Very discouraged, I went back to my *murcha* to unpack my kit and think out how best we could get things ready in the time that was left. I stooped to enter the gloomy, cramped hut and saw a figure huddled in a corner reading. He looked up from his book, introduced himself as Adam Malik, the new Regimental Medical Officer, and apologised for not being there to greet me when I arrived. He explained that he had been sent up to Tawi Atair to look after us until Brian Spice, the senior non-commissioned medical orderly in the regiment, returned from leave in a couple of weeks' time.

Many of the MOs in SAF were on secondment from the Indian Army but unlike us, they were not volunteers and they did a three-year tour. I quickly discovered that Malik was the gently nurtured son of a wealthy Indian Army family in Delhi and ill-equipped by disposition or upbringing to cope with the squalor of life in a place like Tawi. He was very dejected and apathetic and had done nothing to improve his living conditions but I made no comment. He turned out to be a charming companion once he had conquered his depression and I was glad of his company. I had a small chess board and asked him if he could play. He said no, but he was willing to learn, and in a short time he was beating me so consistently that I grew bored with the game.

I started cleaning up the kitchen and the *murcha* with the doubtful aid of my new Baluch orderly, Habib Ullah. Habib spoke not a word of English or Arabic and neither was he blessed with the quickest of intellects, so for a long time my efforts to communicate with him met with total failure. But he was tough, cheerful and a natural soldier and despite occasional lapses we got on well together. He stayed with me until the end of my time in Dhofar.

20 June 1975

The next morning was the first of many such during the *Khareef*. The harsh bright sunlight which had wakened us every morning until now was gone and in its a place a thin, milky light filtered through dripping mist and penetrated all our possessions, spreading black mould onto beds, furniture and clothing. They became damp and stayed that way for almost three months.

I decided to visit the northern picquet on the other side of Tawi Atair and set off in our battered Land Rover. Already the tracks had turned to strips of greasy mud, but going downhill towards the well was no problem. Once we rounded the cattle troughs and tried to climb the picquet, however, the vehicle skidded itself to a halt and slid gently sideways until it was securely impaled on a couple of large rocks. It took most of the rest of the morning to get it off and by the time we had done so, we were covered in mud from head to foot. The simple matter of supplying 12 Platoon, who were less than a mile from Company Headquarters, remained a headache throughout the *Khareef*, and in the end we resorted to man-packing rice and flour across the low ground.

I was worried about the enemy infiltrating our scattered positions in the poor visibility and we set up a number of barbed-wire obstacles across the more likely approaches. I debated whether to mount roving patrols to cover the gaps at night, but knowing the propensity of the Baluch and the *firqa* for blasting away at anything that moved after dark, I decided that they would be at some risk from our own sentries and I therefore discarded the idea. As things turned out, I overestimated the enemy's boldness and to my knowledge the Adoo never approached closer than a thousand yards or so to Tawi during the *Khareef*.

My first really unpleasant surprise was the decaying latrine left by my predecessors. It consisted of an oil drum sunk into the ground, capped by a wooden thunder-box and surrounded by a sagging privacy screen made of rotting tentage. The state of the thunder-box defied description and it seemed that every scorpion in Dhofar had made its home in the voluminous folds of the screen. Imagination unmanned me and in the urgency of the moment no sure protection against the scorpions could be devised, so I took a shovel from the colour sergeant's stores and clutching my rifle, withdrew into the privacy of the mist to crouch soaked and cheerless in the wet, gradually sinking into the soil which by

TAWI ATAIR: JUNE–AUGUST 1975

C Company medic Brian Spice, CSM Bilal, and *firqa* soldiers,
Tawi Atair, post-*Khareef* 1975.

now had turned into a soft, glutinous chocolate pudding. Ah, the joys of soldiering!

Whilst I was coming to terms with mundane problems presented by the wet weather, I was also turning over a more serious plan of action and I came to the conclusion that we had to push forward two projects simultaneously. First, we had to dispel any notion in the minds of the Adoo, the *firqa* and ourselves that the *Khareef* was a time for skulking miserably in our shelters waiting for the dry weather to return. In many places it had been so in the past and until quite recently SAF had been in the habit of withdrawing from some of the hill positions altogether in the wet season, with the inevitable result that much of the previous year's work was lost. It was no way to gain the confidence of the hill people and I saw no reason why the Adoo should be allowed a holiday in my area. Second, we had to use our building materials quickly to make improvements to our living conditions. In particular, we had to make the ration huts as waterproof and rat-proof as possible and construct some firm paths, for even the shortest walk was already becoming a muddy slog. I also had fight against a creeping lethargy in myself and the soldiers induced by the warm humidity and the sheer difficulty of achieving anything in this dripping, turbid world.

We laid out concrete paths and floors in the ration huts and we spread our remaining black plastic over them, using sandbags to channel the rain water into some sort of runoff. The roofs had been laid flat when the huts were built and the weight of water that had fallen the previous year had bent them into a trough so that rainwater collected and squirted under pressure through leaks onto the stores below. I spent many hours in the teeming rain shifting sandbags this way and that, but it was never entirely successful, and in the end we were forced to move stores out of the way of the worst leaks. In an attempt to dry some of our wet belongings and preserve the perishable items of food I had paraffin heaters lit in one of the stores, but the subtle maintenance they required was beyond the Baluch and one by one they went unserviceable.

Visibility was rarely more than a few yards, so when we went out on patrol we had to rely on the compass and I spent many hours practising my NCOs in its use. I employed the *firqa* as guides, but from time to time I liked to go on patrol without them. It was not that I wanted to exclude them as a matter of policy – on the contrary, I made a point of working hard to improve our relationship – but I knew that to get the best out of them, we would have to be seen to be capable of operating independently. Besides, it made a nice change to go for a walk once in a while without having to justify every decision and argue endlessly all day. An equally important factor was that the *firqa* leader and his deputy had both found solid reasons to be in Salalah when the *Khareef* broke, leaving command of the *firqa* to the third in line, Mohammed Daan. Mohammed was a nice man, but a hopeless leader incapable of controlling the unruly tribesmen. Not only was he timid, but he suffered from the crippling disadvantage of being from a tribe other than the al-Amri. His boss, a murderous tyrant by the name of Ahmed Sayyid could overcome the handicap for a while by sheer force of personality, but it defeated even him in the end and caused endless trouble in the process.

I soon realised that Mohammed Daan was a reliable guide to the activities of the Adoo. If I suggested that we visited a particular village or waterhole and he readily agreed, saying that we were sure to find Adoo there, I knew we were probably wasting our time. If, on the other hand, he was reluctant to visit an area there was a fair chance that we would contact the Adoo if we went. Mohammed had a healthy regard for his own safety.

Operating in the *Khareef* was not as bad as I thought it would be. For the first couple of weeks the going was very hard because the mud clung to our boots and weighed us down, but after a while grass began to cover the bare earth and walking became much easier. The Baluch had a simple answer to the mud – they took off their boots and slung them round their necks, going barefoot. Suleiman was about five foot three and very squat and the rear view of him striding purposefully across the Jebel, boots round his neck, trousers rolled up above the knee and thick, brown calves pumping along plastered in mud is a memory I will always treasure. Insects proliferated but were mostly harmless, the exception being hordes of small black flies which bit mercilessly through the fabric of our shirts and trousers. On patrol they settled on us as thickly as a blanket, but after a while we grew accustomed to them. The *Jebalis* were plagued by flies which bred in the rich broth of liquid cattle manure around their huts and settled everywhere in swarms, but our base was some distance from the cattle so we were less troubled by them.

We accepted that we would be soaked to the skin within minutes of starting a patrol and as long as we kept moving it was no problem. But when we were forced to sit around waiting for any length of time the rain and mist became irksome and if the wind was blowing it quickly chilled us to the bone. At night the combination of darkness, fog and difficult going underfoot made progress very slow and navigation had to be exact. One night it was so dark that I could not see my hand even when I brought it to the tip of my nose and only after an hour or so did my vision improve sufficiently to see a couple of feet in the blackness. It was then that we discovered all the sharp edged rocks on our way and they all seemed to be at shin height.

6 July 1975

After two and a half weeks there was a break in the weather and for a while we enjoyed blue skies and welcome sunshine. Morale shot up as we spread our damp belongings out to dry and drew up lists of necessities for the next convoy. We had discovered all sorts of small items that we needed, not least some spares and a mechanic to sort out the generator which had failed on the second night of the *Khareef*. The Baluch were not good at looking after anything as delicate as hurricane lamps and over the next few weeks we gradually lost the battle to maintain a civilised lighting system at night.

9 July 1975

Considering what a quagmire the tracks had become it was astonishing how quickly the sun dried them out. Within twenty-four hours we were able to take the Land Rover across to the north picquet with supplies and after three days a convoy rolled into Tawi Atair with all sorts of goodies on board. There was some very welcome mail from England and Baluchistan, a resupply of whisky and after heart-rending pleas from me to Sher Mohammed the Quartermaster on the radio, some more black plastic sheeting which was like gold at this time of year. Sher had worked a miracle to get it, but the fatigue party had tossed it carelessly into the back of a truck and thrown coils of barbed wire on top, ruining most of it. Such crass and wanton foolishness left me speechless with rage and frustration and when a truck driver reversed over one of the concrete paths a few minutes later destroying hours of work, he was lucky to escape with no more than a tongue-lashing from me.

That afternoon banks of grey fog rolled up the Jebel, blotting out the sun and plunging us back into a damp, pearly twilight. But now tiny emerald stars of life sparkled with bright necklaces of moisture on the brown earth, growing imperceptibly together until they carpeted the ground. One morning the wind rose, sweeping away the mist and unveiling the hills in their glorious new mantle of shining green under scudding grey clouds like the Downs on a rainy autumn day. The sight made me very homesick.

The *Khareef* had wrought a great change in a short time, and it was difficult to believe that not fifteen miles away the land lay under the brassy oppression of an Arabian summer.

It was becoming apparent through conversations with members of the *firqa* that the village of Hayeen might be worth a visit. We had not been there yet and when I mentioned the subject to Mohammed Daan, he gave a violent start, then hurriedly insisted that there were no Adoo in the area and changed the subject. This immediately clinched the matter for me and I began laying plans for an early patrol. Hayeen consisted of a small group of huts about five miles south of Tawi Atair near a waterhole in one of the valleys leading down into the Wadi Hinna. It was a fairly easy approach across rolling grassland and the village lay close under the steep eastern side of the main wadi. Above the huts, the valley narrowed and split into two densely wooded side wadis, one of which petered out on the plateau to the north, whilst the other curved north-west, reaching up towards a small group of huts perched on the rim of the scarp overlooking the coast. Patches of dense scrub and trees on the slopes overlooked the wadis and below Hayeen the valley broadened into a strip of flat pasture on which the villagers grazed their cattle, then abruptly narrowed again and plunged over the scarp in an impenetrable tangle of rock and trees. Evidently it had something of a reputation as a trouble spot and as I had resolved that the Adoo would not be allowed a holiday during the *Khareef*, this particular hornets' nest was due for a stir.

There were a couple of villages on the way to Hayeen and not wanting to alarm Mohammed Daan unduly, I decided that we would take the *firqa* as far as the first one, a small group of huts close by Tawi called Andreydod, and announce that we were going on in the hope that they would be shamed into coming with us. Presented with a fait accompli, Mohammed could hardly refuse without losing face and though it was an underhand trick, it worked.

16 July 1975

It only took us three-quarters of an hour or so to reach Andreydod which nestled under a small wooded knoll at the entrance to the great complex of the Wadi Shuffloon. Unlike many of the wadi systems of Dhofar, Shuffloon was not deep but wide, an enormous grassy network of valleys stretching many miles up to the scarp above Mirbat, its size belied by the small, rocky ravine in low hills by Andreydod through which it drained into a shallow valley leading to the headwaters of the Ghazeer.

We approached the village cautiously, picqueting the wooded knoll and watching the huts for a few minutes before going down to make contact with the villagers. The *Jebalis* kept their cattle in low grass-roofed huts during the daylight hours of the wet season and round these enclosures water, mud and manure gathered in stinking pools, providing rich breeding grounds for millions of flies. I skirted a couple of middens on my way into the village whilst the *firqa* bustled round rousting out the few people who seemed to be at home. I chatted about this and that with one old boy who seemed pleased enough to see us and asked him if they needed medical attention, but they were close enough to visit the clinic at Tawi if the need arose and there was no-one sick. Plenty of rain had fallen and the grass was coming on well, so from the *Jebalis* point of view it looked like being a good season. Although the weather made my life difficult, I was glad for them, for they had very little and they depended on their flocks and herds, which would prosper on the strong new growth of grass.

In one hut I met a gentle, beautiful woman, the mother of two small children who invited me in and gave me a bowl of fresh warm cow's milk to drink. We could only exchange the simplest of phrases for she had little Arabic and so we sat in the gloom making stilted conversation for a few minutes whilst I drank the milk and stole admiring glances at her sweet face. There was no sign of her husband and as we left Mohammed Daan sidled up and in the manner of one imparting a great secret as a considerable favour, told me out of the corner of his mouth that she was the sister of Rajah Masoud, a name that rang vague bells in my mind. They should have been loud ones, for Rajah was one of the most respected leaders of the al-Amri, regardless of the fact that he was also one of the leaders of the Adoo groups in the Eastern area. I reflected that information of such importance should have been mine by right and not handed out in miserly fashion as some sort of special favour and I thought of pointing that out to Mohammed Daan, but he would not have understood what I was talking about, so I said nothing.

As we moved away up a grassy slope I told Mohammed that as a result of what I had seen and heard I had resolved to go on to Hayeen. He immediately threatened to return to Tawi Atair, natural caution no doubt reinforced by a guilty fear that his rash betrayal of information to me was now about to rebound upon him in some way, but when he saw that his threat had no effect, he reluctantly agreed to accompany us. In the event his presence made little difference, for we began to descend into the valley and were soon above the village. Tension suddenly mounted and Baluch and *firqa* alike began to move cautiously across some flat lawn-like enclosures close to the village.

I was unfamiliar with the layout of the valley so it came as a surprise when the beehive-shaped structures of huts appeared in front of us in the fog. Suleiman was slightly ahead of me at that point and suddenly, for no apparent reason, he yelled 'Charge!' and led his men forward at a run towards the village. The fog-blanketed silence was shattered with the clatter of small-arms fire, and I ran forward to where Suleiman and his men had taken up position along a thorn cattle fence and were firing into the village. Women and children were running hither and thither, screaming hysterically as bullets cracked around them and suddenly I saw two figures burst from a hut at the rear of the village and begin scrambling frantically up a steep muddy path leading out of the wadi. They were clearly enemy, and for the first time in my life I raised my rifle and took careful aim at a fellow human being. I squeezed off three or four shots at the pair as they disappeared into the trees without apparent effect, then shouting at Suleiman to stop his men firing indiscriminately into the huts, I ran round them and started up the wooded slope.

Up until now I had been functioning on automatic, but as I scrambled up the path, slipping and sliding in the mud, my brain began working normally again and I was suddenly aware that I was alone and on the trail of a dangerous quarry. I had already spotted blood dribbling thinly down the path in the rain and mingling with the soil, and now the distinct possibility of being ambushed made me pause. Suleiman and his men were some way away and out of sight in the fog and it would have taken several minutes to get them organised for pursuit. There was no alternative but to push on up the path, every nerve straining to catch signs of danger. In a few minutes I came to open country above the wadi where the trail ended and I cast about in the wet grass for clues as to which way our friends had gone, but there was no sign of them. I circled round the edge of the trees and close by the path, I picked up a small black notebook filled with figures and Arabic script.

Just then I heard the sounds of pursuit from below and I called out cautiously, having no desire to be shot by an overexcited Baluch or *firqa*. Suleiman appeared with his men and we held a quick council of war. The enemy could have gone in any one of a dozen different directions or even be sitting in the thick trees close by listening to us, but there was nothing we could do about it. I showed the notebook to Mohammed Daan who said that it belonged to Rajah Masoud, but the name still meant little to me and I thought it was merely being repeated for effect. It was not until we arrived back in Tawi Atair later that day and I was talking about the contact on the radio that I discovered how important he was. When I mentioned it to Ian (Yarpy) Wardle, the battalion intelligence officer, he was incredulous and said that if that was so, then we had just contacted and possibly wounded the most important Adoo leader in our part of Dhofar. When the notebook was eventually delivered to Salalah, Mohammed Daan's assertion was substantiated and we learned later that Rajah had indeed been shot in the leg that day. It was a measure of his toughness and the loyalty he inspired that he was able to keep on the move and recover from a wound that would have immobilised most men for half a year, despite the fact that he had no access to skilled medical attention. From that point on, speculation about his whereabouts became rife, not only in C Company and at KJ headquarters but also amongst the *Jebalis*. We had reports from all sides that Rajah was here. Rajah was there. Rajah was everywhere and if only a quarter of them were true, then he must have established a world record for endurance.

I should have been told about him by the intelligence organisation but it was no surprise that I was not. In spite of repeated requests, information on the Adoo organisation was withheld by the intelligence staff in Salalah, many of whom seemed to think that their work existed in a vacuum unrelated to operations on the ground.

Endless fog and rain turned each day into a featureless, dreary repetition of the one before and the steady erosion of running water sapped at our *murchas* so that working parties had to turn out at regular intervals to shore them up with stone and replace rotting sandbags. I finally grew weary of tramping out with a shovel each day and built myself a little Elsan shelter of old tentage. It was wet and soggy, but better than crouching out in the rain and fog, particularly at night. I destroyed the disgusting, ramshackle structure bequeathed to me by Bills and Ritson by pouring kerosene over it and setting it ablaze, incinerating the scorpions and a host of other bugs of all shapes and sizes, and I sterilised the contents of the oil drum in the same way. Fat white worms that had prospered undisturbed in the foetid darkness until now boiled up in a seething, revolting brew.

20 July 1975

There was another short break in the weather and this time we were promised a helicopter. Brian Spice had arrived back from leave and was waiting to come to Tawi Atair and Malik began to get very excited about leaving. He could not cope with the squalor and discomfort of Jebel life, especially during the *Khareef*, and I was not surprised by the speed with which he crammed his belongings into his bag ready for departure. When the chopper arrived his haste to be off was indecent and he did not even pause to exchange two words with Brian Spice, who was coming the other way.

I had not met Brian before, but I was impressed by the fact that he had spent the previous wet season at Tawi Atair and had apparently volunteered to do the same again. Anyone who would do that must have had a good reason, but it was a long time before I worked out what made Brian tick. He was a fully qualified nursing ex-warrant officer in the RAF and the reason for such high-powered medical cover was that in the *Khareef* there was little chance of getting any serious casualties out to Salalah, so the medic had to be competent to treat all but the most hopeless cases, who presumably would die. Brian was to prove himself as a doctor and midwife many times before the end of the rains, thereby demonstrating a skill and courage belied by his nondescript appearance. He was a short, round middle-aged man with thinning grey hair and thick pebble spectacles who spoke in exaggerated tones, emphasising points with limp-wristed, effeminate gestures.

He was one of the many mercenaries who were in Dhofar for all sorts of reasons unconnected with the war and over the course of many

TAWI ATAIR: JUNE–AUGUST 1975

long conversations with him in the months that followed, I gradually uncovered a tangled family history that partly explained his self-imposed exile. There had been a marriage of mixed blood which ended in acrimony, leaving him alone in his advancing middle age and there were two grown-up children, alienated from him and resentful of the ambiguous status conferred on them. He was, as I suppose many medics are, a frustrated would-be doctor and to my untutored eye he seemed to have the inclination and compassion for it. In Tawi Atair he could (and did) bind up wounds, cut out bullets, deliver babies and carry out all kinds of minor surgery that would have caused him to be struck off the nursing register in Britain for his impudence, but at Tawi Atair in the *Khareef* he was a godsend and so he fulfilled his longings for a while. He was never happier than when he was doing his rounds and he looked after us all, soldiers, *firqa*, civilians and even a cow that received a stray bullet in a shoot-out. He was very conscientious and never missed a surgery in the village, no matter what the weather, and he earned the respect of the tribespeople who addressed him by the honoured title of '*tabeeb*' ('doctor') which naturally he loved.

He tackled every task with great aplomb, most memorably when a sentry shot a cow in a nervous burst of firing one dark night. The *firqa* reported the casualty next morning, chuckling over the incident and saying that it was of no consequence for the cow would live, but I knew that if it was not treated the wound would soon begin to suppurate and the wretched beast would suffer agonies in consequence. That did not bother the *firqa*, but it stirred my tender sensibilities and I suggested to Brian that he might like to take a look at it. He took off straight away, found and repaired the cow and reported triumphantly back to me.

In the evening Brian turned to the bottle, and in it he found not solace, but a deep bitterness against the world which began to focus itself on me as a symbol of everything that had eluded him in his sad life. I was securely married and when the first letters from home arrived I rejoiced publicly over them, unwittingly twisting a cruel knife in his wounded soul whilst he, poor man, waited in vain for word from his latest love, another black woman to whom he had trustingly made over a large portion of his income. I was young and despite the discomforts and discouragements of life at Tawi, I was doing what I wanted to do. I believed fervently in it and I was the boss with considerable power and full of self-confidence. It showed, and Brian hated me for it.

There were persistent reports that the Adoo were visiting the village of Kizetakhayf about four miles west of Tawi Atair and using it as a base during the *Khareef*, safe in the knowledge that SAF did not venture out of doors at that season. Kizetakhayf had a long history of involvement with the Adoo and had been burnt to the ground in the past as a punishment, but it was close to the Darbat and family ties were stronger than abstract ideological concepts. The village could not be left undisturbed for it was in a good position to threaten the road which ran not far to the north and it lay at the head of a number of escape routes into the huge wadi system below Jebel Aram to the south. I decided to take a couple of small platoons and some of the *firqa*, about forty men in all, and pay it a visit.

22 July 1975

The plan was to skirt round to the south and move on the village from that direction, hopefully cutting the enemy off from their usual escape route. To prevent them going north into the equally impenetrable mass of the Darbat, I intended to detach a platoon to occupy a small area of rising ground just north of the village and guard the exits from that side. The route was carefully planned so as to approach the village in dead ground and early the next morning we set off in clear weather. It was the first patrol with more than a handful of the Firqa al-Amri and they were as eager to discover my strengths and weaknesses as I was to see how they performed. The outward journey soon began to develop into a series of discussions and arguments as each member of the *firqa* came up to me in turn to voice an individual objection to what we were doing or offer his own ideas, whilst the Baluch looked on with growing impatience. It was a problem of leadership and under Mohammed Daan the *firqa* did as they pleased. They were feeling mischievous that day and they tested my patience to the limit. I could not possibly deal with each one of them separately and in attempting to do so, I was becoming dangerously distracted from the main business in hand. I told them that they should take their difficulties to Mohammed who would make the necessary decisions and bring any insoluble problems to me, but they would not countenance it, and in the end I refused to listen to them. Some took umbrage, but the point had to be made at the outset or we should have chaos.

The *firqa* were very disparaging of my insistence that we should move along the high ground at the start, picqueting religiously from hill to hill, but I did not yet know the lie of the land and I did not entirely trust their insistence that there were no Adoo around. Later, when we came to know the area intimately, more routes and alternatives would offer themselves, but in those early days I was taking no chances.

As we made our way along the peaks a bank of grey cloud came rolling up the slopes towards us and when visibility shortened to a few yards we abandoned the hilltops and took a more direct line towards our objective. I was unconcerned about the return of the fog, for I had my bearings and it would give us the cover we needed to cross the last few hundred yards of open ground to the village. I began counting off the little finger wadis as we crossed them and kept a constant eye on my compass. At the agreed point, Ahmed Dur and 11 Platoon disappeared into the mist, heading for the top end of the village.

We went down into a wadi and after circling round we picked up the right spur and made our way up again towards the huts. As they loomed out of the mist the platoon shook out into line and leaving a gun on either flank to cover our approach, we moved in cautiously. This was a hazardous moment for we were very exposed as we crossed last few yards of open ground and had the enemy opened fire on us, there would have been very little cover. But the *firqa* seemed relaxed and as usual they had sized up the situation correctly. There were not many people in the village and those who were there seemed friendly enough. Yes, it was a good (wet) *Khareef*. Yes, praise God, the cattle were healthy. No, there was no news, all was well. No, they had seen no sign of the Adoo.

The medical orderly moved round the village dispensing aspirin and other small comforts. One old man was covered in the most appalling sores, but he seemed to accept his lot with the stoicism of his race and declined my offer to get him to Salalah for treatment. When the pleasantries were over we moved forward to make contact with Ahmed Dur and to my surprise I found him just a few yards from the huts. He was unsure of his position and not wanting to make a mistake, he moved in very close. It may have been the right decision, but the Adoo chose that moment to let us know that they had been there by loosing off a burst of automatic fire about a thousand metres away to the south. Presumably they heard Ahmed Dur coming and not wanting to get into a fight, they pulled out along their usual escape route, passing close by us in the fog as we came up in that direction. Had we taken a path a few yards further over there would have been some very surprised people indeed, on both sides. We squelched back to Tawi in the mud.

29 July 1975

The weather stayed closed in and a few days later I took a patrol to the Hount waterhole north of Tawi Atair in order to scout out the land that way. As the patrol was moving along a path through the trees on the side of a wadi leading to the waterhole, I was scanning the high ground opposite when I saw what looked like a small donkey. I looked at it through my binoculars and saw a great grey wolf standing quite still, watching us. After a few moments it turned and trotted over the rim of the hill and out of sight. Wolves were often heard howling in the hills at night but I had not seen one before and it was the high point in an otherwise uneventful day. Later I saw another close by Tawi Atair very early one morning and though it seemed unconcerned by our presence I was glad that it had the sense to take itself off before the *firqa* rose from their beds, for they would certainly have slaughtered it without a second thought. Like pastoral people the world over the *Jebalis* were paranoid about anything which might conceivably harm their cattle, and they were ruthless in eliminating real or imagined predators.

Mansoor returned to Tawi Atair on the helicopter that brought Brian and he immediately set to work getting the kitchen organised again. One evening we were sitting back contentedly after one of his excellent dinners when automatic fire suddenly broke out on the western end of the main picquet. I grabbed my rifle and belt and plunged out into the black, wet night, cursing at the thoughtlessness of anyone who would choose to attack at such an uncivilised hour. The night was very dark, my eyes had no time to adjust, and within a few yards I was totally disorientated. I stumbled into a barbed-wire entanglement that had been laid with the express purpose of stopping people from wandering about at night in places they should not be, and it worked like a charm. As I struggled and bled in my own trap the firing stopped and a flare went up, making the fog shimmer with light. For a moment I had a nightmare vision of my dead body hanging on the wire and I stood very still and prayed that no-one on either side was drawing a bead on such a helpless target. When the light died away I managed to free myself and found my way to Ahmed Dur's platoon where he met me with a garbled story about a sentry seeing a mass of Adoo approaching the wire and opening fire on them. We did a short clearing patrol in front of the position but found nothing. I was doubtful about his story as I had only heard the thumping of our Browning and it was unlikely that the enemy would have held their fire in the circumstances. The crack and thump of incoming rounds is unmistakeable and I heard none. I was not in the best of moods when I got back but Brian dressed my wounds, clucking sympathetically.

The next morning I was standing on the main ridge watching the mist thinning and wondering if we were going to get another break in the weather when there was a storm of firing from a number of different weapons, this time from the *firqa* camp. I called Mohammed Daan on the radio to find out what was happening, but for a few moments there was no response and as I waited anxiously more shooting broke out, this time from the western picquet. I sent a soldier to Ahmed Dur's platoon to tell them to stand to and be ready to send out a section to investigate and just as I was about to start down the hill, Mohammed came up on the radio. I asked him what was going on and he told me gleefully that a wedding was being celebrated in the customary way. As calmly as I could I said how nice that was, would he greet the bride and groom on my behalf, and would he be kind enough to warn me the next time the *firqa* decided to have a bean-feast of that sort. All this time Brian had been down at the village and when he returned he told me that the shooting had started just as he was approaching the huts, making him jump out of his skin. There was never a dull moment in Tawi Atair.

3 August 1975

Early in August I received a signal saying that my new second-in-command had arrived in Dhofar and would be joining me shortly. There was no flying and no vehicle movement on the Jebel, so the plan was that D Company would move out from Arzat to the Darbat, carry out an overnight search and escort a convoy up to the top of the scarp at dawn the next morning. I was to take a small force of two platoons and some *firqa* down to Twin Tits and from there do a dawn search of the village of Ghaday which lay a mile or so east of the old Darbat picquet. We would all meet up at the picquet and the new officer would return with me to Tawi Atair.

The *Khareef* remained as thick as ever and navigation at night would be a problem so I decided to march along the vehicle track as far as Twin Tits and use a compass bearing from there. The night was every bit as dark as we expected and on the way there were times when it was only by feeling with our feet or crouching to catch a faint glimmer from water in the wheel ruts that we were able to keep to the track. We barked our shins on sharp rocks that had been pushed aside when the bulldozer graded the track and as we plodded along the ten miles to Twin Tits seemed an eternity. At about two o'clock in the morning we came to the spot where the track curved sharply to the right and changed to a paler hue as it began to climb the twin hills. It was what I had been looking for and I led the column off the road and up onto the picquet to wait until just before dawn.

We stumbled up a rocky slope to the summit where I posted sentries and settled down to try and get a little sleep. Within moments the air was filled with whining as mosquitoes homed in for a meal and we spent the next couple of hours trying to protect ourselves against them. I pulled a poncho over my head and dozed fitfully.

As the blackness began to pale we moved down and silently surrounded Ghaday and when the inhabitants began to emerge, we moved in. The *firqa* made contact with them and carried out their usual cursory inspection. If there was any prospect of a find they could be quite energetic, for a recovered weapon carried a reward, but usually they considered it a waste of time and made only a half-hearted effort. I was beginning to trust their instinct and in any case, important weapons would not be hidden in the villages but cached deep in a wadi nearby. It had been wisely decided that soldiers were not to get involved in searching which was as well, for the Baluch would have relished such an opportunity. They would have been diligent and destructive and that would have done little to win the trust of the tribespeople. As expected, the search of Ghaday proved fruitless, and at about nine o'clock on an overcast, cheerless morning we moved off to rendezvous with the convoy.

As we approached the trucks I saw Douglas McCully and Major The Honourable Hugh Willoughby, Coldstream Guards, the commander of D Company, who was known to all and sundry as 'Orrible 'Ugh. The third man was a tall, thin, balding captain I did not recognise, but who I guessed must be Peter Willdridge, the new second-in-command. We introduced ourselves and were soon swapping news through mouthfuls of cold mutton washed down with warm beer. A clerk from Battalion Headquarters came up to me with a heavy sack stuffed full of paper which he insisted had to go up to Tawi. I sorted out the personal mail and threw back into the sack triplicate copies of unit orders going back almost two months, lists of equipment, strength returns and similar foolish bits of paper which the chief clerk in his blinkered way imagined that I would bother myself with. I gave the sack back to the clerk, telling him that if his boss thought them that important he could carry them up to Tawi Atair himself because I certainly would not. The lad was upset by my irreverent attitude to his sacred paperwork (clerks were much respected by both Pakistanis and Baluch), but after the trials of the last couple of months I was unable to take such trivia seriously.

Having rid ourselves of the paper, we loaded up with as many batteries as we could carry, all the personal mail and half a dozen bottles of whisky and, saying goodbye to Douglas and Hugh, we set off for Tawi. As the

TAWI ATAIR: JUNE–AUGUST 1975

Peter Willdridge and David Freeman going 'dry' in Tawi Atair, 1975!

convoy disappeared in the mist I remembered the yellow 'bombs' that Brian had given me the day before which were supposed to renew my vigour and put a spring back into my step. Peter had been up all night tramping around the Darbat and we were both beginning to feel jaded, so we took one each. They had absolutely no effect apart from giving us both blinding headaches by the time we finally plodded into Tawi and we never bothered with them again. We arrived back at about midday, stinking and exhausted and flopped down to rest, grateful that the endless marching had stopped. It was already clear that Peter and I had a lot in common with one another and as we sat in pools of water and sweat talking over the events of the morning and discussing the Company I felt instinctively that we would be able to work effectively together, which was as well, seeing that we would be with each other for the best part of the next year. Indeed, there might be times when we would depend on one another for our very survival, but I had no idea that our partnership would be tested quite so soon as it was.

Peter settled quickly into the strange routine of life on the Jebel. He was tall, muscular and fit and he had no difficulty in meeting the rigorous physical demands of operations. His down to earth approach enabled him to cope with the psychological and spiritual strains that our isolated, comfortless way of life imposed on us and his earthy sense of humour quickly endeared him to the soldiers, who loved a joke and never saw in Peter the tetchiness which I occasionally gave way to. It was easy to forgive his little quirks, such as refusing to have anything to do with the *firqa* whatsoever for the first few months on the grounds that his Arabic was not up to standard. He was right, it was appalling, but all the same it irritated me that he never seemed to be around when a file of *firqa* came marching up the hill each afternoon to deliver their latest complaint.

He delighted in shocking people and most evenings he would utter some outrageous remark which never failed to make Brian, who pretended to a certain rather prudish morality, splutter with indignation. It sometimes caught me out as well and I would be ranting away in response to something he said until I noticed the deadpan expression on his face and realised I had been well and truly hooked. He was to become a staunch friend and brother in arms.

5 August 1975

As if to mark Peter's arrival, the next day dawned bright and clear and stayed sunny all day. Yarpy Wardle came on the radio at about lunchtime to tell me that a helicopter was on its way, but when it arrived there were none of the stores that we asked for on board. I was very angry at the waste of money and resources and it was not the only time that a helicopter flew to Tawi Atair without the Quartermaster knowing. It rather negated the point of putting on a flight, which was to get badly-needed stores to Jebel positions during short breaks in the weather.

The blessed sunshine continued for the next two days and by the third morning the muddy tracks had dried sufficiently to take wheeled traffic and Tawi Atair lay shimmering in the heat.

There were three donkeys on charge to C Company, intended for carrying stores to places which vehicles could not reach and I began to take an interest in the possibility of using them on operations. They had already done a little light work carrying rations across to Suleiman's platoon on the north picquet, but if they could be equipped to carry an 81-mm mortar and ammunition for example, it would greatly extend the range and hitting power of our patrols. They could also be made to carry water, thereby increasing the length of time we could remain in an area undetected, should we wish to do so. They had a very easy life, apart from the casual brutalities inflicted on them by the Baluch who would hobble them with wire which cut into their flesh. I only stopped the practice by

Major David Freeman, Dhofar.

An under-strength C Company, KJ, of four platoons, post-*Khareef*, 1975. Note the 81-mm mortar and twelve GPMGs displayed in front of the company.

C Company Sergeant Major, WO2 Hajji Bilal in the C Company main position at Tawi Atair. Note the warm jacket against the morning cold.

Lieutenant Charki, OC 10 Platoon, C Company, KJ, Qisais ad Deen. His good-humoured nature is apparent in this photo.

Staff Sergeant Ahmed Dur Mohammed, OC 9 Platoon, C Company, KJ – KIA 9 August 1975. Note the National radio, used for company-level communications.

Peter Willdridge on patrol, Jebel ash Shawr. Note the FN rifle – a weapon with great stopping power at range. C Company's radio operator is in the background.

Lieutenant Badil Mohammed, OC 11 Platoon, C Company, KJ. Sadly, he and his son were to drown in Oman in a boating accident some years after this image was taken.

David Freeman on patrol, Jebel ash Shawr. Like Peter Willdridge above, he carries an FN rifle, a good weapon for the open Jebel.

Above: A typical improvised sangar overlooking Wadi Darbat, 1976. A sangar like this would take about two hours to build.

Above right: Resupply by Skyvan. This method was never really justifiable, given the small supply packages it could deliver to patrols or the organisation required to execute this type of mission.

Right: Sergeant Gulam Hussein, Platoon Sergeant, 11 Platoon, manning a GPMG on patrol. Body armour and helmets were never worn on operations in Dhofar.

Left: Baluch GPMG gunner, Dhofar 1975. Carrying a small pack, and with the weight of the gun and ammunition, he would have struggled to move fast across the very hot and difficult Dhofar terrain.

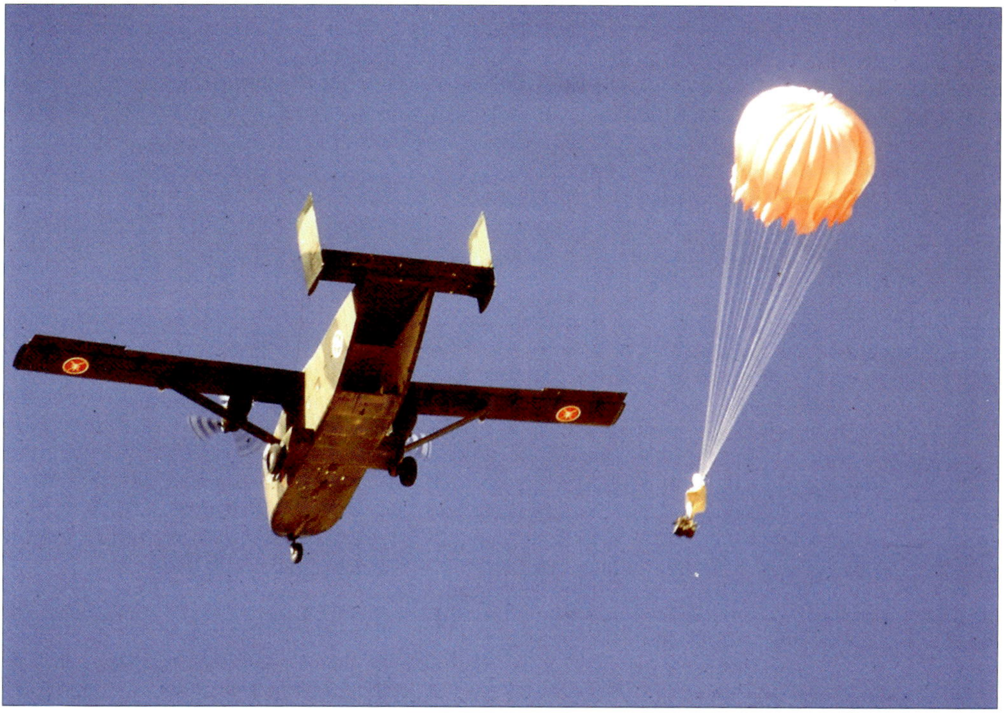

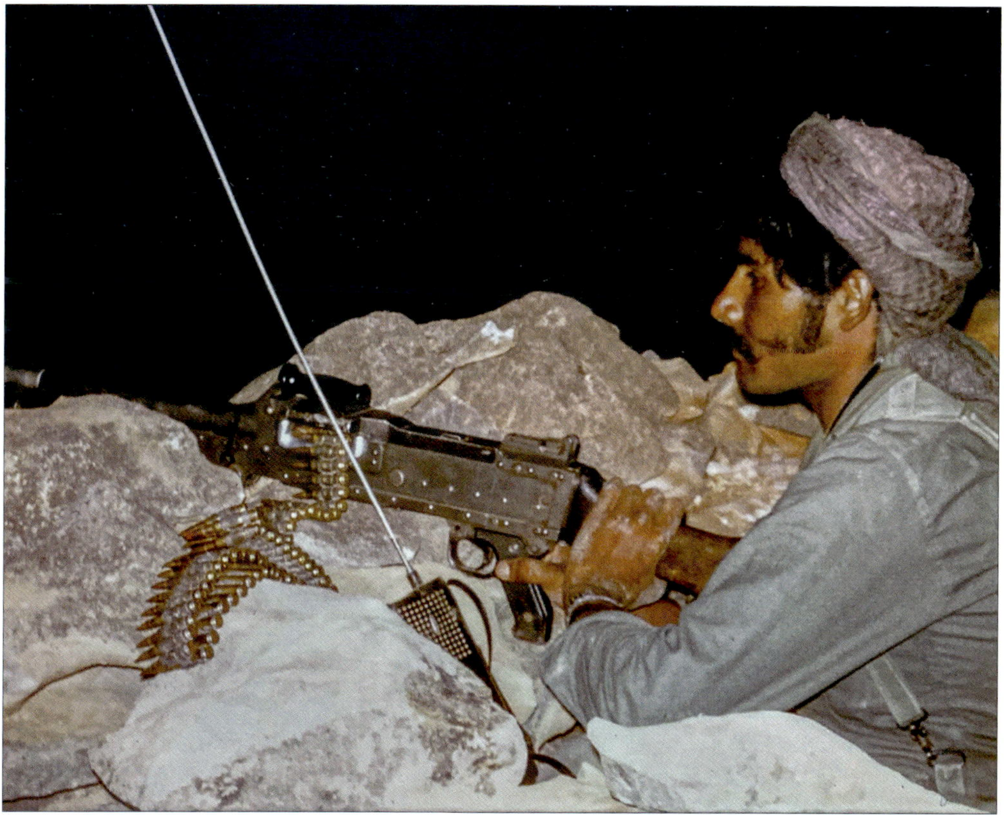

Brian Spice (Company Medic) and Peter Willdridge in the mud at Tawi Atair during the *Khareef*, August 1975.

Lalu the cook, making chapatis on the Jebel in 1975. Rations were basic and food-preparation facilities primitive on the Jebel. Fresh food was a rarity and improved morale and physical condition immensely when it arrived.

C Company helping Jordanian engineers build a road on the Jebel. There was no tarmac available for these backwater roads – just smashed rocks. The roads made it easier to supply positions on the Jebel, but took a toll on vehicles.

C Company, KJ, building sangars, 1976. These are up-market sangars, built with sandbags instead of rocks, and were for the main company base.

Home from home – David Freeman's sangar, Tawi Atair, 1975. The mosquito net helped to keep the rats out as well as insects.

Range day at Tawi Atair. David and Peter placed a high priority on training when not on operations. Peter in shorts and floppy hat and CSM Bilal standing on right.

Firqa al-Amri – Mohammed Said (front centre wearing watch), *firqa* leader. Tawi Atair 1976. The *firqa* were always lightly equipped, very fit and knew the Jebel well.

David Freeman on patrol in 1975. Note his Armalite rifle, chosen for operations in close country. Peter Willdridge had a stoppage in contact with one, which he was none too pleased about!

Ubiquitous rats, September 1975.

The harsh terrain of the Jebel over which C Company operated on foot –
dry, stony wadis cutting deep into the ground.

Larking about. Yanusz Heath (*left*) and Yarpy Wardle, Jibjat 1976.

Christmas 1975. Duck hunting. On the left, David Freeman. Top right Peter Willdridge.
And a young Alex and Nick Freeman!

Winning hearts and minds – schoolchildren in Tawi Atair.
Note the Lebanese or Palestinian teacher and that both boys and girls are being educated.

25-pounder artillery piece, Eastern Dhofar, 1975. These guns provided indirect fire support for C Company on operations on the Jebel.

BAC Strikemaster in action, 1975. Three Strikemasters were shot down over the course of the conflict, including one that was reportedly lost to SA-7 surface-to-air missiles. The Strikemasters were replaced by faster Hawker Hunters, but were sorely missed by the infantry who appreciated their low and steady capabilities – ideal for the close air support role.

C Company on patrol, Jebel ash Shawr. Patrolling was hot and arduous and little more than weapons, ammunition, communications equipment and water could be carried.

Two Strikemasters pass low over Tawi Atair, 1975. Flown by RAF and Fleet Air Arm pilots, Strikemasters provided close air support for operations in Dhofar.

The C Company Land Rover on patrol above Wadi Darbat. Despite the photo, the beloved Land Rover rarely left base. Patrols were always on foot and often inserted by helicopter.

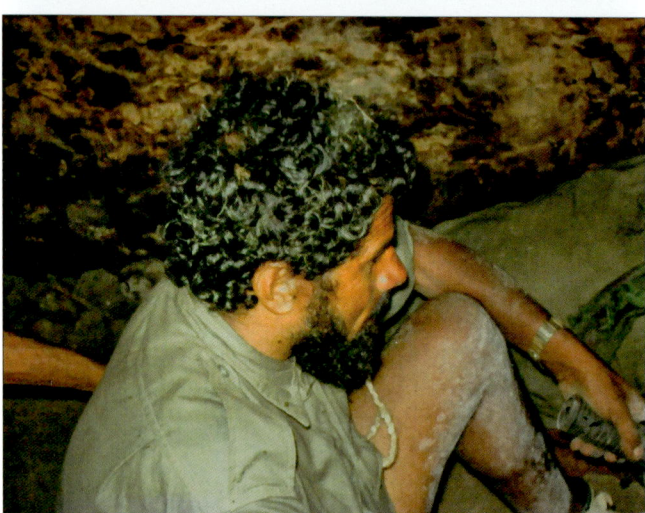

Ahmed Said (*firqa* leader in 1975) searching for weapons in caves east of Tawi Atair. During this search he found intelligence documents and ammunition.

Dawn stand-to, Wadi Hinna, 20 December 1975, the day after B Company was involved in a contact that cost the lives of four soldiers.

Captain Jummah Hussein, Omani Artillery, an excellent observation officer who ran an efficient troop of guns at Tawi Atair.

The good-natured, industrious and very competent Sergeant Jelal of 10 Platoon, C Company, KJ.

Rajah Masoud al-Amri. Leader of the Adoo in the Eastern Area until July 1976, when he finally surrendered at Mirbat.

Peter Willdridge and the KJ shooting team, Dhofar Brigade small arms meeting champions, 1976. The Baluch were naturally good shots and took great pride in their marksmanship skills.

Saladin armoured car.
From left, Peter Willdridge, David Freeman, Staff Sergeant John Perkins, prior to DMF's last patrol in Dhofar.

threatening the direst punishment if it happened again and after that the donkeys lived an idyllic life, feeding on their Army-issue dates and the sweet long grass around them. It seemed to me that they ought to earn their keep.

They were not the meek, gentle eyed little things to be seen at the seaside in England but large, ill-tempered beasts from the Jebel Akhdar in Northern Oman, as big as mules and twice as awkward. By the simple humour of the Baluch they had been christened, if that was the right word in our Muslim society, 'Sergeant Major', 'Corporal' and 'Private' in descending order of size. They had been spoilt by their idle existence and it seemed to me that the first step in incorporating them fully into the Company order of battle was to establish a clear moral ascendancy over them. Hajji Bilal had already come to grief trying to ride one, sailing over the handlebars as it stopped dead under him. Hajji was rather priggish and solemn, and it added spice to the story which was being gleefully told and retold amongst the soldiers, who delighted in the thought of him coming a cropper.

We had no saddlery, so we had to make do with a blanket supplemented with a rope halter and Sergeant Lai Bux, who set himself up as the expert, prepared one of the donkeys for me to ride. A rope securing the saddle blanket was passed under the donkey's tail and pulled so tight that it stuck up rigidly erect like a jackstaff in the sun. The donkey turned its head and glared at those who had inflicted such an indignity and I knew there and then that there was going to be trouble. Conscious as ever of the need for the gallant Major Sahib never to be outfaced (least of all by a donkey) I seized the halter with one hand, put the other on the blanket saddle, and swung myself upwards. The brute turned and began to rotate gently away from me. The soldiers, who could see a good joke coming a mile away, had gathered to witness this momentous occasion and now they began to collapse around me with gales of laughter. I could see the joke as well as anyone, but my laughter had an edge of panic as I tried to get the animal under control.

Eventually I managed to secure a seat and we set off at a jolting trot downhill, straight towards one of the artillery ammunition bunkers, whose roofs happened to be at exactly the right height for a donkey to enter. Unable to stop the beast, I scrambled off as it went into the shelter, just in time to avoid being chopped in half by the sharp tin roof. The donkey had taken refuge as far inside the shelter as it could get and was clearly determined that our ride had come to an end. I was equally determined that it had not and by dint of a great deal of pulling and pushing, I managed to get it out into the sunshine again. I remounted and, giving the other ammunition bays a very wide berth, set off again into the valley.

I had hoped to avoid the *firqa* camp, being well aware of how much they enjoyed mocking just such a foolish situation as the one I now found myself in, but I could not stop my donkey following the other two right through the middle of it, and they turned out to scoff just as the soldiers had done. It was a relief when we left the camp behind and started up the hill to Suleiman's position. He greeted us with his usual politeness, his stern dark face crumpling in a smile when he saw my inept efforts as a cavalryman.

We walked round the position, chatting to the soldiers and then we relaxed in the sunshine and enjoyed the magnificent views all round the north picquet. By now the *Khareef* was well advanced and away to the east the sun illuminated the tumbled, wooded hills of Qisais ad Deen against a deep black backdrop of thunderous clouds. Far away at the very edge of the cloud lay the dry ridge of the Gatn, untouched by the *Khareef* and sparkling golden and white like a shimmering narrow belt on a sombre cloak of grey and green. This was strange, broken country that as far as I knew had not been visited for years by forces of the Government and it was one of the few undisturbed sanctuaries left to the Adoo in the Eastern Area. It was therefore high on the list for a visit.

Presently the donkeys were brought and the three of us mounted. I was not looking forward to the return journey because my bottom was already smarting warmly from the unaccustomed chafing, but once again, duty triumphed. I tried to shut my mind to the discomfort, but the donkeys sensed that they were headed for home and with a resounding chorus of farts, they took off down the hill at an alarming rate. The sight of Lai Bux and Peter bouncing down the track reduced me to hysteria and that, together with the pain in my backside, the tears of laughter coursing down my cheeks and the rifle pounding my back into a jelly, destroyed any coordination or strength I might have brought to bear to control the animal. As large, skull-crushing rocks whizzed past I clung on for dear life and I remember, frozen as though in the frame of a film, the face of one of the Pakistani maintenance men, staring open-mouthed in amazement as the wild cavalcade swept past, howling with laughter. Women watering cattle at the troughs looked on scornfully at men playing boys' games.

The donkeys were easier to control on rising ground and they slowed to a bone-jarring trot, but when we arrived back at the main position I had to concede that whatever moral victory we may have won in riding the donkeys to the north picquet and back, it was Pyrrhic, for nothing would induce me to repeat the experience. That evening, still laughing over the day's events, I happened to remark that my backside was very sore. Without ceremony Brian had me take down my trousers and he applied some soothing antibiotic, accompanied by a string of vulgarities from Peter. The ride had cost me two strips of skin about four inches long from the inside of each buttock.

8 August 1975

The next day was again fine and clear and I added a few more pages to the letters I was writing to Carol and the boys. Adding to them every day or so meant that they could be quickly finished and despatched if a helicopter should suddenly appear, but they were beginning to look more like diaries than letters. The helicopter pilots were very good about letters and would often undertake to post them personally when they got back to Salalah, which clipped a day off the time they took to get home.

Ahmed Said, the *firqa* leader, had returned in the convoy that brought Peter to the Darbat rendezvous and his second-in-command, Mohammed Said, came up to Tawi about a fortnight later. That afternoon they came to see me and we had a long and not very friendly talk. Ahmed Said was the older of the two with a bearded, jovial round face marred by suspicious, rather shifty eyes. He was heavily built and had a fearsome reputation as a former hit-man for the Adoo who specialised in the execution of backsliders and traitors to the cause before he saw the light and joined the Sultan. He was not of the al-Amri and although I did not realise it at the time, there was no love lost between him and Mohammed Said. Ahmed Said was as crafty as a cartload of monkeys, and in a nation of circumlocutors was distinguished for the ambiguity of his utterances. Mohammed was very different. He was an imposing figure, not tall, but straight as a ramrod and looking every inch a soldier. His hair was neatly trimmed and his handsome face was adorned by a short, military-style moustache. He had a ready smile and eventually he become as good a friend as Musalim had been at White City, though not before we went through some painful moments of mistrust and misunderstanding which arose out of the tangle of tribal politics.

A minority group of outsiders, which included Mohammed Daan, coalesced around Ahmed Said, splitting the *firqa* into two quarrelling factions who could barely bring themselves to speak to one other. The reason for Mohammed's prolonged sojourn in Salalah became clear later in the year when the al-Amri succeeded in ousting Ahmed from the leadership. He and his men departed in high dudgeon to form a new *firqa* based in Mirbat and named the Firqa Jebel Ali, after a prominent hill just north of the town. But all this lay in the future and in the meantime I found myself in the middle of a complicated dispute between Ahmed and Mohammed over the leadership of the *firqa*. I should have firmly refused to get involved but instead I foolishly revealed my thoughts by stating what I believed were the important factors in the argument and thereby dug myself deeply into the mire of local politics. First, Ahmed Said was the appointed *mulazzim* (lieutenant) with the Wali's seal of approval upon his leadership. Second, Mohammed had been an inordinately long time in Salalah with his cronies whilst we got on with the job of looking after his area. Third, Mohammed was young, fit and of the al-Amri and Ahmed was not and last, and most important, the appointment and dismissal of *firqa* leaders was firmly the prerogative of the Wali of Dhofar and I had no right to interfere. They were all valid points, but they cancelled one another out and they were not flattering to either party. In the end I had to say that as far as I was concerned Ahmed was the leader until Sheik Baraik pronounced otherwise which upset Ahmed, who rightly discerned that my support for him was less than wholehearted and Mohammed, who believed, incorrectly, that I was set against him. It was a bungled piece of diplomacy.

To make matters worse the *Khareef* returned with a vengeance in the afternoon and by five o'clock that evening it was dark and rain was pouring from the black sky in a solid stream. At about that time a long signal arrived from Douglas saying that the Battalion was going to run a convoy along the coast road to Mirbat the next day and would we please secure the high ground above the point where the Wadi Ghazeer came down to the coastal plain. There the road turned in close under the hills and crossed a ravine and it was a favourite spot for ambushes. We did not have the strength to picquet every high feature properly and it would not have been very effective if we had, because there were plenty of escape routes and it was impossible to see into the wadi from the top. I therefore decided that the best way to protect the convoy was to stir up trouble by some aggressive patrolling on the high ground above the Ghazeer and around the Hayeen waterhole, which would divert the enemy's attention away from the road and onto me.

I made my plan on that basis and later that evening in the dripping gloom of a large *murcha* which served as Company Headquarters, command post and conference room, I gave out orders for the following day, ordering 9 Platoon (Staff Sergeant Ahmed Dur Mohammed) and 10 Platoon (Sergeant Lai Bux) to accompany me. I followed the standard sequence of orders, pausing at regular intervals for questions from my platoon commanders and as usual there were none. When I came to the end I asked, as always, 'Right, before we finish, have you anything you wish to discuss?' knowing what would follow. There would be a short silence, followed by *'Naam, Sahib . . .'* and off we would go into a rambling discussion conducted in a mixture of Arabic, Baluch and English, chewing over the plan until everyone understood what was required of him. That evening Ahmed Dur sat looking very glum and obviously not listening very carefully to what was going on, so I asked him what was troubling him. He poured a long complaint about the lack of fresh rations and how his men were losing their strength as a result. I explained that we were all suffering and that we were trying to get some money to buy fresh food and he and his men must be patient. Although Ahmed Dur was one of life's grumblers I had a soft spot for him and indulged his little weaknesses, but I was angry that he had allowed discomfort to distract him from an important set of orders, and I told him so.

9 August 1975

The next day was dry but overcast. Taking Ahmed Said, Mohammed and a detachment of *firqa*, we set off south, moving from ridge to ridge across the rolling grasslands between Tawi and the Ghazeer. We were about forty in all – two very small platoons of about fifteen men each, Peter and myself and a couple of signallers in Company Headquarters and half a dozen *firqa*. We made good time across country and by about eight o'clock we were nearing the upper reaches of the Ghazeer, above Hayeen. As we came within about 200 yards of the rounded shoulders of the wadi and were to be able to look down into it, we saw women hurrying away towards the huts, a sure sign that the Adoo were in the vicinity.

We rushed forward to the heights overlooking the village and almost at once shooting started. A group of enemy broke from the huts, fleeing north into the densely wooded valleys beyond. Peter gave a whoop as the GPMGs began to clatter and in the noise and confusion I tried to make sense out of what was happening and work out a plan to cut off the enemy's escape routes. Before the radio net became completely jammed by excited *firqa* chatter, I managed to tell Ahmed Dur, who was on my right, to take his platoon to the north, block the main wadi and prevent any Adoo from escaping towards Tawi Atair. Taking Company Headquarters and

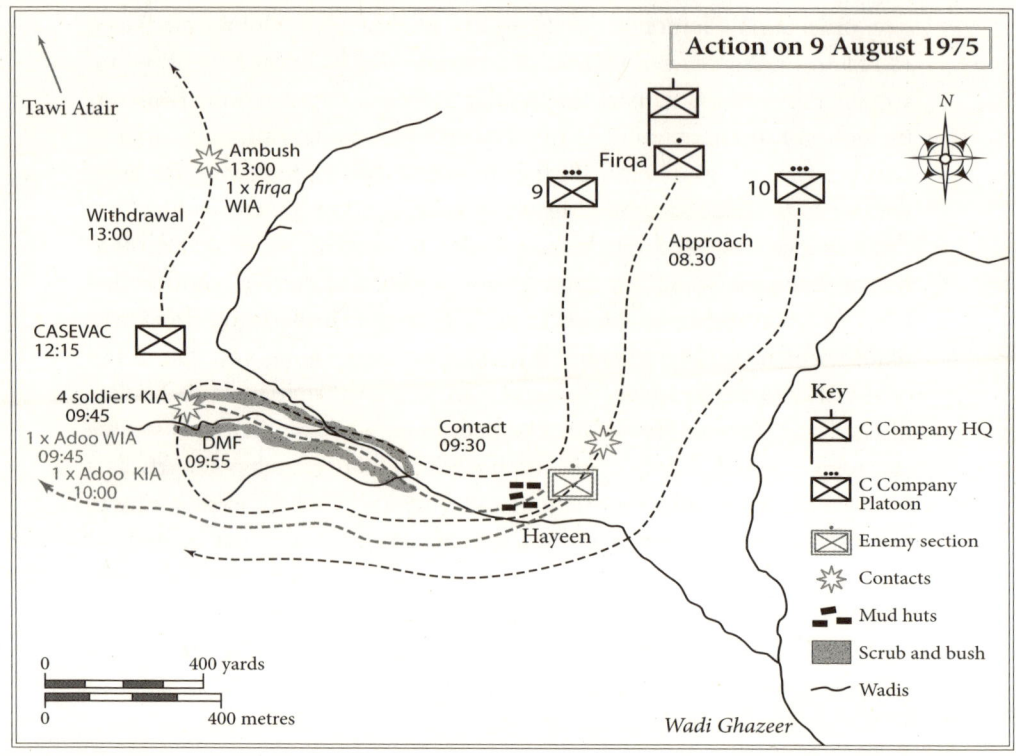

the *firqa*, I ran down into the valley, past the huts where I had chased Rajah three weeks before, and scrambled up the opposite side to a rocky knoll which would give me good observation all round the area and allow me to seal off the other side wadi running north-west from the huts. I sent Lai Bux off to the left and beyond my position to seize the highest point of a ridge overlooking the scarp from which the enemy could have made life very difficult, had he got onto it.

It was an exhausting run, but as soon as our small party was on the knoll I began to assess the situation and try and get some control over the battle, which was now spread over a wide area. The problem was complicated by the fact that communications on the radio were jammed by a non-stop babble between members of the *firqa* which I was powerless to prevent, and a distracting crossfire which opened up on us a moment or two after we reached the knoll. It came first from the south and then from the north, forcing us to scrabble from one side of the rocks to the other. The fire from the south was coming from a group of Adoo who had been too quick for us and escaped over to the scarp and they only stopped shooting at us when Lai Bux secured his picquet and put down some effective fire on them. We searched in vain for the source of the fire which was cracking over our heads from the north.

Whilst this was going on, Ahmed Dur's platoon were making their way up the main wadi, seeming to crawl in slow motion at that distance. They crossed the wadi and begin circling back towards some huts on the edge of the scarp about 500 yards north-west of us. Either Ahmed Dur had decided to do something different on his own initiative or, more likely, he had misunderstood my instructions. Either way, he was abandoning a blocking position and I tried frantically to get through to him on the radio without success. Ahmed Dur had the bit between his teeth and was not answering, even when I managed to get in a word between the babble of the *firqa*. As the platoon reached the huts, my attention was on the southern part of the battle, so I did not see Ahmed Dur and a handful of his men dropping down towards an isolated patch of low trees and scrub just below and across the side wadi from our knoll and neither, in the general firing that was going on at that time, did I register the noise of them circling the patch of scrub and firing at random into it.

The first hint of disaster was when I tried to raise Ahmed Dur again on the radio in a lull and heard only an ominous silence, though he had to be somewhere close at hand. Suddenly I knew something had gone badly wrong and my worst fears were confirmed when one of Ahmed Dur's youngest soldiers rushed up onto the knoll, his equipment and his rifle gone and his eyes wide with shock and terror. He was gabbling incoherently, but there was no need to translate. I began to run down towards the patch of scrub where I now knew Ahmed Dur had disappeared, followed by Peter, Ahmed Said and Mohammed.

Fear gripped me. I began to pant in shallow gasps, my heart constricted painfully and a terrible foreboding came over me as I realised that Ahmed Dur must surely now be dead and that I was as likely as not to follow him in the next few moments as I ran towards the place where he had died. As I crossed the open ground in front of the copse I was alone. The others had dropped back a few yards but I had to go on and see whatever lay in the scrub. The last few yards seemed an eternity. I moved as though in a dream, my mind blank and no longer functioning to protect and control my body. A horrible, bubbling moaning almost unmanned me and as I moved into the edge of the trees I saw the nightmare source of the sound. Leaning against a tree was a man with a ghastly, bloody mask of half a face lolling from side to side on his shoulders, his eyes closed and the moans gurgling bloodily out of a smashed mouth. The teeth of his upper jaw hung incongruously white over the open space where his lower jaw had been, and though his AK-47 was close at hand, he was clearly no longer a threat.

Three more steps took me, numbed, to a scene of carnage. Ahmed Dur and three of his soldiers lay huddled, almost touching, in a small clearing no more than about twenty feet across, their bodies stitched red with machine-gun fire. Wildly, I swung from the scene and in the same instant I saw a second enemy soldier beyond Ahmed Dur's body. Blindly, I raised my rifle and fired. The round took him at close range in the centre of his forehead an inch or so above his eyes, smashing his skull to fragments and emptying his brains on the ground behind him. The hideous shrunken mask of his face flopped back onto his shoulders, lips bared in a last rictus of agony.

Impressions crowded in on me uncontrollably. I looked again at Ahmed Dur, staring sightlessly at the sky in an expression of vacant surprise and the medic kneeling over him, trying uselessly to breathe life back into his cooling corpse. Pieces of skull like broken coconut lay scattered about on the grass and the brain still wobbled on the ground where it had fallen, almost intact despite the impact of the bullet. I stumbled to the edge of the trees and sat down, trembling in shock, and struggling to bring my whirling mind under control.

Ahmed Said, indifferent to death, had already started the work of looting the dead and wounded enemy soldiers. He stole their AK-47s and a money belt from Ali Matook, the man whom I had killed, whilst I, the over-educated, over-sensitive Westerner, sat on the edge of the copse trying to get myself organised. The firing had stopped and I gave orders to start clearing up. I spoke to Lai Bux on the radio and asked him what was happening in his area whilst Peter went up to the remainder of Ahmed Dur's platoon by the huts above us and got them organised under command of Ahmed Ali, the senior corporal. Douglas had arrived at the Ghazeer with the convoy and had been listening anxiously to the prolonged gunfire but he refrained from interfering in my fight and I was grateful. I reported the situation to him and asked for a helicopter to take out the dead and wounded. He offered me reinforcements, but at that moment it seemed as though the remaining enemy had left the area, so I told him they would not be needed.

We began the job of getting the bodies to an area of flat, open ground on which a helicopter could land. As usual, the *firqa* declined to get involved and the Baluch were none too keen on manhandling dead bodies, so Peter and I did most of the hauling, getting soaked in blood to the elbows in the process. Soon the corpses lay in a line on the flat ground, the faces of the Baluch covered with *shimaags* by their comrades. There seemed little point in covering what was left of Ali Matook's face and his erstwhile comrade lay propped against a rock in a semi coma, his face bound with a field dressing through which blood was already dripping.

Whilst we were waiting Ahmed Said came to me and said that there were still Adoo in the wadi and I went with him to the edge and looked into the thickly wooded complex. He could not know for certain and, even if there were, we could not possibly search the area with the few men that we had. Angered by the refusal of the *firqa* to lift a finger to help in the evacuation of the dead and already aware that they had outflanked me by removing the enemies' weapons whilst we toiled, I brusquely invited him to go back into the wadi and do a search if he was that certain. In the light of later accusations that he was to make against me, it was probably a crafty ploy on Ahmed Said's part. It was the biggest mistake I made that day. I should have accepted the offer Douglas made, stayed in the area and carried out a thorough search, but as it was, I handed Ahmed Said an excellent stick to beat me with when I refused his suggestion.

After what seemed like an eternity we heard the distinctive 'whock-whock-whock' of a helicopter and saw the machine coming towards us over the scarp. My Sarbe beacon was giving trouble and we contacted the pilot on the VHF radio with some difficulty. The helicopter landed close by and we began loading, arms and legs flopping about awkwardly. One pilot looked round to watch, but when the headless corpse was pushed in, his eyes went wide with horror above the impersonal flying mask and he quickly looked away again. We piled the bodies one on top of the other and I desperately shoved an arm and a leg into the heap before the door would close properly. It was a grisly task and when the aircraft took off it was as though a weight had been lifted from my shoulders.

The sounds of battle would have attracted enemy from far and wide by now and we would have to move cautiously on our way back to Tawi Atair. I pulled in Lai Bux's platoon and briefed him and Corporal Ahmed Ali at the abandoned huts. I showed them the route back, which was a few kilometres to the east of the way we had gone down and I talked in detail about how we were going to move. As we moved off the only thought I could console myself with was that we had achieved the task we had been given. The enemy's attention had been well and truly diverted from the convoy, which now continued unmolested on its way to Mirbat, but a heavy price had been paid and I mourned Ahmed Dur and his soldiers.

We moved off across the grain of the land, picqueting each ridge before moving on to the next, and we were about halfway back to Tawi when we ran into a well-planned ambush. Ahmed Ali and his men had already crossed a wide, shallow wadi to a small hill overlooking it and Lai's platoon were still on the far side in a defensive position. Peter and I and the gaggle of signallers and *firqa* that made up Company Headquarters were climbing the long open slope towards Ahmed Ali when we came under fire from three or four machine guns concealed in some rocks on a slope about 600 yards away to our right. Long ago I had developed the unconscious habit of noting patches of cover when moving across open ground and without thinking I sprinted to some low rocks about ten yards ahead and dropped into the meagre shelter they offered. My signaller, a corporal who had replaced Saleh Mohammed, beat me by a short head, threw himself into a narrow cleft in the rocks and lay there, face down and hands over his head, sobbing in terror. He had obviously lost interest in soldiering and in that stark moment, a string of mysterious little incidents fell into place. A week or two earlier he had disappeared from his station just behind me in a similar contact, reappearing sometime later when the shooting had stopped and saying that he could not keep up with me. Earlier that day at the Hayeen waterhole he disappeared again, leaving me without communications for an hour or more.

My signaller, our only link with the outside world, was a coward. Whilst I was digesting this information, another enemy position opened up from somewhere down the wadi behind us and when I looked down the slope to where Peter and some soldiers lay motionless under the storm of fire my heart sank again at the prospect of more casualties. I yelled at them, but there was no response.

I started working out another plan of action, going through the options open to me. We had to extricate ourselves from what was becoming a tricky situation, but the enemy had us pinned to the slope like butterflies on a wall and they were too far away for us to hit them, even if we could have manoeuvred to do so. Ahmed Ali and his men were returning a vigorous fire, but there was little he or Lai could do to help us. Peter and the others looked horribly vulnerable as they lay in the open and for a moment I was gripped by black despair at the thought that more of them might have become casualties and that Peter might have been hit on his first patrol. It seemed that I had failed them all and the thought almost overwhelmed me.

Then the moment passed and I was calm again. I felt that nothing would ever again approach the trauma of that morning and even the bullet which neatly sheared off a tall new blade of grass in silent slow motion a foot or two from my nose scarcely interrupted my thought process. I jumped up, leaned over to where my signaller was still cowering in the rocks and told him to get me the guns at Tawi Atair. A muffled, wracked voice sobbed that it was impossible, so I grabbed the handset from him none too gently, changed to the gunners' frequency and in a minute or so the guns began firing. There was a lull in the firing and I was relieved to see Peter move, but a *firqa* lad stood up and was promptly whirled backwards as a bullet took him in the chest. Ahmed Said now redeemed himself for the moment by strolling calmly down the slope, lifting the boy on his shoulders and bringing him back to shelter. Peter yelled at his orderly to throw over his radio and as the set arced across the short distance between them a bullet went through it and a moment later it struck Peter's upturned face, splitting the bridge of his nose. It was the only damage he or I suffered that day.

The renewed fighting was being followed on the radio in the operations room at Arzat and they called up air support. As the first artillery rounds began falling on the enemy position to our right, a Strikemaster pilot came up on my radio. A moment or two later a pair of jets appeared over the horizon and the enemy fire stopped as they began to attack, but the pilots saw nothing for the Adoo had almost certainly run for shelter as soon as the planes appeared. I told Lai to get started and we moved on up to Ahmed Ali's picquet and took stock. The *firqa* lad was losing a lot of blood, but his wound was not yet mortal, so I radioed for a casevac helicopter and told Brian to get ready for him at Tawi Atair. A couple of the *firqa* began to hurry him away and in another astounding demonstration of *Jebali* fortitude, he walked the remaining four kilometres back to the airstrip where he arrived half dead from loss of blood. Brian was waiting with drips and dressings and his efficient care almost certainly saved the boy's life. Just before we moved away I saw that my signaller was without his weapon. I asked him where it was and he replied that he had dropped it when we came under fire. When he refused to fetch it, I told him that I would assuredly shoot him if he did not do so and I meant it, but we were both spared the trouble by one of the *firqa* who produced it at that moment. The jets circled protectively above us as we made our weary way back and I remember looking up at them and experiencing a feeling of warm gratitude. We had been fighting and marching for ten hours and it was good to get a break.

That evening Peter and I visited Ahmed Ali and the men of 11 Platoon, imagining that they might need consolation after the loss of their comrades, but they were cheerful and philosophical about it. As good Muslims they believed that those who had died fighting for the faith against infidels were surely already in Heaven. I wish I could have shared their confidence, but I could not believe that souls survived in bodies reduced to so many lumps of inert meat and in the moment that I looked into Ahmed Dur's dead eyes, my own faith began to crumble to dust.

Until that day at Hayeen, combat had been an exciting business at fairly long range in which, candidly, pursuit of and shooting at the enemy had been a joyous, if occasionally frightening business. At close quarters it turned out to be a messy, stomach-turning affair, conferring neither glory nor dignity on the living or the dead. As Mansoor said, in a rare moment of wisdom, 'It takes such a long time to bring up a child to manhood and such a short time to kill him.' I had mastered fear and done my duty, but more could have been done. The encounter should have been followed up vigorously and the fact that it was not has been a lasting reproach. Ahmed Dur and his men died because they were not trained sufficiently and that knowledge bred in me a serious and dedicated altitude to training that has irritated successive superiors with different priorities ever since. I had mastered fear, the worst enemy, but I had trouble sleeping for some time and it was many years before the bloody, shrunken mask of Ali Matook no longer appeared without warning to haunt me in the wide-awake hours of a restless night, thousands of miles from that small patch of woodland in the hills of Dhofar.

It was not long before recriminations began flying back and forth over the incident. For the first time I heard that Ali Matook was wearing a money belt which disappeared and Wali Baraik naturally wanted to know what had happened to it. I was asked by the Brigadier to send him a written report on the contact and after two summonses, Ahmed Said went to Salalah to explain himself. There he accused me of stealing the money belt and said that if I had followed his suggestion and gone back into the wadi we would have killed another twenty Adoo. His allegations successfully muddied the waters and he even got away without handing in the weapons he had taken, presenting them instead to the Omani ambassador to the Lebanon who visited Tawi Atair the next day. Ahmed Said's fairytales were easily outdone by Radio Aden which claimed that eighteen Government soldiers, including two British imperialist mercenaries (Peter and I, presumably) had been killed in the incident. As if that were not enough, the rumour factory began working overtime in Salalah and soon everyone had his own firm views on what had happened.

TAWI ATAIR: JUNE–AUGUST 1975

The next day Yarpy Wardle flew up to Tawi Atair with Tim Hewlett, one of the Strikemaster pilots who had come to our aid, and they brought with them a plump little Gunner major who had just arrived in Dhofar to take over the battery at Taqah. Yarpy and Tim listened to my account of the previous day's action sympathetically, but after a minute or two I was sharply interrupted by the Gunner, who launched into a detailed account of the day which bore no resemblance whatsoever to what had happened. I had admitted my errors, but now a scarcely credible catalogue of tactical mistakes was being laid at my door and I realised that the armchair tacticians had decided on the sequence of events, apportioned blame and closed their minds. I was less than charitable with the pasty-faced little Gunner, and I savaged him with the sharpest sarcasm I could muster.

It was a warm and sunny day and at last we received a few of the things we had been asking for over a period of weeks, such as radio batteries and spares, new compasses and a new Sarbe beacon. Despite my forebodings about the hatchet job that Ahmed Said and the boys in Salalah had done on me, things were looking up again and when Yarpy asked me to go back to Hayeen the next day I agreed with equanimity.

D Company had been given the task of 'searching' the Ghazeer and the Hinna and we were ordered to assist by once again securing the high ground. It was an optimistic plan, because it would take a battalion several days to do the job properly, but we had to get back there quickly, if only to show that we were undeterred by recent events. We set off before dawn and by first light we were well on our way down the route we had followed a couple of days before. We left Ahmed Said behind to wait for a helicopter which would take him back for another talk with the authorities in Salalah so the *firqa* was commanded by Mohammed Said, a distinct improvement from my point of view.

A few miles out from Tawi Atair we spotted two small figures on the horizon moving rapidly at right angles to the line of our advance. Cautious from our recent experience, we kept them under close observation as they converged and passed behind, ignoring us completely. It was an old man and his wife travelling at an apparently leisurely pace but in fact crossing the undulating ground at a speed which would have taxed our heavily-laden soldiers. The Adoo came from a people used to covering great distances across their native hills and being lightly equipped, it was no wonder that they could move so rapidly.

Not long after daybreak we made contact with D Company and soon we were deploying along the ridges and picquets overlooking the area to be visited. D Company's mortar section began registering targets and I switched in to listen on their company radio net as the first puffs of grey and brown smoke began to blossom on the hillside. Presently we saw a long column of tiny figures wending its way down into the Wadi Hayeen and reappearing a few minutes later on the near side. Then it began to climb the long sloping flanks of a high ridge overlooking the scarp. At the summit of the ridge was a small group of huts and as D Company approached them Hugh Willoughby came up on the radio again, talking to his leading platoon commander. 'I can see some men by the huts on the top. Can you see whether they are Adoo?' There was then a short exchange inaudible to me and the next thing I heard was Hugh passing a fire order to his mortar section, giving a grid reference which I saw from a glance at my map was that of the huts above us. Then I heard 'Oh well, I'm going to fire anyway.' At that point I interrupted him with a sharp query as to whether the men at the huts had been positively identified as Adoo, and my intervention was followed by an embarrassed silence as Hugh realised that his momentary lapse from grace had been marked by a fellow Englishman. No rounds were fired at the huts and the day passed without incident, but it was a chilling reminder of how decent men can lapse into casual barbarism when they control absolute force and there is no restraining law at hand.

13 August 1975

Slowly the weather began to improve and when, a week or so later, the skies cleared and the ground started to dry out, we began training the company in the techniques of searching wooded areas. I selected a suitable densely wooded hollow close to the *firqa* camp and set up a small demonstration. The *firqa* quickly gathered and soon we had one or two of them enthusiastically playing enemy and providing 'bodies' to be searched. Peter was doing the demonstration and he moved in towards a young lad playing dead and placed a large size-eleven boot squarely on the boy's back in order to immobilise him. The technique is sound enough, but it ignored the fact that, to an Arab, it is an insult even to sit with the sole of the foot towards a person, let alone to place it firmly between his shoulder blades. The lad struggled vainly beneath Peter's boot and as soon as the pressure was released he jumped up, screeching with rage and humiliation. Peter looked hurt and puzzled and I quickly apologised for his error, explaining that no insult was intended. To prove my point I lay down and allowed Peter to repeat his performance, which he did with even greater gusto, knocking the breath out of me with his great hoof. The rest of the *firqa* regarded it as a huge joke and honour was restored all round, but I thought the encore a shade too enthusiastic for comfort and said so. Peter affected innocence.

We moved on to the next part of the programme, which was skirmishing. We had no blank ammunition so we used live, thereby dramatically increasing the realism of the exercise. There were no instructors from the School of Infantry on hand to check that we were within the prescribed safety limits and as we moved up the wadi towards the corporal whom I had briefed to put down 'enemy' fire on us, the sound effects were very convincing indeed. It was a successful day's training.

Helicopters were becoming a very sore point with me by this stage in the *Khareef*. We had not eaten fresh food for weeks and we were getting short of vital items, so I expected that the spell of fine weather would be used to bring us up to scratch again, but I was to be disappointed. The helicopter that visited on 10 August brought an Omani Air Force lieutenant to spend a few days on leave at Tawi with relatives, but very little in the way of stores and I discovered that if it had not been for his leave (he being a relative of the Sultan) the helicopter would not have come at all. I was furious at what I regarded as a flagrant abuse, and when a second machine arrived loaded to the roof with soft pink lavatory rolls and, in a crowning insult, a new windsock, I was quite unable to see the humour of it. The task of coordinating resupply with helicopter flights seemed beyond the staff at Salalah and helicopters came and went often without picking up much needed supplies from Arzat. I did not blame our Quartermaster – Sher was doing his best – but it did seem that there was little recognition of our needs where it mattered. My letters home at this time were full of bitter observations on all and sundry on the plain, but in retrospect I suppose they did what they could.

With the warmer weather the barber got started on the soldiers and a number of them opted to have their heads shaved completely. I was beginning to look a little theatrical with locks curling down over my collar, so went along to get a trim as well. There was no finesse in this salon and I was shorn like a lamb, much to Peter's amusement.

14 August 1975

A helicopter was summoned to take our Air Force friend back to Salalah at the end of his leave and with him went Ahmed Said to make yet another report to the intelligence officer. I was glad to see the back of the Air Force officer for he was an ostentatious and flashy young man who flaunted his wealth before the simple folk of Tawi Atair and he had an ingratiating manner which was beginning to get on my nerves.

17 August 1975

Douglas McCully and David Bills came up to Tawi with the first convoy for more than a month and I complained bitterly to them about the supply situation and the fact that C Company was being steadily weakened for lack of men. For a variety of reasons – leave, sickness, transfers, casualties and so on – platoons were down to about a dozen men each and it was becoming difficult to mount operations without amalgamating them, something I was loath to do for a number of reasons. Guard rosters were becoming a burden on the riflemen and I told the Sergeant Major to put the men of Company Headquarters on to help.

This caused immediate resistance. Headquarters staff, particularly the *babu* (clerk), had achieved a position of comparative comfort and privilege by dint of patronage, influence, education and (occasionally) ability, and it was no part of their duties to be demeaned by having to do guard duties. Keeping a tight hold on my temper, I patiently explained to Bilal that someone had to guard the base at night and whilst we were away, after all, the *babu* and the storeman did little work. My words were as water poured into the sand for in Bilal's mind the important thing was not equity, but the principle. No matter that they could all be murdered in their beds and the base overrun whilst we were absent, no matter that the common soldiers could plod for miles in the heat or the rain whilst they sat and whiled away the day exchanging pleasantries and vain chatter, the proprieties had to be observed. But my sense of justice was outraged by his attitude and I was adamant. *Babu* and the others would do guard duties and they could like it or lump it. Bilal and the rest of the company hierarchy were deeply shocked and for days I kept receiving little delegations from high and low to complain about the harsh treatment, but to no avail. Later I discovered to my astonishment that, far from being pleased at the help I had organised, the ordinary riflemen were as aghast as Bilal at the arrangement. In fact, they all looked forward to achieving an easy billet in Company Headquarters or better still, Battalion Headquarters some day and what good would that do them if an awkward officer promptly put them back on a guard roster?

18 August 1975

The weather continued fine for a few more days and we went a couple of kilometres south to do some more training. On the way back I decided to put in a little practice with some of the 66-mm anti-tank rockets we had 'liberated' from a British Army unit in Salalah. The rockets, which were originally intended for the tanks of the Warsaw Pact, were an excellent means of delivering high explosive at short ranges and even shorter notice, and we could have done with a few at the Hayeen waterhole. They had not long been in service and as I had been almost three years out of the mainstream of regimental soldiering, I was not familiar with them, so Peter prepared to demonstrate his skill, taking the old Skyvan hulk at the top end of our airstrip as his target. Enjoying his moment, Peter explained the rudiments of the rocket to the assembled Baluch, turned, raised it to his shoulder and fired. A satisfying bang from the rocket ignition was followed by a hiss of appreciation from the Baluch which died into silence as the rocket flew over the Skyvan and into the blue distance beyond the ridge marking the end of the runway. There was an embarrassed pause which was ended by the echoing thump of the warhead detonating on some far slope. We looked at each other and I struggled to keep an expressionless face.

I lifted a second rocket to my shoulder, sighted on the hulk and began to squeeze down on the trigger. Nothing happened. I squeezed harder, inadvertently jerking the rocket as it went off. There was another mighty bang, another sigh of exhaled breath from the audience, another long pause and another distant thump far away over the ridge. Peter cackled with satisfaction. After a third failure we decided to call it a day, do some intensive training using the three empty launcher tubes which we now had, and try again later. It was not a convincing demonstration of the combat prowess of the British Army.

We drove round the east end of the main picquet in our battered old Land Rover and as we jolted up the rocky track towards Company Headquarters I saw a small, portly Arab in a white *dishdasha* (robe) hurrying towards us, stumbling on the uneven ground in his haste to intercept us. From his clothes and his evident unfamiliarity with the rough going underfoot, I could see even from a distance that he was no *Jebali*. As we drew level with him, Peter stopped the Land Rover and without any of the customary preliminaries, he grabbed my sleeve. 'You are the Colonel? You must get me a helicopter now. I have to get to Salalah tonight.'

He had chosen the wrong subject on which to importune me and his peremptory manner did nothing to help his case. I took his hand from my sleeve and squinted at the clouds rolling up the hillside and blotting out the late afternoon sun. 'Look at those clouds. There will be no helicopter tonight nor, perhaps, for many nights.' 'But I have a wife and children in Salalah. You are the Colonel and you must get me a helicopter.' 'I have a wife and children in England and I have not seen them in many months. There will be no helicopter.'

Impatient with his imperious demands, I told Peter to drive on. 'Shall I tell him we're about to try and set up a record for the longest time without a helicopter resupply?' Peter suggested cheerfully as we drove away, and I laughed. The government vet, as he turned out to be, came to pester us again later in the evening, demanding that we feed him and give him the bed in the sick bay. 'You may feed with us and the Sergeant Major will fix you a bed in the *murcha* next door, but you are not sleeping in the sick bay and I doubt that there will be another helicopter for ten days at least.' His face crumpled. 'Then you will give me an escort and I will walk down to Salalah in the morning.' 'If you do, the Adoo will certainly cut your throat, for I will give you no escort.' He crept away, dispirited and deflated.

19 August 1975

The next day we patrolled westward to the village of Anshaam, close to the bend in the Darbat where I had been ambushed on my visit to Tawi Atair with the armoured cars. Perched on the edge of the great wadi, it was an ideal refuge for the Adoo and it had any number of easy escape routes running from the back of the village into the thick trees below. I did not have enough men to seal off the village and I was ignorant of what lay between the it and the wadi, so on this occasion I was not trying to catch anyone out. It was more in the nature of a reconnaissance so that I could get to know the ground around Anshaam for a future occasion.

As we approached a couple of men moved, casually and without haste, away from the village and down into the Darbat. They were unarmed and too far away to give chase and even if we apprehended them, it would be impossible to identify them as Adoo. The only people who might have been able to do so were the *firqa* and whilst they were happy to take on their relatives in battle, it was quite another matter to expect them to betray them in cold blood. They would never be forgiven for doing so.

Oddly enough, the Adoo often betrayed themselves by their reaction to a sudden descent on their village. If they went calmly about their business and outpaced us, there was little chance that we would identify them, but often they or their women would panic at our approach. There would then be a lot of rushing around, perhaps some gunfire, and so precipitous a flight that their identity was unmistakeable.

On this occasion they played their cards very carefully. Apart from one or two sullen youths who attracted my attention, we found only old men, women and children in the village and after the usual round of courtesies and some ministration to the sick, we moved out and returned to Tawi Atair by way of a great circular, sweeping movement along the edge of the wadi.

24 August 1975

The days of dreary mist and rain dragged on, seemingly without end. Then one evening a wind from out of the desert to the north blew the clouds away and left the air so clear and washed that the pale gold rocks of the Gatn leapt into focus as though it were but a short distance away. The great wooded peaks of Qisais ad Deen stood etched against a fiery sky, illuminated by the evening sun in shades of green from almost black to bright emerald. They evoked half-forgotten childhood images of some lost, legendary land of giants and castles and seemed almost to brood in their far isolation.

That evening Dishdasha Man came up from the *firqa* camp where he had been enduring their rough hospitality and again pleaded for transport out of Tawi. The *firqa* were not overly concerned with the finer things of life and the poor fellow had not been enjoying his stay. His manner was somewhat chastened, and I softened towards him, explaining that I had no control over the allocation of helicopters and that we too had failed to get one when it was needed, but I would do what I could for him. We consoled him by letting him join in a small informal shooting match that had started between ourselves and some of the *firqa*, but we made certain that he kept the pistol pointed well away from either of us. At the start we had teased him by saying that he might have to stay for ten days or more, so when a helicopter did eventually arrive four days later, the prophecy was fulfilled. Like Malik, his haste to depart was indecent and later I reflected that in all the time that he had spent with us, he never so much as looked at a single cow and so an opportunity to do some good was wasted. It was predictable behaviour. A qualification was regarded more as a passport to a plush, air-conditioned office than as an obligation to toil in the countryside amongst those who needed it most. That could safely be left to Europeans on contract.

28 August 1975

Until now I had refused to go to Arzat on the grounds that if I did so, I might not be able to get back, but items for my attention were piling up and the intervals of clear weather were becoming longer and more frequent. This time I received a direct order from the CO to go and in an undignified scramble, I fought my way onto the helicopter against dozens of *firqa*, all of whom apparently had personal appointments with the Wali in Salalah. After nine weeks and four days in Tawi Atair I found myself flying down over the great scarp and along the coastal plain to Arzat.

Lunch in the Mess was excellent and after weeks of poor food I thought of how well they all lived and how nice it would have been if a little of this opulence had found its way onto the hill. In the afternoon I visited the small NAAFI shop at RAF Salalah and, resolved to enliven our brutish existence with some music and a means of contact with the outside world, I bought myself a radio cassette player and a selection of music by Mozart, Schubert, Beethoven and Haydn. At the Mess, by contrast, they were celebrating the installation of a magnificent new hi-fi system, a gift from the Sultan. It would provide unheeded muzak for many a drinking bout, but like so many other arrangements in the Mess, it was of no interest or benefit to the Baluch officers. In the evening I took too much drink and got into a long argument with a newly arrived mercenary lieutenant colonel who was due to take command of the *firqa* and who seemed to my hopelessly biased mind to be talking absolute rubbish about them on the basis of twenty-four hours' experience in Dhofar. Later I discovered that he had spent a number of years with X Company of the Trucial Oman Scouts, which was largely composed of *Jebalis*, so he probably knew a great deal more about them than I gave him credit for. I was becoming very crusty and antisocial, and Douglas McCully took me to task for it, dubbing me 'The Old Man of Tawi Atair'.

31 August 1975

The next day being Jummah (Friday), it was the Muslim weekend and towards lunchtime the Mess began filling up with people from Salalah who had come to enjoy another round of eating and drinking in the KJ Mess. I knew very few of them and found it difficult and tedious to follow their conversation which revolved around matters of no interest to me. After two months away I knew little of the latest Salalah gossip and cared less and after a while I slipped away, ate a solitary lunch and retired to my room.

During the afternoon my stomach decided that this unexpected surfeit of rich food was too much of a good thing, and by evening I was abed and feeling very sorry for myself. I spent a wretched night heaving up until there was nothing left in me and then retching dry on an empty stomach until the dawn, when I slept for a few hours, exhausted. I woke feeling very weak and ate nothing that day, but on the Sunday I bestirred myself and taking a reluctant Malik with me, caught a plane down to Mirbat to see Badil and his men.

Badil met us at the airstrip and took us down to the fort, which had been the scene of an epic battle a couple of years before between an SAS detachment supported by a few soldiers of the Oman Artillery and *askars* of the Wali's guard, and several hundred Adoo who had gathered in the shadows of the nearby Wadi Ghazeer and attacked Mirbat in the only massed assault on a town carried out by them during the war.

The fort and the town were a picturesque and odorous part of old Arabia. Huddled by the sea on the edge of a small flat plain below the towering ramparts of the Eastern Jebel, Mirbat was a jumble of houses crowded together along the shore, all in various stages of decay. One or two were marked only by a pile of rubble, having been destroyed, it was said, on the orders of the Wali of Mirbat as a punishment for disloyalty to the Sultan.

Ancient fishing boats lay on the beach amongst mountains of litter, European and Arab, twentieth-century and medieval, not at all what a tour operator would include in his description of 'unspoilt Arabia' if ever he were allowed to go there. Over all hung the stench of the drying sardines from which the coastal fisherfolk made a living. These were brought ashore in shoals, laid out on the beach to dry (hence the smell) and then transported to the Jebel in great sacks slung on camels, where they were fed to the cattle. They were a valuable food supplement, especially towards the end of the dry season, when the grazing became sparse. Surprisingly, cows devoured the dried fish eagerly and it never seemed to taint the milk they gave. Indeed, the *Jebalis* swore that the milk was creamier and richer as a result of this curious diet. A caravan of camels laden with fish on its way to the hills could be smelled for many miles down wind.

I went round his positions with Badil then we made our way up to the Jebel Ali, a hill about a hundred feet high standing alone a mile or so north of the town where the platoon maintained a small detachment overlooking a dry, rocky cemetery of graves marked only by small upright headstones in the Muslim manner. The detachment was commanded by Corporal Jumma, a large, round soft man who now sported a bushy black beard and affected a grave manner quite different from the joviality which I remembered from only a few months before. Like Badil he had recently caught the religion bug, which bit some men at a certain point in their lives and changed them from laughing, carefree comrades in arms to gloomy, introverted bores who lost interest in everything except prayer. They were fit for very little else and it always depressed me when I saw it happen to one of my soldiers.

Two days later I was back in Mirbat, this time with the CO and Tim Creasey, then a Major General and Commander of the Sultan's Armed Forces. We were greeted by the Wali and taken upstairs in his house where we sat round the walls on carpets, with Creasey and his Omani ADC in the place of honour. Trays of coffee, tinned fruit and '*halwhaal*', the colourless, sweet 'Turkish delight', of Arabia were brought in and for an excruciating hour or so Creasey made halting conversation with the Wali in his execrable Arabic whilst the rest of us looked on, willing the words into his mouth. His ADC, a bright, likeable and quick-witted fellow intervened diplomatically now and then to supply an elusive phrase for his General and had obviously had plenty of practice in doing so. At last we moved out and up to Jebel Ali, via the fort. I had arranged a mortar shoot for the General, entrusting the fire control to one of my best young corporals, but Creasey was not impressed. 'A bit slow' was his gruff comment as he watched the puffs of dust and smoke rising from a wadi beyond the town, ignoring the fact that the NCO was doing better than many officers would in the same circumstances.

We flew out of Mirbat and low over the clear aquamarine sea, passing over a school of sharks basking close inshore by Taqah and I wondered idly what would happen if an engine failed and we were dunked into the water. A year later there was an answer of sorts when a Britten-Norman Defender taking off from Mirbat did plunge into the sea, drowning all on board except the pilot, who managed to get out before the plane sank.

Back at Arzat, it was clear that my welcome was wearing very thin. I had been down five days and Gordon-Taylor was beginning to mutter remarks about officers who spent all their time in Salalah instead of on the hill with their men, glancing sideways at me from under those knitted, black brows of his. I could take a hint, and the next day I flew back to Tawi Atair.

Chapter 9

Tawi Atair: September–December 1975

3 September 1975

The moment I arrived back Ahmed Said rushed up to see me, fearful that I had told my side of the story, thus pointing the finger at him in the matter of the money belt missing after the Hayeen contact. I had a long and very awkward interview with him, dodging the many traps he laid for me with his wily tongue only with the greatest of difficulty. So skilled was he at shifting the focus of guilt that I found myself almost apologising to him over any anxiety I might have been caused and I assured him repeatedly that I had not raised the subject of the Hayeen contact in Salalah. In the end it was I, the aggrieved party, that came off worse from the discussion and from that moment my attitude hardened and I resolved that I would make no further attempt to conciliate him. I took no trouble to conceal the dislike and distrust which I now felt for him and this, combined with his style of leadership and his tribal background (not being of the al-Amri) brought about his downfall as *firqa* leader and I made no move to save him.

Also on that day a young fellow with the sonorous name of Ahmed Said Da'aan Shahri walked into Tawi and announced that he was surrendering to the Sultan after three and a half years with the Adoo. In their pragmatic way, the *firqa* welcomed him enthusiastically, but he declined to go down to Salalah and, short of arresting him, there was no way in which I could force him to do so. Significantly, he did not bring his weapon with him, so keeping his options open if he should decide to go back to his friends. He was not untypical and many *Jebalis* changed sides more than once without incurring any odium on either side for doing so. It was a very gentlemanly way of doing things, but no *Jebali* would understand the term even if it were explained to him.

At this time quite a few enemy soldiers were coming in from the area around Tawi Atair and I liked to think that it was at least partly due to our operations during the *Khareef*, but getting at the truth was difficult. Surrendered Enemy Personnel (SEPs) tended to go through *firqa* channels and although an authoritative-looking fellow had been hanging around Tawi for some weeks calling himself a '*seeyasee*' (strictly, 'political agent', but used loosely in Dhofar to mean an intelligence officer), there was no feedback from the intelligence system in Salalah and it came as no surprise when he told me that eight SEPs had come into Tawi within the last month. It looked as though it was becoming fashionable to give oneself up, but as always in Arabia, sorting out truth from fiction was next to impossible.

The next day the wet weather returned with a vengeance but the mist and drizzle did not deter Jumma Hussein, our agreeable Omani FOO, from having an outdoor lunch and inviting us to join him. The Gunners had bought and killed a cow and in Omani fashion, they boiled it up and piled the pieces on tin trays. Ignoring the rain, we squatted together in the wet grass and tucked into the piles of meat and rice. Great glistening coils of entrails were pounced on eagerly and devoured with gusto by the soldiers so Peter and I were able to get some reasonably lean meat, although it was tough and took a good deal of chewing. I never saw the eyes of either sheep or cattle eaten at any meal during my time in Arabia, for which I was profoundly thankful.

6 September 1975

At about this time all our lighting systems finally gave up the unequal struggle against Baluch ham-fistedness and, as the rain poured down and the fog billowed about us, our evenings were at last illuminated by a humble candle. To add to our troubles Ramadan began.

Ramadan is the month of fasting laid upon the Faithful once a year and during it they may neither drink, eat nor smoke during the hours of daylight. It offered endless possibilities for argument and discussion and we explored them all. Patiently I explained that, in accordance with the word of the Prophet, dispensation had been given them at the highest level since they were soldiers fighting against the enemies of God. They should eat and drink whilst on operations and so be stronger in the fight for the Faith. But it was too good an opportunity to miss. Bilal groaned in religious ecstasy at the sheer martyrdom of it all, and the *firqa* declared that they would probably not be able to go on operations. Men whom I had never seen on their knees now professed themselves bound with hoops of iron to their sacred duty as Muslims to observe the feast, no matter what the Sultan's mullah might say.

The poor soldiers had no option: they had to do as they were told, though Bilal protested loud and long and for that month did even less than usual, becoming almost completely immobile in his tent and passing each day in endless gossip with his cronies. I rarely took him on operations for he was more of a hindrance than a help, distracted as he was by his religious fixation.

Now the mountains of Bird's Eye custard that had been flown into Tawi just before the start of the *Khareef* came into their own. As soon as the sun went down the Baluch would fall upon the custard and devour it by the gallon, smoking and chattering endlessly through the night. It never ceased to amaze me how they talked, as though every day was packed with exciting new experiences, instead of being the fairly tedious routine that it usually was. By this time Peter and I had exchanged most of our information and although we were on the best of terms, our conversation tended to be limited to the occasional cryptic grunt, but the Baluch talked on and on and on . . .

Two days after the start of Ramadan I decided to visit the village of Qunf, an isolated group of huts some miles to the east of Tawi on the edge of Qisais ad Deen. The night before I had sent a curt word to Ahmed Said inviting him to join me on the patrol and telling him to rendezvous with me by the artillery compound early the next morning. I did not tell him where the patrol was going and this he rightly took as a calculated insult, so that when we moved out just after dawn we found a small group of them sitting in a sullen, resentful huddle. Without any preliminaries, Ahmed began to berate me for not taking him into my confidence and saying that, in the circumstances, he could not go with us. Shrugging my shoulders, I told him that it was all the same to me whether he came or not and turning on my heel, I walked away from him and back to the patrol, who were squatting in the grass and watching the proceedings with interest.

I half expected to hear Ahmed's AK-47 being cocked as I walked away, for I had seen the fury in his eyes at the humiliation which I had deliberately inflicted on him, but the *firqa* were outnumbered by the Baluch, who would have welcomed the chance to have a go at them, and even Ahmed would not be so stupid as to risk the consequences of killing a British officer in public. I had no conscience about provoking the rift, for I already knew that a split between Ahmed and his cronies and the al-Amri element of the *firqa* was on the way and I felt we could manage without him. It was a cynical attitude, but in Ahmed I had found a good teacher in cynicism.

So we set off without him and for once it was quite pleasant to stride out up the long slope towards Qunf without the endless running discussions which always seemed to go on when he was with us. We were soon wet to the waist from the heavy dew on the long russet grass, but it was a beautiful morning and a million spider webs danced in the gentle breeze, the sunlight sparkling on tiny droplets of water caught on their threads.

Three hours of hard walking brought us to the hilly, sour land on the edge of Qisais ad Deen where, in contrast to the lush pastures around Tawi Atair, the grass was still thin and stunted, even after months of mist and rain. Even so, as we approached the hamlet of Qunf, we could see herds of white goats and sheep dotting the hillsides, industriously stripping what little grazing there was. The mist cleared and from some high ground close by the huts we could see a seemingly endless succession of ridges and valleys which made up the Wadi Shuffloon complex stretching away to the scarp above Mirbat.

There were not many people in the hamlet and they were surly and indifferent to our presence, although we must have been the first representatives of the government to visit them in years. The huts were surrounded by the usual lake of cattle dung mixed with water bubbling away, and the flies crowded eagerly around in their millions. I peered into the gloom of a hut where a woman sat, sunk in lethargy, on a floor carpeted with flies crawling unheeded over cooking utensils, food and the children. It was small wonder that the villagers were listless and as sour as their land. We asked for the news, but as usual, 'God be praised', there was none and it was clear from the outset that we were going to get little from the villagers but polite phrases, so after tending some of their more obvious aches and pains, we reorganised ourselves and started back.

Jelal volunteered to navigate on the return journey, but the weather began to close in again so I kept a close check on our progress, especially as visibility shortened to a few yards and we began to blunder around in the familiar milky-white opacity of a Jebel mist. I was not going to interfere in what Jelal was doing and Peter and I clambered patiently in and out of wadi after wadi until at last we came out close by the well at Tawi, having walked several kilometres further than necessary. I took Jelal to task for assuring me that he knew where he was each time I asked him, when patently he did not, and he was suitably chastened.

We plodded wearily up the hill, hot, wet, stinking and covered with small black flies that bit mercilessly, even through the fabric of our shirts and trousers. Bilal had spent the morning lounging in his tent and Peter greeted him in jocular fashion, remarking that all the soldiers had been drinking whisky on the patrol. Bilal, sunk deep in his religious obsession, stiffened with outrage at such flippancy, but some of the less reverential soldiers chuckled at his discomfiture.

After so long on dried and tinned rations we were all beginning to look decidedly peaky, particularly now that Ramadan was on us. Patrols that would have been an easy jaunt in May or June were now quite a trial and the desire for fresh rations, particularly meat, had been a constant theme in my conversations with platoon commanders and the soldiers. With so much meat around us, the problem should have been easily solved, but the view at Battalion Headquarters seemed to be that we had been issued sufficient rations for the period of the *Khareef* and that was that. Prices were high on the Jebel, but even so I was on the point of forking out the money for a cow from my own pocket when, after weeks of pleading, Peter was eventually authorised to spend 196 rials to buy a calf for slaughter. The *firqa* drove a very hard bargain, although they knew that we had been living on dried and tinned rations for months, but we were desperate and eventually Peter concluded the deal. A black bull calf was dragged up to the camp and tied to a Land Rover bumper to await its fate.

10 September 1975

A nervous debate now began on who should slaughter the animal, led by Bilal. I was quite surprised that the Baluch should have been so squeamish and I offered to shoot it myself, knowing full well that the offer would be refused. To be acceptable, the wretched beast must be slaughtered by Halal – having its throat cut in the prescribed manner. Appropriately, the barber eventually agreed to do the job and the calf was tied and dragged, bellowing fearfully, to the place of execution. A large sheet of polythene was laid out on the grass and without further ado, the barber stretched its head backwards and began sawing industriously at its throat with his blunt knife. It was a sickening spectacle, for the animal did not die until its neck was almost sawn through and snapped backwards, but the Baluch were gathered round expectantly and I knew they were watching me to see what my reaction would be, so I forced myself to look on impassively.

The carcass was quickly butchered and the prospect of steak for dinner quelled my feelings of revulsion for the moment. There was much jesting over 'fresh meat', Baluch slang for an effeminate individual, and there were howls of laughter when I announced my intention of taking back a warm handful of the stuff to Mansoor, he being the butt of much ribaldry on that subject. When Corporal Ibrahim sliced off the still twitching penis and suggested that I should take that up to Mansoor as well, the soldiers collapsed and rolled about on the ground in hysterics.

The same morning Ahmed Said came up to see me. He was in a much less truculent mood and clearly chastened by my rebuff of two days before and I received him with a distant politeness. That evening we invited Jumma Hussein to join us for dinner and we had a thoroughly convivial time.

The next day the weather cleared and I obeyed repeated summons to go to Arzat again. I made a determined effort to mend my fences with the CO, though it took some effort of will to do so. Fortunately David Bills was also at Arzat, so the drinking bout that evening, which was mandatory if I was to make any headway with Gordon-Taylor, was more congenial that it might otherwise have been. Even so we consumed vast quantities of whisky and by eleven o'clock I could take no more. My tongue was lolling uncontrollably in my head and the room was beginning to spin, but Gordon-Taylor was about four or five drinks ahead of me and he talked on and on, apparently unaffected by almost five hours of drinking on an empty stomach. Affecting a bonhomie I did not feel, I dragged him into the dining room, collapsing into a chair with relief and hoping that food would rescue me from collapsing utterly. Then in came Dinn, the Goanese steward, with a tray full of the whiskies I thought had been left unnoticed on the bar. I had hoped that Dinn would quietly dispose of them being, as I thought, a friend, so it was with a deep sense of betrayal that I watched as he solemnly lined up six glasses in front of me, almost making me heave up on the spot. How I got through that meal I shall never know, for I have no memory of it or of what happened after.

Bills and I went into Salalah the next day and on the way back we took up a long-standing invitation to visit the government official I had met on the plane down to Dhofar at the beginning of my tour in Oman. It being Friday, he could reasonably be expected to be at home and I was curious to see inside the luxurious new flats then being constructed on the road between Umm al-Ghawarif and Arzat.

We knocked on the door and after a moment we were let into a cool, palatial house with expensive tiled floors and curtained archways adorned with modern furniture of the very highest quality and my thoughts turned involuntarily to the rat-infested hovels we inhabited on the Jebel. By this stage in my tour I had totally lost the facility of making polite small talk, so for the next half hour or so Bills did most of the talking whilst I sat back, thoughts wandering in and out of my head and interrupting the thread of conversation. After a while another visitor arrived, a beautifully barbered and immaculately dressed merchant from Salalah, who greeted our host warmly. We introduced ourselves and the conversation turned naturally to the war and affairs in Salalah. Clearly, they knew little and cared less about what was going on within a few miles of their well-upholstered lives and I could not help but remark upon the contrast between the poverty of the hill people and the newfound wealth which was so conspicuous in and around Salalah. I observed that it was an imbalance that would have to be redressed if the progress we had made so far in the war was not to be lost, for if it was obvious to me, then it would certainly not escape the notice of the sharp-witted *Jebalis* who frequently visited Salalah.

At that, the atmosphere cooled abruptly and our Omani friend rose to leave, presenting as he did so a large, expensively wrapped present to our host which he accepted without a trace of embarrassment. Bills and I also left and on the way back to Arzat I wondered aloud if, in my usual diplomatic way, I had put my foot in it again. 'Not at all,' chortled Bills in his jovial fashion. 'These Salalah lurkers, they're all the same – in it for all they can get!'

In the evening we went back to the Brigade Headquarters mess to see *From Russia with Love* – delightful dated nonsense, but great fun.

14 September 1975

The next day I felt sick again, something that happened on most of my visits to Arzat over the next few months, so it was as well that I was unable to get a helicopter back to Tawi until the day after, when the CO came up and stayed for about an hour. It was a beautiful day made better by Ahmed's departure to Salalah on the pretext of illness. In the afternoon we saw the first of the Hunter jets that the Sultan had acquired from Jordan. The pilot came in over the picquet once or twice, waggling his wings in acknowledgement of our waves and disappearing to the west. A few minutes later he swept in again, streaking up the airstrip so fast and so low that we were able to look down on him from the picquet. Trapped in the grubby daily round of life at Tawi Atair, there was a fleeting moment when I envied the glamorous, carefree existence of our friends in the Air Force.

16 September 1975

A couple of days later the first fixed-wing aircraft landed at Tawi since the beginning of the *Khareef*. It was an important day because (we fondly imagined) it marked the long-awaited end of the rainy season at last. I sent Peter to Salalah for a few days' rest and made preparations to receive 11 Platoon who were due to come back from Mirbat the next day. Although it would have been nice to have kept Mirbat in my area so that we could rotate platoons through in order to give them a break from the Jebel, there was no longer any tactical reason for doing so now that the *Khareef* was almost ended and we desperately needed the extra troops at Tawi, for we were beginning to look very thin on the ground indeed.

17 September 1975

The next day was foggy and damp in the morning, but at noon there was a brief clear spell. In that interval a Skyvan shuttled our men and their belongings up from Mirbat, making the brief trip three times. On the second trip I discussed the fog, which was beginning to roll back up the hills, with the pilot, an indefatigable Australian, but he dismissed the obvious dangers with a light shrug of his shoulders. As he took off, we established contact on the Sarbe and a nail-biting twenty minutes or so followed. The distinctive boom of his engines reached us as he cleared the scarp above Mirbat and approached the airstrip for the third time, but by now the approaches were almost totally obscured by cloud. I warned him of the fact and advised him to abort the flight and return to Salalah, but his cheerful voice came back announcing that he would 'tool around for a bit' until he found a hole in the clouds. It was a hazardous plan, considering the many small hills and picquets all around and we listened anxiously as he droned overhead, invisible above the murk. Then he turned and headed west and after a minute or two I saw him drop steeply through a small hole in the clouds no wider than his wingtips, bank sharply towards Tawi and thump down on the airstrip threshold. Before the aircraft had stopped rolling, the tail door was open and the last of 11 Platoon was scampering out, scattering baggage and kit onto the grass, for by now a sense of urgency had well and truly gripped us all.

Within moments the Skyvan was taxiing back to the top end of the strip. Turning, its engines roaring, it accelerated downhill, tearing through the advancing tendrils of mist and disappearing into the gloom as the runway was finally enveloped. It would hardly have won the approval of the Air Officer Commanding at Salalah, but it was a magnificent piece of flying.

Badil and his platoon had become thoroughly domesticated during their stay at Mirbat, but they were as pleased to be back with the company as we were to see them. We gossiped away, admired the chickens they had brought with them, and generally made them feel welcome. The brood included one magnificent rooster whom we promptly christened Chanteclair and he made the top of Bilal's tent his perch, though who woke whom first thing each morning became a matter of debate.

18 September 1975

The next day a Defender brought in Tim Burls of the Parachute Regiment, a newcomer to Dhofar, who was to spend a few days with us getting the feel of life on the Jebel, and a couple of photographers on a government-sponsored project who had come to take pictures of the rather limited development that had taken place at Tawi so far. It was very crowded in the *murcha* that evening, and although visitors were always welcome, the extra mouths were a heavy imposition on my small food stocks which were not easy to replenish.

Almost as soon as the aircraft took off the heavens opened and it began to rain as never before in that season. The gloomy afternoon thickened into night and the five of us (Spice, Burls, the two cameramen and myself) huddled together over dinner, dodging the drips. The civilians had that awed, lost look that people always assume when faced with impossibly harsh conditions and when I told them that Brian and I had lived like that for months, their eyes widened with horror. Burls stolidly chewed on his dinner, unmoved by his surroundings.

Later that evening I briefed three of my platoon commanders, Badil, Jelal and Suleiman, for a second patrol to Qunf, starting before dawn the next day and we retired to bed with the sound of rain hammering on the roof.

In the darkness of the early morning I swung my feet out of bed and onto the old blanket which served as a floor covering and to my surprise they sank into a billowing, wet morass. I was sleepy and confused, but when I shone a torch I saw that my little den was several inches deep in water. It was the first time that the water had come in and the slight biliousness of early morning together with my cold wet feet made for a bad start to the day. I swore feebly, dressed reluctantly and splashed out into the wet gloom to greet my equally introspective soldiers. We set off in the rain.

After telling him about the miseries of the people in Qunf, Spice had said that he would like to come with me to see what he could do, so taking him, and Burls as my company second-in-command I led the patrol round the edge of the *firqa* camp and up the slope towards the village. Brian was unused to walking in the hills and after a kilometre he had fallen so far behind that I told him as kindly as I could that it would be better if he returned to base. He was mortified by his own weakness, but he was much older than the rest of us and not a soldier, so I did not reproach him, but rather was grateful for the thought behind his effort.

As the morning wore on the weather cleared and by about ten o'clock it was cloudy, but bright and pleasant. The *firqa*, led by Mohammed Daan, were cheerful and cooperative for a change and I began to enjoy myself. On our previous visit we had seen little of the ground, but now we could see that our route took us close to the Gatn and on this side of it stretched a tumbled mass of thickly wooded, dark green hills and valleys with conical peaks thrusting up into the lowering grey sky and looking very Germanic. The view had been totally hidden on our last visit, but what we were now seeing was Qisais ad Deen at a different angle than that visible from Tawi Atair. Whichever way it was looked at, it was superb.

Once again, our reception in the village was cool and as we made our way back, the thought struck me that Qunf was ripe for development as a forward base from which to strike into Qisais ad Deen and the Wadi Shuffloon. These were the last two remote parts of the Eastern Jebel and a base was eventually established at Qunf, but not until long after I had gone from Dhofar.

As we came near to Tawi Atair I saw a Defender taking off from the strip and later I heard from Spice that our two photographers had risen very late, taken one look at the wet, grey vista and retired within, where they sat in silent misery until the plane came to rescue them from the living hell of Tawi Atair.

Peter arrived back from his short holiday and I was glad to see him again. We began to make plans for the reception of David Bills and B Company who were to stay for a week or so at Tawi and do some training in the hills before taking part in the annual post-*Khareef* operation in the western area. I was looking forward to having Bills around and although we saw eye to eye on most things it did not prevent us from having vigorous arguments on any and every subject.

Just before Bills and his men came to Tawi Atair, Ahmed Said returned, bringing with him a British officer from the Firqa Headquarters in Salalah. Very tall, solemn and thin, Blackburn had been a trooper in the SAS and returned to Dhofar on contract as one of a small band of ex-soldiers who had been given the job of getting the *firqa* organised. Lofty, as he was dubbed in the Army's unoriginal way, had been told to investigate the trouble in the Firqa al-Amri and report back to Firqa Force Headquarters. He was in the same difficult position as me, for any action he took would be interpreted by one faction or the other as a move against their interests and he had to be particularly careful not to be seen to be hobnobbing with me. He did, however, stay long enough for me to give him an account of recent events at Tawi Atair, then he went down to the *firqa* camp where he spent the next few days. I deliberately avoided him during that time so as not to complicate his task unnecessarily and after about a week he began making preparations to leave. I had not pressed him for his views, but I was naturally curious to know what impressions he would take away with him, so just as he was leaving I put it to him that, although I respected the confidentiality of his mission, it would be nice to know in general terms what he thought of the situation at Tawi Atair. He looked at me for a moment and said simply, 'I see now what you meant,' and went on his way. It was not long after that Ahmed Said left Tawi Atair for good, taking most of his followers. Mohammed Da'aan remained behind with the rest for a while longer.

22 September 1975

B Company came up by convoy and it was good to see them. It was rare for two companies to be in the same place at the same time and when the trucks rolled in there was much slapping of backs and swapping of news amongst the Baluch. I always got on well with Bills and I knew that in spite of his jolly, rather avuncular manner, he was a fit, hard soldier with the simple but effective philosophy that the quickest way to win the war was to be forever on the march, patrolling the hills endlessly and keeping the Adoo on the move. 'You've got to move 'em on, lad, you've got to move 'em on,' he used to say, in his comic London bobby tones, but I had seen him leap from a helicopter under fire and lead his men straight at the enemy.

Bills wasted no time in getting out and about and a couple of days after his arrival both companies made a sortie in strength, B Company to the ridges north of the Wadi Shuffloon and C Company to the small hamlet of Kizit to the north-east. It was a crystal-clear day and from the positions we took up in the hills we could see the ant-like figures of B Company as they crawled across the great expanse of rolling, grey green downs south-east of Tawi. Towards noon, the distant sound of gunfire was borne on the wind from their direction and shortly afterwards the guns at Tawi began to thump. I could not raise Bills on the radio, so it was with some relief that, a short time later, I picked out his figure striding resolutely across the hills amongst his men. When we got back to Tawi I asked David what had happened. 'Oh,' he said, in his off-hand, jovial way, 'A couple of jokers opened up on us so we plastered 'em with the guns.'

Later, the *firqa* complained bitterly about the fact that the guns had been fired, saying that we could have set the pasture ablaze. I had some sympathy with them, but I insisted that we retain the right to use our supporting weapons when the need arose and I maintained that position thereafter.

26 September 1975

We decided to celebrate the end of the *Khareef* by holding a joint sports day consisting of a football match, a shooting contest and a series of donkey races. B Company won the football match and, by some mathematical sleight of hand, the shooting. Although we won all the shooting events, they came out best in aggregate, so Bills declared a victory and being a good host, I declined to argue. The donkey races, on the other hand, were an undisputed victory for C Company. Ridden bareback down the airstrip, they were the most hilarious and popular event of the day. Sitting well back on the donkeys' rumps, their legs wrapped tightly round, the Baluch careered down the strip accompanied by howls of appreciative laughter from the audience. Inevitably, the Sahibs were invited to race each other but strangely, Bills refused adamantly to participate, so Peter, John Moody and I leaped onto our steeds and charged off. It was a short race as one after the other we crashed to the ground in a welter of dust and flying hooves like Indians in a second-rate Western. Painfully, but laughing feebly, I dragged myself to my feet to see the soldiers literally prostrate on the ground with helpless laughter. Bilal, normally so grave and solemn, was rolling around actually slapping his sides and it was some time before they all recovered their composure. It was just the sort of slapstick humour that the Baluch delighted in, and the story went on for months. Doubtless it is still repeated in Baluchistan when veterans of the Sultan's Army gather to talk over old times.

Fresh food and better weather quickly made us fit and patrolling the hills in the long, clear days became a joy again. Mansoor was happy and he revelled in the unaccustomed praise he was getting from Bills and

TAWI ATAIR: SEPTEMBER–DECEMBER 1975

Donkey racing, 26 September 1975.

Moody – my grunts of acknowledgement were becoming ritualistic after almost a year in his company – but he disliked our demands for food at irregular hours and I had to speak to him fairly sharply after one of his tantrums. It was very hot at noon and after three weeks, the observance of Ramadan was becoming patchy. Surreptitious swigs of water were the order of the day on patrol for the soldiers, which was a relief, for I had resolved not to drink, eat or smoke in the presence of my men during the fast.

Early one morning before the moon rose, the two companies set off to visit the Wadi Ghazeer. The move began with a leg-breaking descent down the side of the main picquet and as all the rocks were covered in long grass, there was much cursing and groaning as knees and shins cracked against unseen obstacles. We sorted ourselves out on the level ground by the airstrip and the two columns swished away into the night, moving parallel through grass lit silver by the moon which had now risen. Considering that almost 200 men were on the move we made little noise until Bills walked straight through one of the low drystone walls encircling a small area of cultivation, setting lumps of rock crashing and ringing together. We crested the last ridge before the Ghazeer, where the *firqa* announced that they would go no further. Nothing I could say would persuade them, so we moved on without them.

We moved onto the high ground overlooking the Hayeen waterhole and soon had parties of soldiers ferreting around in the valley below. Towards noon Suleiman reported enemy movement in the caves across the valley from the waterhole, so we called up Strikemaster jets and they began to plaster the caves with rocket fire. They flew more cautiously than before, swooping down from high level to deliver their armament and climbing swiftly away again, rather than circling lazily around a few hundred feet above as they used to do. The change in tactics had been brought about by the arrival in Dhofar of SAM-7 ground-to-air missiles, which had downed several Iranian and one or two SOAF aircraft in a few days after their introduction. The Adoo could have scored a devastating victory if they had kept the new weapons secret until a major opportunity such as a large-scale operation with lots of air activity presented itself, but they chose instead to fire them off in ones and twos, thus giving the airmen time to introduce effective countermeasures such as new tactics and decoy equipment.

Getting the Adoo out of caves was always a risky business for there was no escape route and they tended to go down fighting rather than surrender. A number of soldiers were killed in similar situations, so when the airstrike was over, 12 Platoon moved cautiously towards the caves, but on reaching them, they found nothing. The enemy, if there had been any, had evaded Suleiman's cordon and escaped.

28 September 1975

The next day B Company returned by convoy to Arzat, taking Brian Spice with them. The need for him to remain on the Jebel had passed with the *Khareef* and in a way I was glad to see him go. His drunken tirades most evenings had become tiresome, but I had developed a great respect for his dedication to caring for the tribesmen and a lot of aches and pains would now go untreated, since most of the old folk refused point-blank to go to Salalah for treatment.

During the day we had another dust-up with the *firqa*, who accused us of stealing rations that had been delivered for them by helicopter. I checked back with the Quartermaster and after some discussion, it transpired that some *firqa* rations had come up with ours, but he had not known about them and assumed they were all for us. It was an understandable muddle and I apologised and returned the rations, but the incident did nothing to improve our relationship with them.

Charki Faqir Mohammed, my erstwhile Company Sergeant Major, arrived in Tawi on the transport which came to fetch Bills and his men.

Charki had successfully completed his commissioning course and was now a brand new Second Lieutenant. I was delighted to see him again and his lined, grizzled face lit up in a broad smile as I shook his hand. He was a lot older than Badil and Suleiman and I wondered how he would get on. The other new arrival was Captain Ashley Loxton of the Royal Artillery, who was to be the second FOO in the Tawi gun troop. The next day I had nothing planned and I was looking forward to a little peace and quiet, but Peter and Ashley decided that they would go down the well shaft and when they put it to me that, as Lord of the Well, I could hardly pass up an opportunity to explore this marvellous corner of my parish, there was no room for manoeuvre and I had to agree.

It was a fairly easy scramble down the first hundred feet or so over fallen rocks and tangled bushes, but after that the only way that we could see was down the pipes which had been dropped into the well by some intrepid Royal Engineers when they installed the pumping facility a couple of years before. The pipes were fixed to the rock face for fifty feet or so below the rock ledge where the path ended, but for the last 150 they hung in space in front of a huge cave opening onto the floor of the shaft. They swayed back and forth like thin pieces of rope and although rungs were welded to them at intervals, some of them had rusted away and fallen into the chasm, which meant a monkey-like shin down six or eight feet to the next foothold and a mighty heave up the same distance on the way back. I tried not to think what would happen if a rung gave way whilst one of us had his weight on it.

All in all, it looked a distinctly dicey proposition, but as the gallant leader, I had no choice but to go first. I lay on the rock ledge, swung my legs over the side and began to climb down, my eyes firmly fixed to the rock-face about two inches from my nose and my knees shaking. Everything went well until I reached the point where the pipes left the rocks and dangled out in space, where I began to feel very exposed indeed. By some miracle I made it to the bottom, where I sat sweating and exhausted on a rock and wondering how on earth I was going to get out again. Peter swung his long frame easily down the pipes, apparently unconcerned, and I was sufficiently recovered to take a photograph of him, dwarfed in mid-air against the great dark mouth of the cave.

After a short rest we began to explore the bottom of the shaft. It was covered with large boulders and thick bushes and looking up, we saw a myriad of birds wheeling against the blue circle of the sky and now we knew why it was called 'The Well of the Birds'. There were three caves opening onto the floor of the shaft. Two had high ceilings but did not extend far back and these had little of note, but the third, on the north side of the shaft, was filled with deep blue water stretching back into impenetrable darkness. Around and above the entrance, the limestone had assumed fantastic shapes and colours. There was a great bas-relief on the side of the cave like a man standing, his head bent in prayer, whilst an enormous yellow globe of rock protruded out of the water perched on a narrow collar and looking for all the world like a giant discoloured Christmas pudding on a plate. Many of the rocks were tinged with vivid greens and blues.

Without boats, however, we could go no further, so we scrambled back to where the pipes turned at right angles to begin their dizzy ascent. I was terrified by the idea of climbing out, but the only way was up and it was not a good idea to sit around thinking about it. I shinned up the pipe at high speed and collapsed thankfully on the rock ledge, swearing solemnly to myself that nothing would induce me to do the journey again.

I was pestered mercilessly by the *firqa* to produce aircraft to get them to Salalah in time for Eid which would mark the end of Ramadan, but I had recovered my zest for life, which had sunk to a low ebb during the last weeks of the *Khareef*, and I made a effort to get on well with them which began to pay off. The wildlife that inhabited our *murcha* was augmented by a bat which flapped its leathery way around at night, shitting on our kit, and the little garden which we planted hopefully with seeds that Carol had sent out was quickly ravished by pests which relished the unaccustomed delicacy of English radish and lettuce, but nothing could detract from the joy and pleasure I drew from the beauty of the Jebel, which I had come to love deeply.

The rats continued to provide a nightly horror show and I never came to terms with them. On my first leave I bought some large steel rat traps and at the beginning of the rains we had an incident which reduced Malik and I to nervous giggles months afterwards whenever we spoke of it. I set a trap in one of the head-high air shafts in my part of the *murcha* and one morning, just as we were having breakfast, there was the unmistakeable snap of a trap springing. We rushed into my cubicle and in the dim light I made out the silhouette of a very large rat, crouched by the trap making curious sobbing noises. It had obviously sprung the trap without getting caught in it and not surprisingly, it was now in a state of shock. I told Malik, who was standing behind me, to get me something to hit it with and he passed me a handbrush. I swung at the rat, which leapt out of the shaft, bounced off my face and onto the floor. We both shrieked and I cannoned backwards into Malik, who scrambled out of the room as fast as he could go. The rat crouched under my bed, still sobbing and bleeding from the blow I had dealt it. I yelled at Malik for something heavier to hit it and he passed me the next thing to hand, which was a large tent peg. I hit out again and again but, horribly, the rat would not die and it was only when I kicked it out into the open and broke its neck with the sharp edge of the tent peg that it finally succumbed. After that neither of us managed to finish our breakfast.

I had steadily increased the sensitivity of my traps and by the end of the *Khareef* setting them was a real hazard. They closed with a vicious clang that could break a finger quite easily, so I approached the evening trap-setting ritual gingerly. The interval between putting out the light and drifting off to sleep was just long enough for the rats to come sniffing around and it was always just at the moment between consciousness and sleep that a trap would shut with a snap and the scream of a trapped rat would jerk us back into sweating reality. At that point horror would pile upon horror, for no sooner was one caught than it would be ripped open by its fellows and in the time that it took to get out of bed and deliver the coup de grace, the animal would be disembowelled and torn.

6 October 1975

I marked the end of Ramadan by patrolling to Anshaam on the assumption that no-one would expect a patrol to be out and about in the early hours of Eid. A few *firqa* came with us and carried out a very half-hearted search, grumbling all the while about the effrontery of infidels who worked on a Bank Holiday. We found nothing except a number of sick people whom we treated and we made our way back to have our own celebration. The Baluch sat in lines with large platters of rice and goat meat between them and two cans of soft drinks each, paid for out of Company funds. When the meal was finished, Peter and I rose, thanked the Sergeant Major and shook hands with each soldier in turn, using the two-handed clasp favoured by the Baluch. I noticed again how few we were, perhaps no more than about sixty-five all told and watching them crowding round, laughing and congratulating one another, I thought that they looked more like a reunion of long-lost friends than a group of people who had been living cheek by jowl with one another for months. My heart warmed to them, for they were always so cheerful, and their simple, full-hearted greeting made Peter and I feel like kings.

9 October 1975

Next day I paid a fleeting visit to Arzat for a conference, but though the CO was in a jovial frame of mind and pressed me to stay, I managed to get a helicopter back the following morning after the usual bout of nausea. A couple of days later I sent Peter down for a well-deserved break and to my joy, we finally got the generator going again after a break of almost four months from the first night of the *Khareef*.

We started the work of repairing the damage wrought by the wet season, but it was briefly interrupted by a hot, dry Shimaal which began to blow, enveloping the hills in an opaque gritty mist which blew dust into everything. This time it was short-lived but later in the year it would blow for days, fraying everyone's nerves.

12 October 1975

One evening a couple of soldiers from the British Army information team in Oman came to Tawi to show us the film *The Omega Man* starring Charlton Heston. They set up a screen in the open and we invited the *firqa* to bring up their folk to watch. Set in the aftermath of a biological war which had devastated the earth, it was a bizarre choice of film and halfway through I saw one old boy wandering off into the darkness, shaking his white head in bewilderment. Still, we had no repetition of the occasion when, during a tense moment in *Zulu*, it was said that a *firqa* decided to intervene on the side of the beleaguered British and emptied an AK-47 magazine at the screen, bringing the show to a premature end.

Later in the evening as we sat eating together, I sought peoples' views on the film. Suleiman looked at me, his dark face alight with mischief. 'Film no good Sahib,' he said 'No jig-jig.'

I decided that we needed a track up to the top of the main picquet. It was only a short distance, but it was blocked by a number of large rocks and for the next few days Tawi Atair echoed to the thunder of demolitions as we blasted our way towards the summit. We discovered that even a small charge slipped deep into one of the round holes which fissured most of the slabs could produce a satisfying quantity of shattered rock, but the biggest charge merely scorched the surface if it was not properly placed. I rediscovered the simple truth that the Baluch worked with a will if we were there with them and I swung a pick enthusiastically, revelling in the hard exercise.

One moonlit night we put in an ambush on the junction of the Wadis Darbat and Gharr which seemed a likely place for any Adoo travelling from east to west and back to pass. We moved out in the late evening across ground still warm from the sun, past staring cows and slumbering huts, the familiar smell compounded of dust, woodsmoke and cattle dung in our nostrils. Already the cattle had eaten off all the grass around the huts and a low cloud of dust rose at our passing. We crashed noisily into a small, steep-sided wadi and down to a broad circle of white sand marking the wadi junction. I set the Claymores, withdrew a short way up the slope into some bushes and settled down to wait. The sand in the killing zone gleamed like snow in the moonlight and I found myself wondering what would happen if, as had happened to Harry Fecitt months before, a dark file of silent figures should come striding down the wadi.

The night wore on and from time to time I shifted silently to relieve a tortured extremity or move my flesh from a sharp stone pressing into it. Above me, a wolf began to howl somewhere close to the edge of the wadi and the dismal refrain was taken up by another somewhere further down. The hair on the back of my neck prickled at the sound. Towards dawn we lifted the ambush and trudged back empty-handed in the light of the sinking moon, our shadows long on the ground beside us in strange, beautiful mimicry of the sunset.

At this season, the very early mornings were a time of cool beauty and I often woke before dawn to watch the sun rising over the hills, painting the world in changing hues of rose and orange and turning the long waving grass into a sea of flame. Only in the early morning or at sunset was there colour in the landscape, for when the sun rose towards the zenith its fierce brightness washed the hills in dazzling pale pastel shades of grey, silver and yellow.

We patrolled and ambushed regularly, but after the alarms and excursions of the *Khareef* the Adoo seemed to have disappeared completely from the scene. We visited every corner of the area and I never tired of the variety of Jebel scenery that it contained, but of the enemy we saw nothing. We trained vigorously, practising everything from mortars to hand grenades and we worked on improving the position. The days seemed to fly by.

22 October 1975

One day Mohammed Said appeared in Tawi Atair after a long absence, accompanied by a crowd of new faces and announced that he was now the new *firqa* leader and that Ahmed Said was superseded. Within minutes of his arrival Mohammed Daan appeared at my door demanding a plane and the next day he and the remainder of Ahmed's followers departed in high dudgeon, saying that they would not return until Ahmed had been reinstated. No-one, least of all myself, made any attempt to change their minds and so Ahmed's star wavered, guttered and went out.

25 October 1975

When the pumps at the well broke down a few days later there was, predictably, pandemonium. With their usual ill nature, the tribespeople began by harassing and threatening the wretched Pakistani operators who could do nothing about the problem and I moved them up into Suleiman's platoon position for their own protection. Next, I went down to the well to talk to the people and explain to them what was being done. I hoped that Mohammed Said would be on hand to help, but he could not be found and thus escaped any risk of being associated with failure whilst I was left to face the unreasoning anger of the herdsmen on my own. It was very worrying because the guarantee of water was one of our ace cards which had to be maintained, especially since, by the very provision of it, we had concentrated the herds and put them at more risk than they were before when they were scattered around a host of smaller waterholes. For some days the problem took priority over everything else and I badgered and pestered Battalion Headquarters until eventually, to the relief of all, the pumps were repaired and life resumed its even tenor. It was a good illustration of the fact that, although technically the operation of the pumps, like any other aspect of civil administration, was strictly speaking no concern of mine, it became my responsibility because the goodwill of the people was a concrete asset in our fight and therefore it was my duty to foster that goodwill by all means at my disposal. There was also the stark consideration that if I did nothing about it, no-one else would. Whether or not we gained any goodwill by looking after their interests so assiduously was hard to say, for they always seemed utterly indifferent to our presence whatever we did until, of course, something went wrong.

We caught a glimpse of the enemy late in October when we went down to the Jebel ash Shawr which overlooked the coast south of Tawi. This high ridge was separated from the rest of the plateau by a wadi, not long like the Darbat, but surprisingly deep and wide, particularly at its western end where it swung round ash Shawr and debouched onto the coastal plain in a wide, wooded amphitheatre. Above its source, at the eastern end of ash Shawr, it was possible to cross onto the Jebel over a narrow saddle. We had not been on the ridge itself so I was keen to see it and I said that we would leave at dawn. This was a departure from our usual practice of setting out in the night and appearing unannounced miles from Tawi when the sun came up and Mohammed Said said that in his view such a late start was a waste of time as the Adoo would see us coming. He was right and I began to feel guilty about taking such a lazy course of action, but I mumbled something about wanting to have a good look at the route and confirmed my plan.

26 October 1975

The next day was clear and bright and we made a leisurely start at dawn. On the way south, the russet gold grass waved in a soft early morning breeze like ripening wheat, throwing the fresh green foliage of trees crowding the hollows and small wadis on our way into sharp and striking relief. As we approached the scarp, momentary glimpses of the ocean between folds of high ground gradually broadened and lengthened until, on a knoll commanding the saddle linking ash Shawr to the Jebel proper, a breathtaking panorama of sea and mountains revealed itself, stretching eastwards as far as the eye could see and southwards across the blue vastness of the Indian Ocean. We paused and for a few moments Peter and I lost ourselves in the beauty of the scene. The *Jebalis* and the Baluch were quite unmoved by such abstractions and assumed we had stopped for a rest, which made the former impatient and the latter grateful, as always, for the respite.

We climbed onto the spine of the ridge and strolled along the summit with the ocean on our left hand and the mountains on our right. Immediately about us, the land had a contented, well cared for look and but for the hot sun and the little, beehive shaped grass huts dotted about on the gently undulating pasture, we might have been strolling on a common anywhere in England. Perhaps the beauty of the morning and the landscape around put me into an unusually mellow frame of mind, but the huts looked neater and the people seemed friendlier than any we had encountered before. There were no flies and even the omnipresent tang of woodsmoke and cattle dung seemed less pervasive than usual.

At about noon we reached the end of the ridge and looked out over a huge wooded amphitheatre more than a thousand feet below us. A mile away to the east the ground rose again steeply on the other side of the wadi to a wide, long ridge and further still beyond that Twin Tits and the high ground of the Darbat Picquet could be seen clearly. Here we sat down to brew tea, eat some food and relax for a while before turning back. Sentries were posted and Jumma, Mohammed Said, Peter and I were chatting and eating when Mohammed suddenly stiffened and stared across the wadi. He asked for my binoculars and a moment later uttered that electric word: 'Adoo!' Grabbing the glasses from him I searched the ground he indicated and sure enough, there was a patrol of four enemy soldiers, rifles over their shoulders and packs on their backs, striding south down the ridge towards the scarp and blissfully unaware that they were now being watched with great interest from above by about sixty pairs of eyes.

It was a strange feeling to be watching the enemy in that detached way. They were fleeting, often invisible adversaries and usually the only sign of their presence would be a burst of automatic fire which was extremely difficult to pinpoint accurately. The moment they were threatened either by encirclement or accurate fire in reply, they would disappear and it was unusual to catch so much as a glimpse of them. It was rather like stalking, or being stalked by, a rare and extremely dangerous animal but now we studied these four almost at leisure. The enemy patrol was two kilometres away, far out of range of the weapons we carried and beyond an obstacle which would take at least an hour to cross, but with luck we could hit them with the guns at Tawi Atair. Jumma and I quickly agreed on the map position of the enemy and he passed a fire order to the troop. A minute or so later the first salvo crashed around the Adoo and they ran for their lives towards the trees as more followed. Whether we killed any of them is unknown, but we certainly frightened them. As Peter put it on the way back, 'Now that's the sort of contact I enjoy.' Perhaps it had some effect, for we had a number of SEPs from that area shortly afterwards.

We were visited the next day by Sher Mohammed, who had taken over as Quartermaster a few months before. Sher was a delightful man, always ready with a grin and ever conscious of the needs of the rifle companies and I knew that if some piece of equipment I had asked him for did not arrive, it was because it did not exist in Dhofar. I never asked Sher how he balanced his books, but he would lie, beg and steal for us and he was not a man who believed that stocks were to decorate shelves in a store. I was delighted to see him and I feted him like a king, making sure that he was happy and comfortable. He was a refreshing change from the usual run of sour, grudging Quartermasters that we suffered from in SAF, so I was dumbfounded a few months later when Gordon-Taylor effectively demoted him, subordinating him to another contract ex-British Army QM of the old style. It was a withering insult to an energetic, dedicated and charming officer.

Harry Fecitt, who was now on contract with the Dubai Defence Force, had invited me to visit him there, so I managed to get a few days off and started making arrangements. On my way through Arzat, there was the usual party, this time to see Yarpy Wardle off to the UK where he was getting married. The evening was much enhanced by the prospect of Yarpy's imminent departure for an indefinite period and at a late stage in the evening he was standing on the tiled veranda at the rear of the officers' living quarters by the swimming pool, his face flushed and eyes gleaming behind pebble spectacles and a bottle of Glenmorangie malt whisky in each hand. He was haranguing all and sundry when suddenly he let go of the whisky bottles. They smashed on the tiles and Yarpy let out a yelp of mortification followed by a stream of foul oaths, for he loved whisky above all else.

Yarpy was an odd fellow who earned a special place for himself in the history of the Dhofar campaign. He was Rhodesian-born, hence the nickname, and I discovered years later when I visited the country that he had been a bank clerk in Bulawayo when the Rhodesian Army had claimed him for its own in the early years of the bush war that was to end white rule in that country. In an organisation that cherished its roughnecks, Yarpy gained a unique reputation for his loud, foul-mouthed and uncontrollable behaviour. Fuelled by his favourite beverage and encouraged by the atmosphere in which he found himself, the bank clerk turned into a wild man. Eventually his antics became too much even for the Rhodesian Army and they suggested that he find employment elsewhere. After a while, like so many of his fellow countrymen, he made his way to Oman and the Southern Regiment, where as a mercenary, he enjoyed the protection of Gordon-Taylor, who saved him from the consequences of a string of major and minor gaffes. He once suggested to the Brigade Major, a prim and ambitious officer, that he should 'fuck off' and he infuriated the Baluch with his insulting ways. He was open in his contempt for blacks, and that included Baluch. It took a lot to provoke them, for by and large they trusted European officers and they returned a little care and respect with interest, but Yarpy managed to do so at frequent intervals.

He consumed prodigious quantities of whisky and was known to turn up for a briefing in the middle of the afternoon the worse for drink, yet he could leap into a helicopter at a moment's notice, fly to the Jebel and march twenty kilometres across enemy territory to extricate a wounded *firqa*. His language was foul beyond description, yet he loved Beethoven, Brahms and Wagner. His conversation was coarse, inarticulate and repetitive, yet his bookshelves were lined with serious works which he appeared to cherish. Squat, round, almost Japanese-faced, with pale skin, black eyebrows and close cropped, crinkly black hair, he was a difficult man to work with and we had many acrimonious exchanges, but there were moments when I found myself almost liking him.

My feelings were less ambivalent towards another contract officer who arrived in the Regiment at about this time. One day I came into the Mess to see a thin, sharp-faced individual sitting silently at the bar. I ordered a drink and introduced myself as he stretched out a powerful hand. After a short exchange of pleasantries his side of the conversation winded to a series of curt remarks heavy with significance and intended to convey that he was an old Dhofar hand with much more experience of active service than I was ever likely to acquire. He was a chum of the CO, as I might have guessed, and it only took a little longer to discover that he was one of those tedious people who become aggressive and paranoid when drunk. There was a wide range of peculiar drinking habits on the bizarre social scene in Dhofar, but he had the strangest of them all. All week he would abstain totally from alcohol, standing by himself in a corner of the bar or not appearing in the Mess at all, but on Thursday at lunchtime, when people on the plain finished work for the Muslim 'weekend', he would begin his serious drinking. By mid-afternoon he would be semi-comatose and would remain so until Saturday morning when work began again, often slumbering on a barstool all Thursday or Friday night. In the early stages of drunkenness he could be very difficult, challenging anyone who offered him a real or imagined insult to 'come outside'.

Early one Saturday morning Douglas McCully and I drove into RAF Salalah and just after we passed the gate I saw what looked like a bundle of rags lying in one of the storm ditches by the side of the road. We stopped and identified it as the contract officer, head all bloody and snoring away oblivious to his wounds. I suggested that perhaps we should pick him up. 'No,' said Douglas cheerfully, 'Let him come to on his own – he'd prefer it that way.' Sure enough, when we drove out an hour or two later he was gone, to reappear afterwards in Arzat, looking not much the worse for wear. We heard later that he had reached the aggressive stage the previous evening and challenged a Frontier Force officer to 'come outside'. This man, a small, wiry veteran, was a genuine hard case, unlike so many of the bogus tough guys who hung around the bars in Salalah, so when he was invited to 'step outside' he agreed amiably. 'After you,' he said, with one motion sweeping a gin bottle from the bar and bringing it down on his opponent's skull, knocking him senseless and turning back to his drink without so much as another word.

TAWI ATAIR: SEPTEMBER–DECEMBER 1975

30 October 1975

I flew up to the North and spent a couple of days with the Desert Regiment before flying to Dubai. Their CO came to the airport to meet me and after we had introduced ourselves, we set off for the regimental station in the hills at Bid Bid.

In days gone by the journey between Muscat and Nizwa could take days and was fraught with the danger of attack by the fiercely independent tribesmen of the mountains, many of whom owed allegiance to the imam whose power base was the fortress town deep in the fastness of the Jebel Akhdar. The war in the late 1960s that finally established the supremacy of the Sultan started with a running battle along the length of the road between a battalion of the Sultan's army and tribesmen loyal to the imam and the soldiers suffered heavily. But now a broad new metalled road linked Muscat and the Batinah Coast with the towns of the Jebel Akhdar and it was an easy drive of a few hours to Nizwa.

Leaving the flat, tedious coastal plain, the road followed the bed of a large wadi draining the mountain range and as it climbed into the foothills each bend revealed a new vista of bare red mountains, their jagged tops etching successive bands of fading purple and blue against the pale sky. The sandy floor of the wadi threw back the afternoon sun in a fierce white glare, but as we approached Bid Bid the valley walls closed in on either side and suddenly, in welcome contrast to the dazzling monochrome landscape, a cool green plantation of palm trees came into view between the road and the hillside. Sustained by the ancient system of *aflaj* which bring water from the highest parts of the mountains, these date palm plantations stretch for mile after mile along the valleys of the Jebel Akhdar, providing the villagers with their main source of wealth and offering cool green glades of respite from the glare of the day.

We arrived shortly after dark and the officers of the regiment made me feel at home straight away. The camp was one of a number which had been built in recent years to house the extra units of the expanded army and its layout and appearance was familiar. It consisted of several rows of white, single-storey buildings with flat roofs surrounded by a straggling barbed-wire fence the purpose of which was more to delineate army property than to keep anyone out. The officers' quarters were at the rear of the camp, overlooked across a broad, shallow wadi by a steep, bare mountainside. There was a small swimming pool and a stone patio shaded by a trellis entwined with greenery.

One of the nice things about the Sultan's Army was the hospitality and friendliness which was invariably extended to visitors and the Desert Regiment was no exception. Led by Lieutenant Colonel Jim Shepherd, a large, fatherly figure with a kindly manner, they looked after me very well indeed, and when I told Shepherd that Carol and the boys were coming to Oman at Christmas, he insisted that they stay at Bid Bid. It would certainly be pleasanter and cheaper than accommodating them in dusty, overcrowded Muscat and Bid Bid would be a much better base from which to explore the Jebel Akhdar, so I gladly accepted his offer.

Before breakfast the next morning I went out across the wadi, through the palm trees to the foot of the rocky slope. In this part of Northern Oman the mountain slopes are almost completely devoid of vegetation other than the occasional lifeless, grey-green ball of tumbleweed and the naked red rock looks unchanged since the dawn of time. There is no soil and even the ants are few and far between, yet somehow little lizards survive, scampering among the rocks or lying motionless in the hot sun. The slopes are so steep as to be impassable in places and the ridge-lines are jagged, irregular fangs of rock which at dawn or evening are silhouetted against the sky like shattered ramparts of basalt.

On the slope I climbed past an ancient, crumbling watchtower built of mud and stone and up to the first ridge. From there, high above the dust haze in the valley, far images were sharp in the dry desert air and I could see for miles up the wadi to the west where it disappeared round a bend. A long, shimmering sliver of water drew the eye to the middle distance and across rank upon rank of hills marching away to north and south, fading from purple to powder blue with each successive ridge. I was reluctant to leave, but there was much to do that day, so I climbed down the hill to the edge of the plantation where a tightly packed huddle of yellowish grey houses crammed into a small piece of flat land between the slope and the trees. Close by was a tiny cemetery with a scattering of small, uneven headstones and the effort required to hack out even those poor graves from the rocky ground must have been considerable.

I was already aware that travel around the Gulf was fraught with bureaucratic obstacles and later that morning at breakfast I discussed with my new friends in the Desert Regiment ways and means of getting to Dubai for my visit there. Opinion seemed unanimous that it would take several weeks to obtain the required visa, but I had already made up my mind to go and I decided to take a chance. I went into Muscat, bought a return ticket to Dubai and drove to the airport.

TAWI ATAIR: SEPTEMBER–DECEMBER 1975

My passport was stamped with a 'No Objection' certificate, without which it was impossible to get into Oman and as ill luck would have it, the certificate expired during the few days that I would be in Dubai. By the time I discovered this little difficulty it was far too late to do anything about it and I smiled weakly as the policeman at the exit desk laughingly clapped an enormous red cancellation stamp across the precious certificate, assuring me that there would be no problem when I returned. By now I had sufficient experience in the East to doubt the reliability of promises like that and I tried to commit his number to memory so that he could be called as a witness on my return, but failed dismally.

When I landed at Dubai my passport was surrendered in return for permission to stay in the country for ninety-six hours and I took a taxi to Harry's house. The taxi driver, who seemed happy with the instructions that I gave him, drove round and round in ever-increasing circles until eventually I stopped him and asked a Pakistani labourer for directions. None of my letters or signals had arrived so Harry and his wife Thelma were surprised to see me, but they welcomed me and made me feel very much at home.

In those days the markets in Salalah and Muscat were just beginning to emerge from a way of operating unchanged for centuries and although some Japanese goods were being imported, they were displayed in the tiny, intimate cosiness of small shops converted by adding a glass window and a counter and fixing an illuminated Sony or Olympus sign to the wall. Apart from a few stalls selling watches, Salalah was still largely innocent of the glittering gewgaws of the late twentieth century, so Dubai came as something of a culture shock. Its broad avenues were lined by gleaming halls crammed with the very latest treasures, some of which had not even reached Britain, but I was more attracted to the magnificent carpets of Iran and Kashmir and I returned to the same shop several times for the sheer pleasure of haggling over heaps of splendid rugs. I spent hours in various 'antique' shops which ranged from smooth, upmarket establishments selling high-priced silver artefacts of the Gulf to cheerful, scruffy one-room booths piled at random with battered Omani brass coffee pots and ancient, decrepit firelocks held tenuously together by their brass wire decorative work. The proprietors were invariably Indian or Pakistani and in the best suk tradition, they would start the bargaining by naming an outrageous price, displaying deep sorrow mixed with astonishment when I countered with a figure somewhere around a third as much.

After hard bargaining spread over two days I eventually bought a beautiful close-woven Kashmiri rug which earned high praise from Carol for my discerning taste, an unusual if not unique achievement, but I jibbed at the 40 rials I was asked to pay in another shop for an Omani *khanjar*, smugly telling the shopkeeper that I could get a better one in Nizwa for 20. It was a mistake, for later in Nizwa I was offered a *khanjar* of lesser quality for 200 rials and the merchant was unmoved by my protestations that I was a poor servant of the Sultan and not a wealthy oilman.

Dubai lies on a flat, featureless stretch of coast and is divided in two by the Creek, a deep water inlet where dhows still unload cargoes of rice and fish at old wharves overlooked by glittering towers of opaque bronze and silver glass. In those days getting from one side of town to the other meant a lengthy detour by road or a short trip in a rowing boat to an ancient flight of steps leading into the old suk and we chose the latter. Although many of the shops now sold watches, cameras and electronic goods in great quantity and variety, the suk still retained a bustling, exciting character of its own, underscored by the hissing light of pressure lamps and the charcoal fires of stalls selling samosas and other fried titbits.

I met several British and Arab officers of the Dubai Defence Force and they led a very different life to that in the Sultan's Army. The British contract officers lived with their families in comfortable houses in the suburbs whereas almost all of us were unaccompanied and many in Dhofar lived in *murchas* on the Jebel. Round the dinner table in Dubai, service in Dhofar was regarded as something akin to an almost certain death warrant (which of course it was not) and rather like Northern Ireland, those not immediately acquainted with its troubles tended to magnify them out of all proportion. I quite enjoyed playing the hero and did nothing to discourage peoples' misconceptions.

Harry invited me to stay for longer than the four days allowed in return for surrendering my passport and so began the tortuous process of securing a visa. It soon became apparent that I was in a tricky situation, for the immigration authorities would not issue a visa unless I produced my passport and officials at the airport would not release my passport unless I had a visa. For two days I drove around various ministries and departments in the city, but though I was treated with unfailing courtesy at each office, no decision was forthcoming. The situation was unprecedented and in the obstinate manner of officialdom the world over, no-one was prepared to stick his neck out on my behalf. When I said that the intervention of one of the many princes in the Army might solve the problem, the suggestion was gravely considered and it was then intimated that yes, that might help and off I hurried. I asked a British contract officer to introduce me to one of the exalted, but he was reluctant to interrupt any of them at their work and suggested that I might like to go along and make myself known, which I did. Accustomed to the cheerful informality of SAF, I did not intend to be overawed by rank or ceremony.

Stepping round the large white Mercedes parked one behind the other outside the headquarters, I knocked on the door of the second-in-command and went in. The 2iC was seated at his desk, surrounded by desert grandees, all immaculate in their white linen and all with hawks on their wrists. Obviously, I had interrupted a very important conference on military matters, but the prince listened politely to my tale, considered for a moment and replied at length to the effect that I had his deepest sympathy, that it was ridiculous that the immigration people should be making such a fuss over a simple matter and that of course I had his full support. He then smiled and turned to discuss some technical detail of hawking with one of his companions, making it clear that the interview was at an end. My case was no further forward.

In his bluff way Harry told me not to worry about it, that I was to fly from Sharjah and he would collect my passport from the airport on our way there. His plan worked when I returned to Oman a couple of days later, but my troubles were not over. Having assured me that there would be no difficulty over the cancelled 'No Objection' certificate, the police now decided not to let me back into the country. Several hours of argument followed and it was only when I claimed that I had to be on operations in Dhofar in two days' time that they allowed me out of the airport. Again leaving my passport as hostage, I fled thankfully back to Dhofar.

7 November 1975

Before I went back to Tawi Atair I was invited to join a beach party at a small cove a few miles west along the coast from Raysut. We posted sentries on the surrounding hills and spent the day snorkelling in the clear, warm water. Turtles swam lazily near the boat and further out, giant rays hurled themselves into the air, falling back in an explosion of spray which boomed across the sea like a cannon shot. Diving was a new experience and I was enchanted by the underwater world it opened up, but the idyll was somewhat tarnished for Johnny Gorman and myself when the helicopter taking the party back to Salalah left without us.

We were obliged to hike back across the hills in our swimming trunks with a speargun as our only means of defence if the Adoo should decide to attack us. As we crested the last ridge above Raysut we were met by Douglas McCully who belatedly realised that we had been stranded and was coming back in a Land Rover to pick us up. Everyone except Johnny and I seemed to think it was a huge joke.

The wildlife which was an almost unnoticed part of our existence still flourished in the aftermath of the wet season and in the evening of my return to Tawi I surprised a large badger in the cubicle of old canvas and concrete which served as our bathroom. He was taking a drink from a permanent puddle under the pipe outlet which we used as a shower and he gave me an indignant look before turning round and squeezing under the canvas screen, his fat bottom and short legs disappearing last. I did nothing to hurry him along, for the badgers of Dhofar are fierce in defence and they possess extremely sharp teeth. Bright green chameleons and gerbils seemed quite unperturbed by our presence, the latter scampering in and out of the *murcha* with only a passing glance at us to make sure that we were not of a mind to challenge their passing. The days were hot and bright and the nights so clear that millions of stars blazed in the sky, their brilliance only dimming when a huge moon rose in the east, brown, grotesque and distorted at first, then brightening to a glowing white disc. It illuminated the slopes of Qisais ad Deen in monochrome image of the familiar daytime backdrop and was so bright that a man could be seen at almost half a mile on the open hillside and a map could be studied without difficulty.

During the bad weather people and their cattle tended to stay close to the villages, but now there was more movement on the Jebel which made it difficult to practise the mortar and gun crews. We obviously could not afford to risk injuring herdsmen or their animals, but the crews badly needed practice and a number of targets around Tawi Atair had to be re-registered because we had moved the mortars. It was almost impossible to persuade the *firqa* of the need for training, but after protracted negotiations it was agreed that an hour after first light each day would be set aside for practice. So each morning I found myself up on the ridge above Company Headquarters as the first grey light of dawn crept over the far peaks of Qisais ad Deen, map, compass and radio in hand, drilling the crews and waking the world with the sharp coughing of the mortars. Peter declined my invitation to join him in this early morning work and I did not press the matter, for I loved the peace and solitude and some mornings I would delay firing to watch the rising sun paint the landscape in successive waves of pink, red and gold until it rose fully into the sky, draining colour from the earth like blood from a shocked face and setting the hills shimmering with searing light.

The humdrum routine of patrols and ambushes continued and now that communications were fully restored we found ourselves inundated with paperwork. Orders, returns, requests for this and that and a hundred other matters which we never seemed to bother about before now took up a lot of my time and contributed to periodic fits of irritability on my part.

After many weeks of hopeful rumours and promises a consignment of M16 Armalite rifles arrived which included several fitted with grenade launchers. Although there were not enough weapons to equip the whole Company, they went some way to filling the gaps in our armoury and the launchers in particular provided us with an accurate, short-range means of delivering explosive more portable than the 66-mm rockets. For some time I had been convinced of the need for a weapon which could put down a heavy weight of automatic fire like the AK-47 which every Adoo soldier now carried. In a fleeting contact in close country it was vital to overwhelm the enemy immediately and accuracy was not so important at short range as the weight and speed of fire which could be delivered. The aim was to kill the enemy or force him to take evasive action before he could devastate us with a burst of automatic fire. Our FN rifles were single-shot weapons incapable of producing the response we needed and the M16s were a big step forward.

Infantrymen will argue endlessly over the merits of this or that weapon, but the fact is that different situations call for different weapon characteristics which cannot be combined in a single rifle, so all designs tend to be compromises. The M16 was an excellent weapon at close quarters, at night or in thick bush, but I decided to keep my FN for the open plateau, where its hitting power and range would be an advantage.

The new toys were a source of keen interest amongst the soldiers, the *firqa*, and the tribesmen round about, so when we gathered on the airstrip to fire the grenade launchers there was a good audience. We were luckier than on the previous occasion and there was much acclamation as each grenade went off with a satisfying bang at roughly the appointed place.

Whilst we were discussing the new weapons later that evening Peter made a chilling observation. 'You know,' he said, 'if the Adoo had trained a couple of dozen marksmen to use a sniper rifle properly and they'd gone for the company commanders we'd be in the shit by now.' What he meant was that the number of company commanders and seconds-in-command on the hills was quite small, never more than about thirty or so at any one time and it was very much a company officers' war. Our casualties, although few in total, had been running at quite a high percentage level, sufficient to make the small band of brothers pause for thought from time to time.

Barring an ambush or sudden contact in thick bush or at night, the hundreds of AK-47s in the hands of the Adoo and the *firqa* were noisy and could be frightening, but on the open slopes of Dhofar they were not as effective as they might have been. We gave thanks that the AK-47 was universally regarded as a far more prestigious possession, no matter how badly battered or maintained, than a mere old-fashioned, bolt-action sniper rifle. The fierceness of the battle and therefore the valour of its participants tended to be gauged by the volume of noise and not by the single deadly bullet which killed a man half a mile away.

Ammunition for the new rifles was in short supply so I was pleased to find a few boxes of 5.56-mm rounds at the back of one of our bunkers and I decided to use it for target practice on the rudimentary range which Peter had paced out in the grass beyond the airstrip. It was the first time I had used the weapon and inexplicably, it began to jam repeatedly. This was very discouraging, for a weapon which jams in a contact is useless. I changed magazines, checked and rechecked the weapon, all to no avail and it was only when I examined the ammunition more closely that I noticed a minute difference in the case pattern. It was a repeat of the mistake I had made with the mortar ammunition in White City and it was fortunate that it happened in Tawi Atair and not on patrol, where it could have been fatal.

15 November 1975

Shortly after the delivery of the new weapons I received a radio message from the Battalion operations room to the effect that a BATT team would be coming to Tawi Atair. I had the greatest admiration for the team and its achievements, but I was annoyed that they were being foisted on me without consultation. I looked upon Tawi Atair as being very firmly 'my' area and I had no wish to see the system which we had laboured for months to establish with the *firqa* disrupted by newcomers. An added problem was that the team reported back to Salalah through their own chain of command, so that I would no longer be certain of what was going on in my own back yard. My protests to Gordon-Taylor were in vain, for the team had the ear of the Brigadier and when they wanted something they usually got it.

TAWI ATAIR: SEPTEMBER–DECEMBER 1975

To add to my troubles one of the pumps at the well broke down again, reducing the flow of water to the cattle troughs and producing an immediate and angry reaction from the tribesmen and the *firqa*. The Pakistanis were again besieged in their tent and I went to the well to try and calm things down. As I approached women watched, their bright, insolent eyes flashing and their dark beauty framed in the startling reds and greens of their saris like so many exotic birds. Herds of cattle and camels were bawling and stamping around the troughs and sunlight slanted through the choking clouds of dust swirling like smoke under the trees. The men surrounded me immediately, jabbering angrily and waving their cattle sticks as I tried to explain that the problem was understood and that everything was being done to get the engineer up to fix the pump as soon as possible. Not a whit mollified, they became more and more excited and deciding that my presence was only making matters worse, I pushed through the crowd back to my Land Rover and drove the short distance up to the operators' tent. They welcomed me with some relief, but when I suggested that they should move up to Suleiman's platoon again, they would have none of it. It was very awkward of them, but I had to admire their courage, or at least their firm conviction that if they did move out there would be nothing left when they returned. We had a cup of tea together and I made some encouraging remarks, then drove up to see Suleiman. The idea of protecting Pakistanis did not appeal much to him, but ignoring his mutterings, I told him to provide a small guard with a radio at the well, after which there was plenty of grumbling from the tribespeople, but no more threatening behaviour.

I was summoned to Arzat again to attend a conference and in the afternoon of 19 November a few of us drove down to the magnificent white beach which stretched all the way from Taqah in the east to Raysut in the west, a distance of about forty miles. In the absence of tourists we considered that the beach was getting crowded if we could see as much as another person through binoculars but that day we had it to ourselves. As we drove past a little guard hut which marked the seaward end of the protective wire fence strung around Salalah, the toothless old *askar* who was employed to ensure that the Adoo did not outflank Salalah's defences gave us his customary grave salute. We raced down to the sea, sending myriads of white crabs scuttling for their burrows, and plunged into the warm blue water. The Sultan had been shopping recently and, as we bathed, the first of his new Jaguar strike aircraft barrelled along the beach at about 500 knots and over our heads at rooftop level. It was very impressive but I wondered how relevant it was to the real needs of the people of the Jebel.

It was a difficult evening and Gordon-Taylor could barely bring himself to speak to me, but next day the conference went well and in the afternoon we had a long, civil discussion. I tried to mend some fences by dropping conciliatory remarks into the conversation but although he was cordial enough, he gave no sign of recognising my flag of truce. It was his birthday that day and in true KJ style another lavish party was organised in the evening to celebrate. One of the guests was Andrew Dunsire, the Brigade photographer, and we talked at length about his plan to come to Tawi Atair and use it as a base to explore the great waterhole at Teyq, some miles to the north-east. To my lasting regret we never made the journey, but Andrew came to Tawi Atair a few days later bringing with him the means to carry out a proper exploration of the caves at the bottom of the well.

The following day we went back to the beach west of Raysut which was becoming a popular picnic spot. On the way Bills and I had a good moan together about the shortcomings of the gilded staff, but our ill humour was quickly dispelled by a perfect day on the white sands. This time we took good care not to get left behind when the party ended.

The BATT team arrived at Tawi Atair whilst I was away and shortly after getting back I talked to the team leader, a small, lean and sallow-faced staff sergeant. Within a few minutes it was apparent that we would get on well together, but whatever happened I knew that relations with the *firqa* would be affected by the new situation. After all the trouble we had gone through to rebuild mutual confidence it was a pity, but there was nothing I could do about it and I set about making the best of what I considered to be a bad job.

In between patrols and ambushes a steady stream of visitors came and went. Early one morning an American by the name of James Horgan arrived and listened patiently for almost an hour whilst I poured out the old familiar litany of problems. He then went down to the *firqa* camp and asked a host of penetrating questions in Arabic good enough to embarrass both Mohammed Said and myself and I remember noting in a letter home how refreshing it was to receive a visitor who really seemed to care about the hill people. Many officials and politicians from the Omani Government and overseas visited Tawi Atair, but for all their promises, we never seemed to get any further forward. Horgan seemed genuinely concerned with our difficulties and I said to Mohammed Said that I felt sure that this time we would see some result. Horgan left, and we never saw or heard of him again.

Humbler folk, on the other hand, rendered us good service. In the same week as our sincere American, a small, gnome-like figure appeared on my doorstep and announced himself as Wally Ramsey of Halcrows, the drilling company. He was especially welcome as the plumbing had gone on the blink and getting water up to the south picquet was becoming something of a trial. Wally was an enthusiast and although I only met him once during the whole of my time in Dhofar, after two hours of non-stop Geordie monologue I felt that I knew him (or at least his views on the relative merits of 2-inch and 2½-inch water piping in distributing water around Tawi Atair) better than I knew myself. Still, he did fix the system and as the sun was sinking rapidly by the time he finished, I felt that the least I could do was to offer him an evening meal and a bed for the night, even at the risk of another lecture on the intricacies of water pressure, but he declined the offer and flew out of Tawi Atair before sunset.

The next day the flying doctor arrived, accompanied by a nurse who chatted brightly, enjoyed a can of beer and went off to visit the sick. The same plane brought Andrew Dunsire and Peter Sherrington, armed with whisky, steak and sausages and a pile of equipment with which they proposed to explore the caves.

I made them most welcome and explained how sorry I was that I would not be able to go with them because of pressing Company business the next day, a wobbly knee, a poor stomach and every other excuse I could think of. There was some truth in the last of these: my stomach had indeed begun to churn at the thought of that vertiginous descent into the pit and I was determined that once was enough. Nevertheless, my feeble excuses were firmly brushed aside at a very early stage in the evening and I was soon committed to the adventure.

28 November 1975

Considering how much whisky we had consumed, the three of us rose at a creditably early hour the next morning and quickly loaded the ropes, boats, lamps and other paraphernalia that Andrew had assembled into the Land Rover. By 9:30 we were at the edge of the hole and I was beginning to look forward to the trip, despite the flutterings in my stomach.

Carrying the two heavy inflatable boats on our shoulders, we scrambled down the first 200 feet or so of heaped rubble and dense, jungle-like vegetation. We piled our equipment on the rock ledge overlooking the final stage of the descent and again I decided that the wisest course was to go first rather than hang about at the top of the pipe thinking about what might be. Once I started I was less afraid than before and in a short time I was down the pipe and carrying equipment across the uneven floor of the pit to the mouth of the first cave. Above our heads a brilliant circle of blue sky was ringed with a ruff of green foliage and white rock round which the birds wheeled endlessly. It looked very small and a long way away.

We sweated and grunted as we heaved the boats over the rocks to the cave entrance, but the job was finally done and we inflated them, loaded our equipment and pushed out onto the faintly shining, basalt black surface of the first subterranean lake. The light faded rapidly because of the low entrance to the cave but once our eyes became accustomed to the gloom and we mastered the business of operating the powerful flash-lamps, details of the cave walls and ceiling became clear. It was not easy to gauge colours accurately, but my impression was of rough, mottled brown curtains of rock hanging in folds to the water's edge, streaked here and there with lighter stains of limestone where small rivulets trickled down the surface. The muddy bottom shelved steeply away from the cave entrance and in a few yards could not be seen even with the aid of a flashlight. Further in, the walls curved away below the surface, creating an overhang above a curtain of rock dropping twenty feet or so before cutting back yet again to a second overhang, below which the lamp beam, powerful as it was, dissipated into the depths, creating an awesome, almost menacing sense of fathomless space. The water was very clear and a few small, colourless fish swam in and out of the light beams.

We paddled around the perimeter of the first cave which measured perhaps seventy-five metres in circumference and up to the furthest corner where a small opening just large enough for a man to pass through crouching offered a passage into the next chamber. We hauled our boats out onto the mud and rested for a while with a solitary candle for light and when I looked at my watch I was astonished to see that it was already noon. We had been so absorbed in our surroundings that none of us had counted the hours passing. Nervous giggles echoed round the caves as we joked like schoolboys about the dire possibilities that could befall us in that infinitely black tomb, but Andrew was an experienced caver and had seen it all before and after a while he put an end to the foolishness and got us moving again.

The second chamber was much bigger than the first. It was a rough L-shape with a ceiling perhaps a hundred feet above the surface of the

TAWI ATAIR: SEPTEMBER–DECEMBER 1975

Trish Sole (Civil Aid) at the well at Tawi Atair – note the single-strand ladder just visible at the top left of the image, 1975.

water. Each arm of the L was about seventy metres in length and as wide again and the water seemed to be even deeper. Again the sides of the cave curved away under the surface to black infinity and it echoed to the splashing of a number of small streams which ran down the walls on the northern side. We paddled into the edge to sample the rock which turned out to be soft and crumbly, so we were careful not to go under a huge chandelier of rock which hung from the ceiling almost to water level. The water in the cave was about six feet lower than a previous, obviously long-standing high-water mark, which seemed to me to be an ominous sign. The good monsoon which had just ended should have meant a full reservoir, but it looked as though the people and cattle of Tawi Atair were taking water out of the great cistern faster than it was flowing in.

We searched above and below the surface for a second exit, but although many of these subterranean systems stretched for miles below the Jebel, we found none. Time was passing and after a last look round, we made our way back to the first cave. The bottom of the pit was now in deep shadow and high above the light was fading quickly from the sky.

It was six o'clock by the time all the equipment was loaded in the back of the Land Rover ready for the drive back to the south picquet and I had a momentary twinge of guilt at the length of time that I had been out of contact with the company. But all was peaceful and the soldiers had probably enjoyed a day without either of us nagging them to complete this or that chore. We talked over the events of the day, speculating on what else might lie hidden in the caves. I was exhausted and fell into bed not long after dinner to sleep soundly.

A couple of days later I received a signal saying that a staff sergeant commissioning candidate would be on the next convoy to be sent to Tawi Atair. He had been wounded some months previously and had spent a long time convalescing and filling a succession of sedentary posts. As he was to be entered for the next officer selection board, the CO decided that he should get some experience of operations on the Jebel with C Company. A reinforcement draft of recruits from the training centre at Raysut was coming on the same convoy so I was pleased to have him because he could help to train them before they went out on operations.

The day before the convoy was due I gave orders for picquets to move out in the morning and occupy the main features along the convoy route. After they left the rest of the company got on with preparations for receiving the convoy and as a matter of routine, Suleiman's platoon was on stand-by on the northern picquet.

We made radio contact with the convoy as it came over the crest of the scarp above Taqah. It was a tranquil morning but at about 10.30 the peace was shattered by a distant thump. I scrambled up to the top of the south picquet and saw a column of dust rising into the air far away on the shoulder of the Darbat so I did not need the garbled contact report which followed to tell me that a vehicle in the convoy had hit a mine. Saleh, Habib Ullah, Mohim Khan and I piled into my Land Rover and we roared off in a cloud of dust. I saw Suleiman's trucks lurching down the track from the northern picquet and without waiting, I told him on the radio to follow as quickly as possible. We made good time round the west picquet, weaving between small walled fields and out onto open grassland beyond. Just as we crested the last gentle slope onto the plateau overlooking Anshaam and the Darbat, my eye was caught by something black and white on the track ahead and I motioned to Mohim Khan to slow the vehicle. As we drew near, I saw with disgust that it was the dismembered wings of a stork spread-eagled across the track and between them, stuck into the soil by its beak, the bloody head of the wretched creature, staring sightlessly down at the ground.

TAWI ATAIR: SEPTEMBER–DECEMBER 1975

I realised instantly that the best way to deal with this particular piece of nastiness was to display complete nonchalance, so I kicked the pathetic remnants out of the way and told Mohim to drive on. In view of what had already happened the incident was baffling and disturbing and the Baluch, who were usually so phlegmatic, were clearly unhappy about it. I wondered if it was intended as some sort of warning or whether it was a child's malicious trick. None of the Baluch could offer an explanation nor could any of the soldiers who had gone out earlier in the day recall seeing it and when I asked Mohammed Said about it later, he was equally mystified.

Events were soon to take our minds off the little exhibition of malice or witchcraft or whatever it was. A mile or so further on, the track descended again towards the edge of the Darbat and became much rougher as it twisted and turned between circular patches of cultivation close by the village of Anshaam. This was the scene of one or two brawls in the past and in view of the landmine that morning it took no great powers of deduction to work out that another ambush was a strong possibility. I should have waited for Suleiman before pushing on past the village, but all I did was to warn my crew that we might be attacked and tell them what I wanted them to do if we were. Sure enough, as we accelerated away from a particularly tight chicane between two walled fields, the familiar 'crack-crack, thump-thump' of an automatic weapon started up from over on our right-hand side by the Darbat.

Luckily the track was fairly level at that point, so when we leaped out onto the red dirt, the Land Rover rolled gently to a stop a short way away, whilst we sought out fire positions and tried to locate the enemy. It was very difficult to do so and every time I raised my head it provoked a burst of fire. The enemy obviously had us in their sights and they had placed themselves well. I knew from the sound of their fire that they were perhaps 300–400 yards away on the edge of the valley where there were several good escape routes and I assumed that they must be close to the edge of a patch of cultivation there, but I could not be sure. If one thing was certain, it was that our paltry fire was having no effect on them whatsoever. At this point Habib Ullah provided a little light relief by asking if he could loose off one of his grenades at the enemy. It could do no harm and might conceivably give us a moment's respite so that I could get a clearer picture, so I said yes and off went the round to crump harmlessly somewhere down the hill.

All this time Saleh had been chatting away in his imperturbable manner on the radio with Suleiman, who had arrived on the other side of the village and was presumably gazing down from the high ground onto the pantomime going on below. From where I was I could not see Suleiman and my chances of getting into a better position looked fairly slim, so I tried to indicate the enemy position to him and get his platoon moving down the valley side to take them in the flank. Suleiman steadfastly refused to comprehend what I was trying to tell him and after a few minutes I decided to try and extricate myself by other means. I called the guns at Tawi.

We had recently been training the guns to fire airburst and I directed their fire onto the Adoo position, bringing the rounds closer and closer in. Several detonated in spectacular fashion above their heads, but still their fire persisted and it was not until a couple of Strikemasters arrived to spread general havoc along the valley side that they gave up and presumably escaped into the Darbat. The Strikemasters set fire to a long stretch of the valley shoulder, but for once I was unconcerned and let it burn. It might discourage the inhabitants of Anshaam from allowing any more adventures around their village.

It was pointless to follow up the contact because I knew by now that the enemy would have scattered into the many small wadis in this very broken bit of countryside or even cached their weapons and returned to the role of innocent herdsmen. So we collected ourselves, met up with Suleiman and continued on to the spot where the truck had been mined that morning. The only casualty, who had been evacuated by helicopter some time before, was the unfortunate staff sergeant who had come to get some 'Jebel experience'. He was back in hospital with two broken legs, having been catapulted out of the open cab of the truck when it struck the mine and not being a well-trained paratrooper, he forgot to keep his legs together when he returned to earth.

The damaged vehicle was to be recovered the next day, so after making arrangements to picquet it overnight we made our way back to Tawi Atair. The sight of the mine crater had made us all very thoughtful, but one thing was certain – we could only use the existing track and hope that no more mines had been laid. It was good to see the new recruits. Before they arrived the Company looked like an oversized platoon, but after a short period of training they would fill out our ranks and make more ambitious operations a possibility. I handed them over to Suleiman with some broad directions as to what I wanted done with them and let him get on with it.

All this time I had been working quietly away on the construction of a new loo. I was sick of the twice-weekly ritual of emptying the horrible

Elsan and I decided that something more grandiose was in order. The improving tactical situation broadened the range of sites available and it seemed that we could now meet a number of desirable criteria. A good view of the surrounding countryside was high on our list, but not in such a prominent place that it would wantonly provoke the Adoo into a sniper attack at an inconvenient moment. We did not often suffer from tummy upsets but when we did they tended to be virulent, so it should not be too far away, but on the other hand, it could not be too close for obvious reasons. After careful deliberation I chose a splendid piece of ground just along the ridge from Company Headquarters, sheltered from the prevailing wind and with a splendid view to the north and east over the valley of Tawi Atair and away to the blue green hills of Qisais ad Deen. I found an old sentry box complete with wooden thunderbox that would serve very well as the main structure and a couple of large oil drums and I sat down to draw up the plans.

We set to digging with a will in the hard soil and we got down to about six feet below ground level when we encountered the first obstacle, which was a solid slab of rock blocking any further progress. Out came the explosives and the hills echoed to the thunder of repeated digging charges, but we made little headway. At about this point in the operation one of the young *firqa* lads strolled up and with the incredulous curiosity that the *Jebalis* reserved for anyone stupid enough to get himself involved in physical labour, asked us what we were about. In the most elaborate Arabic that I could muster, I explained that in the event of a mortar attack, this was to be my personal shelter. He looked straight at me as I struggled to keep a straight face, muscles twitching with the effort, and after a moment's thought he said with a grin, '*Laa, abadan. Haatha minshaan t'bull.*' ('No, never. That's for you to shit in.')

Eventually I was forced to admit defeat and concede that we would not get both oil drums below ground level and after a moment's thought I hit on the simple solution of building up round the upper drum which protruded some three or four feet above the ground. The result was a most imposing edifice with an even better view than we anticipated and our loo became quite a tourist attraction.

6 December 1975

Douglas McCully came up to see me early in December to talk about operational possibilities in the area. He was obviously keen to do something positive whilst the CO was away on leave and I thought that there was still useful work to do in the Ghazeer and the Hinna so we spent some time discussing them. Douglas always listened closely to what I had to say on the tactical situation on the Jebel and he went back to Arzat looking very thoughtful.

We were all working hard now and Peter had been away on leave for some time, so every piffling matter was being referred to me for a decision, which did nothing for my sense of humour. Things were not improved by the hot, dusty winter Shimaals which were beginning to blow and when one morning I asked Mansoor for a glass of water and he volunteered the suggestion that, 'The mess is closed and it is very inconvenient,' I finally exploded and told him to get his bags packed. The next day he was on a plane to Arzat. It was a mistake on my part and I missed his expert administration for the rest of my time on the Jebel, but it could not be helped. I could no longer live with his petty ways.

After Douglas' visit I had a feeling that we would soon be taking a closer look at the Wadi Hinna. It was unfamiliar territory to me and, I suspected, to the *firqa* as well, so I asked Andrew Dunsire if he could help out by providing us with some air photographic coverage. The Skyvan that took Mansoor out brought Andrew in, laden with Glen Grant and an excellent set of photographs covering, from a slant angle, the whole route from Tawi Atair to the scarp where the Hinna debouched onto the coastal plain in one of Dhofar's spectacular natural amphitheatres. There were also some excellent vertical shots of the main waterhole in the wadi in which I was particularly interested, and we spent a couple of hours discussing and analysing the invaluable topographical information they displayed. They were so good that with the aid of Andrew's stereoscopic binoculars I was able to see the exact shape of the land and pick out tactically significant features without difficulty and, using the knowledge I gained from them, I was later able to lead the company down to the Hinna at night without once referring to a map. I astonished Mohammed Said by predicting exactly when we would arrive at the spot I had chosen as the C Company base position, which was a small patch of open ground in the middle of a densely wooded area. Andrew was an expert in his field and his work instilled in me a lasting respect for and trust in the art of aerial photography.

The photographs arrived in good time for the operation that Douglas had decided to do in mid-December in the Hinna. In broad terms, his plan was that C Company would march out overnight from Tawi Atair and covertly secure the high ground overlooking the vast bowl formed by the wadi where it broke through the rim of the scarp whilst B Company, then temporarily under the command of John Moody, would come up

TAWI ATAIR: SEPTEMBER–DECEMBER 1975

from the coastal plain and thoroughly search the broken ground in the bowl, with the idea of driving the Adoo up onto our unseen positions in the woods above. It was a simple plan, but sound enough provided we could remain undiscovered long enough for B Company to flush out the enemy.

By this time the Dhofar Brigade, under the command of Brigadier John Akehurst, had dealt the insurgents a crushing blow in the western part of the Jebel area of operations. In a short, brilliantly led battle, Akehurst had, as he himself put it, 'thrown three months planning out of the window' in the middle of the fight by abruptly shifting the weight of his attack in order to reinforce what had started as a diversionary ploy down the scarp from Simba, the embattled border fortress under siege by the rebels. After repeated failures to do so, this move suddenly offered the chance of effectively cutting the enemy supply route across the border and capturing their main stores dump just inside Dhofar at the Shershitti caves. Akehurst's gamble succeeded brilliantly and almost overnight, the rebel campaign in the west collapsed. The battle, which is described in detail in the book which Akehurst later wrote, was followed shortly afterwards by an announcement to the Sultan and the world press that 'Dhofar was now ready for civic development'. For the present, however, these dramatic events made little difference to our private feud in the east where the Adoo continued to fight on, although less numerous and worse equipped. They were soon to remind us sharply of their continuing ability to resist.

I was sleeping badly again, waking every morning at one or two o'clock, my head whirling with uncontrolled thoughts of things past and things to come, foolish and inconsequential but banishing sleep. Even the nightingale which sang each night in the great tree above our *murcha* could not lull me and I grew daily more tired and irritable. Things were made worse by having to grub about in the kitchen trying to make something palatable of my unattractive mixed bag of rations and Peter was still away so I was on constant call at all times of the day and night with not a moment's privacy. The peace of mind which I had enjoyed a few weeks before seemed to have deserted me and I was getting up each morning appalled at the thought of another day and very dispirited.

After five months in Tawi Atair I felt the need of a break, but in these gloomy moments the Jebel would often provide solace. The restlessness of spirit which afflicted me often meant that I rose long before the day and I would go up onto the highest point of the ridge to await the dawn. On a clear morning it was as though I could see from there almost beyond the rim of the world. The new day would touch distant slopes in the west, picking out the slow-moving shapes of cattle against the soft, rounded hillsides and lighting up the toylike boxes and spires of Salalah almost forty kilometres away. The great sweep of the bay leaped into focus, magnified and foreshortened in the clear morning air as if by a giant telescope and even at that range the water's edge could be seen bright and sharp, glowing like molten copper as it lapped the dark shore.

These glorious mornings alternated with days when a cold wind would begin to blow out of the north, rustling the leaves of our tree in the velvet dark hours of the early morning and heating up as the day wore on, picking up a choking mixture of churned dust, straw and dung and making life miserable. Douglas McCully decided on mid-December as the starting date for the Hinna operation and since Carol and the boys were to arrive in Oman at about that time and Peter was due back from leave, it was agreed that I would hand over the company to him on the second day of the operation and go up to the north to meet my family.

Using the air photographs that Andrew had provided, I drew up a detailed plan covering the move down to the Hinna and the occupation of blocking positions above it. I decided to leave one platoon behind in Tawi Atair and the afternoon before we were due to start I briefed Charki, Badil and Suleiman, the resident FOO, Ashley Loxton and Peter, who had returned from leave.

19 December 1975

We set out on a clear, moonlit night and went down past Andreydod in a long snake, following the skeleton remains of the Wadi Shuffloon in a south-easterly direction. We skirted the little group of huts without arousing the dogs and rejoined the faint track a few hundred yards south of the village. Shortly afterwards we came to the first hazard identified from the air photographs, which was a narrow defile where the track crossed a small gulley marking the exit of the Shuffloon from the rolling lands to the east of Andreydod. In the moonlight, the white dust of the crossing place seemed a vast expanse, a bright screen against which our silhouettes would stand out more clearly than by day to an observer on the far side. To reduce the risk I decided to take a couple of *firqa* and scouts across first. Leaving the rest of the company settled amongst the bushes and rocks, we crossed swiftly and silently to the other side.

The path disappeared into patchy bush and we moved cautiously forward, stopping to listen every few yards. Suddenly someone belched loudly a few feet away in the darkness and moved, rustling the long, dry grass. My heart almost stopped. Slipping off the safety catch of my rifle, I crept forward another few paces, then jumped and almost burst into hysterical laughter as the camel which had been watching our approach suddenly shied, belched again and lumbered off into the bushes. I paused for a moment to get control of a fit of the giggles, then went back across the defile to collect the remainder of the company. There were some anxious moments as we threaded our way through an open piece of ground studded with low hillocks, an ideal ambush site also picked out from the photographs, but we reached the spot which I had chosen for my headquarters without further incident at about three o'clock in the morning. After checking the platoon positions along the ridge to the right and left of Company Headquarters, we settled down in our small clearing to wait for daylight.

The dawn was as spectacular as any I was to witness in Dhofar. The first pale glimmer of day in the eastern sky silhouetted the enormous shoulder of the wadi, outlining it sharply against the milky blue early morning sky and the darker face of the sea below. For the first time I began to see how enormous the amphitheatre was, with innumerable hillocks and ravines, all thickly wooded and jumbled together below towering cliffs. High up on our right was a great picquet marking the edge of the scarp where Douglas planned to make his headquarters and to our left, beyond the position at the end of the line held by Charki's platoon, trackless hummocks stretched away to the Shuffloon. I began to have serious doubts about the size of the task facing B Company and I wondered if we would be able to do any more than stir up the hornet's nest which we all believed existed there.

The day began to brighten and the radio net crackled into life when B Company started their long climb up from the coast road. By early afternoon they were well established in the lower part of the valley and spreading out to search, whilst we had little to do except extend our line as far as we could manage. We anchored our left at Charki's end overlooking a spur running down to the sea which separated the Hinna from the Ghazeer and our right on the floor of the main wadi where we had turned up onto the ridge. The day was uneventful and later in the afternoon I went across the Hinna and climbed up to see Douglas in his eyrie where, typically, he had set himself up with all the comforts of home and was brimming with good spirits.

As the sun went down Charki's platoon was engaged at long range by a small group of enemy from the Shuffloon which meant that we had not been as successful as I had hoped in remaining concealed. I was going around checking the platoons when the attack flared and died away and as darkness fell I made my way back to a small sangar which had been constructed for me during the day, from which I could look down into the bowl. There had been no sleep the night before and we had done a lot of walking but although I was very tired, sleep eluded me. I regarded the Hinna with the same respect as I did the Darbat and it was not a place in which I could sleep easily. I was wide awake and staring down into the wadi when at about eleven o'clock I saw a series of bright flashes from B Company's area followed a few moments later by the unmistakeable clatter of a GPMG.

There was some more desultory firing, then silence. The radio net stayed quiet, so I assumed that a nervous sentry had loosed off a few rounds into the night as sentries sometimes did and I called up John Moody and chaffed him in a bantering way about the negligent discharge, which is the Army's quaint way of describing what I thought had just happened. There was no reply and assuming that John had taken umbrage, I thought no more of it, but a couple of hours later he called Douglas who answered immediately. The next moment I received a considerable shock as I heard him reporting that the Adoo had mounted a bold attack on one of his platoon headquarters. No-one knew exactly what had happened because there were no survivors to tell the tale, but it seemed as though a group of enemy, looking for a way through the lines that encircled them, stumbled by chance upon the position. No alarm was raised because all the sentries were asleep and the Adoo, using one of the platoon's GPMGs, had there and then shot dead the platoon commander, the platoon sergeant and two soldiers as they slept. They then calmly picked up the other weapons and walked on down the track and out of the company area, explaining en route to an incurious sentry who saw them that they were *firqa*. These were the shots I had seen and heard and the thought that I had been an unwitting witness to the deaths of four of our men was not a pleasant one.

John's report was followed by a great deal of coming and going and some speculative firing as B Company and the armoured cars down on the coast road attempted a belated follow-up, but the enemy by that time were probably miles away and predictably, there was no result. Once again the Adoo had demonstrated how quick-witted and audacious they could be.

The next day I went back to Tawi Atair. My part in the operation was over, but I could not help reflecting once again that we needed something more imaginative than the usual lumbering operation if we were to kill any more of our increasingly elusive and resourceful opponents. There followed a blissful six-week break from the rigours of life at Tawi Atair. I met Carol and the boys when they arrived in an RAF transport at Masirah and we flew to Dhofar in a Skyvan, landing late in the evening at Salalah. John Gordon-Taylor had given me permission to use his house whilst he was away on leave and I spent a glorious week showing them all the sights which had become so familiar to me. On the first morning Habib Ullah peered cautiously round the door of the boys' room whilst they were still sleeping and stared at them in amazement, obviously finding it difficult to believe that I could be the father of two such small, vulnerable beings. The first couple of days were marred for Carol by a stomach upset which laid her low for a while, but she soon recovered and joined in the various pre-Christmas entertainments that were laid on. There was an amazingly acrimonious Christmas dinner in the Arzat mess at which so many insults were hurled around the table that by the time the port and nuts arrived there were only half a dozen stalwarts left. Carol was astonished at the bizarre society in which she imagined I had been living and it took some time to persuade her that life in the hills was much more peaceful, despite the Adoo. The boys loved every moment of it and revelled in the drunken antics with which the day was celebrated and it did not seem out of place when John and Shirley Akehurst arrived at teatime having been shot down over the Hayeen waterhole on their way back from Tawi Atair, the last stop on their Christmas tour of the Jebel positions. They ate their Christmas cake calmly and joked modestly about the affair, but their pilot sat against the wall and said little.

I had planned to take my family up to Tawi Atair the next day, but as a result of the incident I was forbidden to do so. Although it was a great disappointment to them and they never saw the place where such dramatic events in my life had been enacted or met the men who had shared those events, it eliminated a risk that had been worrying me very much. I made up for it by filling a Land Rover with weapons and ammunition and taking the boys down to the range where they blasted away happily for hours under Peter's benevolent eye. We went down to Taqah and drove cautiously out towards the Darbat, but not too far. In my mind's eye I kept seeing the Engineer truck that had been crippled by a mine along that road and no amount of sightseeing was worth that kind of risk. Even so, we managed to see an eagle and a wolf in the space of a few minutes.

In the second week of the holiday we flew to Muscat and went on to Bid Bid where we were looked after most generously by the Desert Regiment.

We toured the North in a borrowed Land Rover, visiting the hot springs at Rostaq and the great fort at Nizwa. We went into the interior of the Jebel Akhdar and spent half a day at the fortress at Jabreen, with its famous painted (and decidedly rickety) ceilings and ancient Portuguese cannons. Carol was enchanted by it all and almost overwhelmed by the endless hospitality of the villagers who bid us '*Tagahwa, tagahwa*' ('Come and have coffee') wherever we went.

After a false start at Masirah, where we were told that there were no seats for us on the plane, room was eventually found and we flew home together. I enjoyed being back in England and had a very lazy month, savouring the simple pleasure of lunchtime drinks in the local pub and dozing by the fire through rainy afternoons. It was a welcome and total change from the heat, glare and dust of the mountains of Dhofar and I enjoyed every moment.

Chapter 10

Tawi Atair: January–March 1976

My face, which had lost much of its deep tan after a month in the English winter, blistered and peeled several times in quick succession and burned painfully in the first few days back on the Jebel.

On my return Mansoor presented me with a garish beer tankard encrusted with red, green and blue glass beads presumably as a peace offering, but Peter and I had already arranged for Ionnestu John, an individual of indeterminate but vaguely Pakistani origin, to go up to Tawi Atair and look after the domestic side of things. In the event, it was the worst possible arrangement, for John turned out to be weak and unreliable and a hopeless drunk to boot. In the beginning I was foolish enough to give him a bottle of whisky, thinking that he was an amateur tippler who enjoyed the odd tot now and again but I quickly discovered that he was a dedicated drinker in a class on his own. Each day he was drunk by nine o'clock in the morning which perhaps explained why he never mastered the art of coming in through the low entrance to the *murcha* at breakfast time without cracking his head painfully on the wooden lintel. At first Peter and I were sympathetic, but after it had happened a number of times in quick succession, it provoked first heartless laughter and then indifference. I had to keep a very close eye on our supply of hard liquor and I threatened John with the direst of penalties if he was caught stealing, but he managed to arrange a supply from somewhere sufficient to keep him in a more or less permanent state of inebriation.

He got into the habit of going for a lunchtime stroll to walk off some of the alcohol he had taken on board during the morning and one day whilst Peter was away from Tawi Atair he decided to go for a walk along the track leading down to the scarp. About two miles out he met a new drilling rig lumbering up towards the base. Manned by John's fellow

Pakistanis, the rig was a cumbersome, slow-moving piece of machinery, and the figure in waiter's whites reeling down the track towards them obviously struck the crew as a person as some significance, because they shouted at him to ask where the new well was to be drilled.

'No sweat man,' came back the reply in John's curious, American-accented brand of Pakistani English, 'Dig right here.'

So it was that a couple of days later, when Peter happened to go up on the western picquet and look that way, he was amazed to see the rig busily thumping away, if not actually in bandit country, at least perilously close to the fringe of it. It was the one positive thing that John contributed to life at Tawi Atair and we laughed about it for weeks afterwards.

Whilst I was away on leave, C Company acquired quite a farmyard of domestic animals. Hajji Bilal discovered a cache of hens' eggs and from these a dozen or so chicks hatched. A couple of goat kids were bought from the *firqa*, one of which acquired a taste for the hairs on my legs, which it ripped unfeelingly from me when I was least expecting it. The kids quickly discovered that climbing up one side of the tent which I used for routine administrative work and sliding down the other was enormous fun and I was often distracted from some boring chore by a small pair of hooves striking me sharply in the back through the canvas wall. The badgers were doing their best to help along the process of natural selection and started killing off our stock of chickens so rapidly that regretfully, I had to authorise the execution of a couple of them. This had no effect whatsoever and our little flock of chickens dwindled and vanished, despite all our efforts.

Peter had grown a bushy, Mexican-style moustache and as it covered a fairly large part of his face, I had to agree that it was a marked improvement in his appearance.

21 February 1976

We were threatened with an outbreak of foot and mouth disease in the *Jebali* cattle, but to everyone's relief, it did not materialise. No great effort of imagination was required to envisage the reaction of the *firqa* if it was suggested to them that they should slaughter their precious herds of cattle for the common good. Since taking command of the company I had exercised close control of the soldiers' pay, rations and leave in order to protect them from the various abuses of the system which occurred elsewhere and not long after getting back from England I was down in Arzat again to collect the month's pay. I still hoped, for the sake of the company, to get on better terms with the CO and we discussed our problems and plans in a meeting lasting almost two and a half hours. The atmosphere was wary rather than amicable, but when the talk was over I could not remember a single concrete statement that he had made. It was a virtuoso performance in which he had committed himself to nothing and made no decisions.

Later I was dismayed to discover that he had put my name forward to Brigade Headquarters as a liaison officer with the Iranians, which explained his reluctance to discuss the future of C Company in too much detail with me. He would have given much to get rid of me to make room for one of his mercenaries, but that solution was a bit too terminal for my liking and I was relieved when nothing came of it. I would take my chances with the Baluch, but service with the Iranians (or anywhere near them for that matter) could be hazardous to life and limb. If I was going to be killed, I preferred it to be with my friends around me and at the hands of the enemy, not as a result of a map-reading error by a half-trained Iranian gunner.

A couple of days after I returned from England Peter and I went out on a patrol to the north of Tawi Atair. I deliberately kept it fairly short, but even so I was chagrined to discover how unfit I had become in six weeks away from the Jebel. The countryside seemed impossibly rugged and the wadis horribly steep and it was clear that I needed to go for some long walks to get back into training. Peter was much amused by my discomfort.

Peter's first UK leave was now due and he left, looking very happy, late in February. It was not so lonely on Tawi Atair as it had been during the early months of my time in Dhofar because I had come to know the Baluch well and enjoyed their company much more as a result. Badil still kept himself very much to himself, but I counted Charki and Suleiman as close friends, and Jelal, Imam Din and the other sergeants and corporals were always welcome at the *murcha*. We patrolled vigorously and I quickly regained my Jebel fitness, which was as well, for an operation was being planned in which we would see some prodigious marching. Early one morning we saw another wolf, this time close by the *firqa* camp at Tawi. It looked at us for a moment, then trotted heedlessly down into the thickly wooded wadi to the north of the camp. I was surprised to see the animal so close in because the *firqa* would have shot it without a moment's hesitation if they saw it.

The Wadi Shuffloon had not yet been visited in strength and at Battalion Headquarters the feeling was growing that it ought to be soon. As usual there was little hard intelligence on which to base an operation;

it was mainly a feeling that, if there was a substantial number of Adoo left in the Eastern area, that was where they were most likely to be found. It was decided that the operation would be based on Tawi Atair and the whole of KJ and the Firqa al-Amri would be deployed, reinforced by two companies of Frontier Force, commanded respectively by Peter Isaacs and Donald Douglas and backed up by helicopters, Strikemasters and artillery.

The operation was preceded by a grand briefing session at Arzat which was memorable not so much for the tactical genius of the plan which unfolded, as for the joint antics of Gordon-Taylor, who urged us at frequent intervals to 'Rip 'em out' and 'Bring back skulls', and Yarpy Wardle, who burst through the flimsy flynet door in the middle of the briefing, scattering papers right and left and muttering 'Christ, I'm still pissed.' In the midst of it all Douglas carried on his calm briefing, neatly following each of the CO's interjections with a smooth phrase such as 'From this, gentlemen, you will see that the Colonel's intention is to . . .'

29 February 1976

The night before the operation was due to start, troops began arriving by road, half a dozen helicopters settled on the airstrip and a large and comfortable 'tactical' headquarters was set up close by, complete with bar, mess tent and other conveniences. I decided to invite the CO, Douglas and the Adjutant, Johnny Gorman, to dinner that evening, but when I went to find John and brief him on what was wanted, I found him lying drunk in his tent and muttering about being ill and unable to do anything. I stood at the entrance to the tent, fighting down the urge to drag him out and hit him very hard indeed, then turned on my heel and walked away, leaving him to it. My guests had to make do with my own poor culinary efforts that evening. At sunset I was walking down to the airstrip when I encountered an enormous black snake coiled in the warmth of the rocks and enjoying the last rays of the sun. In the best Wild West tradition, I drew my trusty pistol, fired – and missed. I fired again and missed again. The snake slithered disdainfully away, bored with my silly game.

1 March 1976

The operation opened with two platoons of the company marching up to the high ground overlooking the Wadi Ghar, north of Tawi Atair. Ghar was the name given to the upper reaches of the Darbat and it was the logical place at which to block any movement from Qisais ad Deen into that wadi. Having sited the platoons on either end of a ridge which commanded superb views to the east and west and briefed them on their tasks, I returned to Tawi with my small Company Headquarters to start the next phase of the operation, stopping only to argue for a full half-hour in the bottom of the Ghar with an old man who demanded that I bring him a transistor radio on my next visit, for surely the Sultan was generous and would he not provide one?

At Tawi we picked up the third platoon, leaving one to guard the base and made our way south past Andreydod to begin the search of our allotted area, which was the lower reaches of the Shuffloon and the broken countryside around Jebel Harr overlooking the Ghazeer and the Hinna. We carried out a short reconnaissance to the south-east of Andreydod and that evening we climbed up to a massive natural fortress of rock a mile or so south of the village overlooking the path we had followed on our way to the Hinna before Christmas. Huge granite boulders formed by the shattering of a large pinnacle stood on a ridge above the valley, two or three of them about 150 feet high and sixty feet across the top. The approaches to them and the spaces in between were filled with dense trees and brush which made movement difficult, but the view from the top was magnificent and commanded the countryside for many miles to the west. On the side of the ridge facing east, the approaches were less steep and it was here that we laid out our defences for the night. As I sat on the rocks with a couple of the *firqa*, scanning the scene with my binoculars, helicopters clattered past below us, flying low down the valley on their way to relocate another company further south. They presented an easy target for anyone in a similar position to us and I warned Douglas about it in veiled terms on the radio, but my caution was ignored.

I had insisted that Bilal should come on the operation this time and as darkness approached I ordered stand-to and prepared to make my rounds with him. The *firqa* sat as usual in their own tight little group, scoffing alike at my insistence on such tedious details as stand-to and Hajji's insistence on evening prayer which as always, conveniently coincided with it. Halfway through the tour of inspection I excused Hajji to go and say his prayers and as I went on round alone it became apparent that far more than the usual number of the faithful were on their knees. Although I had long ago compromised with my military conscience by allowing true believers to pray when they should have been watching, I felt that on this occasion my tender-heartedness was being taken advantage of. So when I returned to Company Headquarters to find Hajji relaxing comfortably in a euphoric afterglow of self-righteousness, I told him that in the morning he would accompany me for the whole of stand-to and take the names of all those who were praying. They would then swell his congregation by attending prayers five times every day thereafter back at Tawi Atair. The numbers of the faithful were back to normal by the next morning.

We set off eastwards the next day into the open, gently rolling grasslands of the lower Shuffloon and although we spent the next few days beating back and forth, we saw and heard nothing, except towards evening on the fifth day. We had reached the Jebel Harr after an exhausting climb out of the wadi below Hayeen, built our sangars and were preparing for the night's ambush in a nearby wadi, when the sound of small-arms fire, muted to a stutter by distance, was borne on the wind from the area around Jebel ash Shawr. Jerry Blatch and D Company had a fleeting contact with the Adoo which ended as abruptly as it began without loss or damage to either side.

Major Karim Bux, the senior Baluch officer in KJ, visited us that afternoon and impressed me by clambering effortlessly up a steep wadi despite his girth and age. In the bottom of the wadi, which formed part of the headwaters of the Hinna, we unexpectedly found a spring of clear water gushing from beneath a huge boulder in the tangled undergrowth. Our route took us down a steep slope dropping about 1,500 feet in about 800 yards before we came across the waterhole, where a woman was filling a goatskin weighing perhaps thirty-five pounds. She would make the journey twice or three times daily from the village above and it struck me as an arduous existence, even allowing for the toughness of *Jebali* women.

The nights were clear and cold on the high plateau and early one morning I saw what looked like a comet moving slowly across the sky, its fiery tail clearly visible. I was now lean and very fit and beginning to rejoice in my ability to march for long periods up and down the rugged hills by night and day with little effect on my reserves of strength. My beard was coming along nicely and I was enjoying myself, despite the smell of my own body which rose around me like a miasma whenever I stopped. We ambushed various waterholes without success, including one murky little sink at the bottom of a rickety ten-foot shaft in a small side wadi below Jebel Harr where we waited all night at the edge of the glittering silver sand bottom until a roseate dawn began to creep over the black sides of the hill above us and the sun shafted into the gloomy depths, restoring some cheer to our frozen bodies.

The operation came to an end after ten days and the company commanders were summoned to Arzat to be debriefed. On the face of it the operation had not achieved much, but it had kept the pressure on the Adoo and made their lives more difficult, thereby hastening the process of disillusionment that seemed to be sapping their strength. Later I came to the conclusion that they were present in some numbers, but had evidently chosen not to take on such a large and well-supported force for later, when we went back in a smaller group, they had no hesitation in doing so. It was also a valuable opportunity to get to know the area better and after tramping around it for ten days I felt I knew it like the back of my hand.

I went to my room to divest myself of my stinking clothes and have a shower and one look in a mirror convinced me that my beard was not nearly as glamorous as I thought it was. I spent a painful half hour scraping away the leprous looking grey and white foliage.

After the busy days on the operation, the next couple of weeks seemed very flat and dull. Shahbaz Khan managed to get himself bitten by a very small snake and made such a prodigious fuss about it that I called up a helicopter and had him lifted out to hospital. The young goats kept everyone busy by upsetting rubbish bins and scattering the contents over the hillside but despite their painful habit of pulling the hairs out of my legs, I enjoyed their gentle butting as they grew accustomed to me and treated me as one of the family.

We were now in the last few days of our time at Tawi Atair and I knew that a very important part of my life was coming to an end. In the hills I had enjoyed a freedom and degree of responsibility that few people in our supervised and centralised world could ever know and Tawi Atair had been the scene of much joy and some profound grief and pain. It would be forever part of my consciousness in a way that no other place could be, for there I had been the effective master of 400 square miles of some of the most beautiful country in the world and I knew a deep sadness at leaving it. Never again would I be able to set my own time of rising and sleeping, of eating and drinking or working and resting and I could see that the brotherhood which sprang from isolation, danger and hardship would soon be lost to us, dissipated by the pettier distractions of life beyond the mountains.

Chapter 11

Arzat

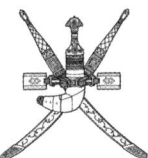

13 March 1976

B Company took over Tawi Atair and we moved to Arzat early in March. Permanent accommodation there had been in the offing for some time, but although government buildings of every sort were being constructed in and around Salalah, shelter for the soldiers seemed to be a lesser priority and we moved back into rotting tents no different from those that had been there when I arrived in Dhofar almost a year and a half before.

There were two major tasks to be completed in the four months before I finished my tour in SAF. First, C Company had to be retrained from scratch, filling in gaps in our knowledge and skills and visiting the Jebel regularly to stay fit and maintain our operating techniques. Second, we had to provide ourselves with some better accommodation.

Life proved considerably more complicated than it had been on the Jebel and because we were the only rifle company in station, all eyes were on us and every little mistake became common knowledge within minutes. Shortly after we arrived in Arzat we decided to have a Company party and the CO was invited. I assumed that attendance would be 100 per cent as it always had been before, so I was dismayed when about half the soldiers found better things to do, leaving embarrassing gaps in the places that had been set for them. To make matters worse, some of them began drifting off before Gordon-Taylor and I had finished eating and later I had to assemble the company for the sort of collective dressing-down that somehow had never been necessary in the hills.

Drill was to prove another trial. It had been both unnecessary and impractical at Tawi Atair, but at Arzat we had to fall in on muster parade in the mornings and move about in formed bodies during the day and though I considered drill to be largely a waste of time, I had to concede that some practice was in order. Hajji Bilal was posted when we left Tawi and Faqir Mohammed moved up to take his place as Company Sergeant Major, so drill was firmly his responsibility. KJ had been promised its Colours and I was very keen that C Company should have the honour of representing the Regiment when the Sultan presented them, so we had a strong incentive to smarten ourselves up, but it turned out to be an unfulfilled promise, which was just as well, for none of the soldiers from Faqir Mohammed down had the slightest notion of rhythm or technique. We spent many a hot morning marching up and down the dusty square with me calling out the time and Faqir marching beside me, swinging his arms and legs always a fraction of a second behind mine so that I grew steadily more and more frustrated. The drill remained a shambles.

24 March 1976

The Sultan was to be married and a four-day holiday was declared in his honour. Representatives from each group of *firqa* made their way north to take part in the celebrations in Muscat. They stayed in all the best hotels and departed, in grand *firqa* style, without paying any of their bills. In Salalah the celebrations were rather more modest, each of the tribes providing a contingent to parade in the square on the day of the wedding. A large crowd of butterfly bright *Jebali* women watched the show, ululating incessantly to encourage the shuffling ranks of warriors. Each group advanced across the square in three ranks, the front rank made up of the senior members of the tribe, skinny, wizened old men with white beards dressed in the characteristic blue woollen kilt of the hills, their lank hair bound by a black rope headband. They all carried a curved *khanjar* in their belts, their social standing denoted by the amount of gold or silver wirework decorating the handle and sheath of the weapon. In one hand they carried bundles of knobkerries which they used to control their cattle like the nomadic herdsmen of East and Southern Africa and in the other they waved their most prized possessions, their rifles. In the dusty, sunlit haze above the bobbing heads I identified AK-47s, FN semi-automatics, Lee-Enfields of great vintage, Garands and even a Martini-Henry or two.

Escorting the leaders in the place of honour were the smart town cousins of the tribe, immaculate in white *dishdashas* and brightly-coloured Omani turbans. They too carried rifles and wore the *khanjar*, but they were somewhat thicker round the middle than the spare men of the hills and they had discarded the humble badge of the herdsman in favour of dark glasses as a mark of their transformation to city sophistication. Each rank of grave dignitaries was supported by one or two lines of younger tribesmen who were considerably less self-conscious. Their shiny black hair bounced in the sunlight and their eyes and teeth flashed white as they laughed, waved and called out to friends in the audience.

I arrived when the dancing was well under way and for the first hour or so I photographed the scene and enjoyed the heat and the festive atmosphere. As the dance went on it began to dawn on me that we had seen hundreds of warriors and since there were many more in Muscat that day, the male population of the Jebel must have been considerably greater than I thought. Then I noticed something familiar about the face of one old boy approaching across the arena at the head of a rank of warriors and I realised that I had seen him several times before that afternoon. The serried ranks that had so impressed me with their numbers were in fact the same group of men going round and round, entering and leaving the square like a stage army.

The officers of the brigade celebrated in different ways and a seven-a-side rugby tournament was played on an old airstrip just outside the gates of the KJ camp at Arzat. The temperature and the dust rose, the partisanship grew fiercer and the abuse and encouragement hurled at the sweating players became more and more explicit. As one gallant CO was hit with a bone-crunching tackle and went flying in the dust, the Brigade Commander was heard to murmur 'That's the only contact — has been in since he's been here.' The Baluch fielded a team captained by Sher Mohammed which fought bravely, but it was overwhelmed by greater experience and sheer weight.

I missed the peace of the hills. The Mess had acquired radios and hi-fi systems and seemed always to be filled with strangers, so that there was an endless cacophony which jarred on ears attuned to the tranquil, rustic murmurings of Jebel life. The week was sharply divided between working days and days off, whereas we had never bothered much about Jumma and I found the daily routine and living by the clock burdensome. The CO's ever-changing moods cast a pall over our lives and made our jobs more difficult than they might have been. One minute he would be all bonhomie and good cheer and the next, his beetling black brows would descend and he would barely be able to speak to us. He loved the Mess garden dearly and spent many hours tending the shrubs in it and when, as sometimes happened, the wilder young officers damaged something after an energetic dinner party, he would go into a black rage for hours.

At about this time Michael Jacks arrived in KJ. Michael was an intelligent, quietly spoken former officer of the Parachute Regiment who had given up a career in the British Army in order to seek excitement and adventure elsewhere and he gave the impression that Dhofar was merely the first stop in his search. He was an impressive figure, not particularly tall, but powerfully built and very fit. His face was strong and square and he had a ready smile and a sophisticated wit which rivalled that of Douglas. He eschewed the bawling exchange of profanities which passed for debate in the Mess and employed instead a quiet, questioning method of argument that silenced the most bombastic bonehead in a few seconds. After one clash I realised that I would have to muster my thoughts very carefully indeed before engaging him a second time, but we saw eye to eye on most matters, so I could sit back and enjoy the spectacle of him demolishing others. He had an arresting line in party tricks and would astonish the waiters at dinner by calling for wine, drinking it and calmly crunching up the glass in his mouth when he had finished. One evening after a dish of tough meat he asked for a pin, stuck it through his cheek and picked an irritating morsel out of his back teeth with it.

Not unnaturally this technique fascinated us and one evening when Douglas was quietly sleeping off a hard day in the corner of the bar, Jacks offered to demonstrate that his technique would work with anyone. Taking a pin, he walked quietly over to Douglas and sank it into his knee. Poor Douglas shot upright with a howl of rage and pain whilst we fell about with helpless laughter.

Peter arrived back from leave and one afternoon we went down to the beach together. When we arrived we saw fishermen struggling to haul in one of the large, semicircular nets they used to catch sardines. We joined in the task, hauling away with a will and I found myself giving thanks that I was a soldier and not a fisherman, for the net was very heavy. As the semicircle grew smaller and smaller, thousands of fish boiled the surface of the water and a few lucky ones escaped over the side. It was a good catch and would soon be laid out to dry on the beach, stinking to heaven but providing valuable fodder for the herds of the Jebel.

As the battalion reserve company we were often called upon to follow up leads and hunches and when, early in April, a former guerilla presented himself at Brigade Headquarters and offered to lead a patrol to some arms caches in the Tawi Atair area, we were told to go and investigate. Some of the weapons were alleged to be in Qisais ad Deen and one, an 84-mm Carl Gustav anti-tank weapon captured from SAF, was supposedly in a wadi south of our old stamping ground on the scarp near Kizetakhayf. I briefed Peter and sent him off with the ex-Adoo and two platoons, but he had not been gone long when contact reports began coming in from him and I decided to go up and have a look myself.

I arrived in the remote, dry bush country to find Peter ensconced on a steep picquet overlooking wooded hills to the south. He had seen several small groups of Adoo and exchanged long-range fire with them, but without effect. In contrast to the wet humidity now blanketing Salalah, it was very hot and dry and it was good to be back on the hill again, but the search had not yielded much and our man was much less sure of himself than he had been in Salalah. Shortly after my arrival there was another sharp but brief contact with the Adoo and we spent another day scratching about fruitlessly before I decided to go back to Tawi Atair and have a look at the second option.

There was no sign of Peter Harris when we arrived, but B Company had evidently been hard at work rebuilding the rather dilapidated *murchas* we had left them. Seeing the remains of the blockhouse where we lived for so long produced a curious empty feeling and I wished we had not come back to see the changes that were being made. Peter and I often joked that when we received the building supplies that I asked for so many times, we would rebuild the Company headquarters as a splendid villa with every comfort that civilisation could afford, but the supplies never came and now Tawi was being rebuilt in the same old haphazard way.

We set out along the familiar rutted track, dismounted a few kilometres south of Kizetakhayf and pushed down a broad, grassy spur on foot. As we approached the little hamlets of Enthelaan and Kudoore overlooking the steep wadi between us and the Jebel ash Shawr, we saw a small herdboy running for all he was worth towards the huts and once again the adrenalin began to flow. We charged down the slope as two Adoo burst from the huts on the other side, running desperately for the shelter of the wooded valleys below. Rifle fire thundered round the hills as I seized the high ground overlooking the action and sent Peter off in pursuit into the wadi.

If we could get some stops into the lower ends of the wadis below us there was a slight chance that we could trap the Adoo and soon two platoons of B Company were on their way by helicopter, Harris having been picked up from Arzat by the leading aircraft. As usual the messages which passed between me, the operations room at Arzat and the helicopters were thoroughly garbled and I was unable to make the Baluch platoon commander at Tawi understand what I wanted before he took off to join the fun, so my plan died stillborn. Gordon-Taylor decided that it was time to take charge of things and he drove up from

Arzat in his Land Rover. The two companies crashed around in the wadi bottoms for the rest of the day, their activities punctuated now and again by bursts of fire from one side or another, but as darkness drew on it was clear that we were into a wild goose chase and one by one our various groups made their way up onto the open ground. Harris met me at last light and asked rather forlornly if I had any 9-mm pistol ammunition as he had lost his magazine a while ago and was now defenceless, but I had none to give him because I always carried a rifle on operations.

We found Gordon-Taylor sitting by the side of his vehicle in the darkness and we discussed what we should do next. In his indefatigable way, he was all for 'holding the contact' and continuing the operation at first light the next morning, but I pointed out that the Adoo were probably miles away by now and even if they were not, they would hardly be likely to sit around, AK-47 in hand, waiting for four platoons to resume chasing them the next day. The others agreed with my line of reasoning, but Gordon-Taylor accepted it with very bad grace and there was a hostile silence at the meal in Tawi Atair later that evening.

The next day the CO was in a foul mood, scowling and muttering away to himself and when the time came to go, the tension between us exploded into open conflict.

'Colonel, we're ready to go when you are.' I said. Silence.

I repeated myself, more loudly.

'I'll come when I'm ready.'

'Suit yourself.' I replied, and swung myself into the seat of my Land Rover. Gordon-Taylor moved suddenly towards me and banged his open hand on the bonnet of the vehicle.

'Who the hell do you think you're talking to?' he ground out between clenched teeth. I boiled over.

'Look,' I hissed at him, 'I've had about as much from you as I can take. My Company has been on the hill longer than anyone else and has put away more of the enemy than anyone else. I've worked my balls off for you and still I can do nothing right in your eyes. Now if you're coming, come, if not, please get out of my way.'

I told my horrified driver to move off, hearing Gordon-Taylor snarl as we did so, 'I'll fix you when we get back to Arzat.'

I was shaking with anger and adrenalin for several minutes, but when it wore off bitter depression settled on me and I thought of the consequences my outburst might bring. The thought of being sacked from KJ did not worry me unduly because I doubted that the CO had the courage to take it that far, but it grieved me to think that Peter and the company might suffer from my bluntness. I was sunk in gloom by the time I arrived at Arzat and even Peter's sympathy and support did little to help. When a summons arrived later in the afternoon to report to the CO's office I braced myself for the worst and I was correspondingly flabbergasted when he greeted me more affably than ever before and we sat down to a long and animated discussion of tactics and policy as though nothing had happened. The man never ceased to amaze me with his mercurial changes of mood.

In between visits to the Jebel, my plans for building some rudimentary accommodation for the soldiers were getting under way. Taylor Woodrow was one of the biggest contractors in Salalah and they had a large depot where building materials were sorted and stored. Next to it was the Public Works Department which owned some splendid six-wheeled dumper trucks and not far from that was Umm al-Ghawarif camp where the resident squadron of Royal Engineers lived. All my potential allies were thus neatly grouped in one place.

I drew up some rudimentary plans, marked out the ground and went off to wheedle and scrounge the necessary supplies and stores. We needed a daunting quantity of sand and gravel but we made a start and a friendly sapper squadron commander lent me a few lads to help instruct the Baluch in basic building techniques. I soon found that whilst we worked for long hours in the hot sun, it proved much more difficult to persuade the Baluch to do so. Mysteriously, the tents which had been full of idly chatting soldiers emptied in a flash when I appeared looking for labour and it was only after one or two fairly severe lectures and quite a long period of education that the Baluch got down to working without me being there every moment of the day to supervise them in detail and prevent them from slipping away on this or that pretext. It saddened me that they were so unwilling to help themselves to improve their own lot or acknowledge the effort that I had made on their behalf and I began to wonder if it had all been worthwhile.

We received another draft of recruits, taking the company to a strength of 140, a splendid command and a great advance on the sixty or so we had in April of the previous year, but it further diluted the comradeship we enjoyed on the Jebel and I reflected again that leadership in adversity is sometimes easier than trying to hold together a group of men distracted by matters other than the task in hand.

12 April 1976

It had been raining intermittently on the plain and one night there was a spectacular climax to the showers. Peter and I went to see an open air film show at the Brigade mess in Salalah but even before it began we could see lightning playing round the hills and hear the roll of thunder. The first fat warm drops put a premature end to James Bond and we all scuttled indoors as the rain began to thunder on the roof. Peter drove back to Arzat at about a third of his usual speed, the windscreen wipers swishing back and forth, vainly trying to cope with torrents of water, whilst the headlights barely pierced the streaming gloom. The going was not too bad until we passed beyond the Salalah boundary fence gate, when the road disappeared under a brown flood of water sweeping all kinds of debris towards the sea. A slight ripple where the water flowed over a drainage ditch was our only guide to the edge of the road and as we approached Arzat we were greeted by the mournful spectacle of the Jordanians in full retreat from their flooded camp. The main gates were open to admit an eighteen-inch deep torrent and most of the camp was under water.

The rain stopped as we drove in and the next morning dawned hot and clear, giving everyone a chance to dry out. Apart from the Ayn Arzat *falaj* which had been breached in a couple of places, there was remarkably little damage, but there must have been some spectacular flash floods in the wadis.

Late in April I won a seat in the lottery on one of the Sultan's BAC 1-11s which was going back to England for some routine servicing. I could hardly believe my luck, especially as I had been let down on a similar trip almost exactly a year before, but this time the system worked and I had a glorious ten days in England.

When I arrived back in Dhofar the weather was building up towards the *Khareef* and it was getting hotter as each day passed. The Shimaal blew fiercely, whipping up the dust and sifting grit into everything.

The CO announced that a contract officer whom I considered totally unsuitable would be given command of the Company when I left, which meant that Peter would only get a few months in command at the end of his tour. I was furious and argued with Gordon-Taylor for more than an hour, but he would not be moved, and justified his position by repeating that he 'had to be kind and give everyone a turn'. It seemed an odd basis on which to choose a commander to say the least and I was bitterly disappointed.

10 May 1976

Charki got himself into trouble with the Sharia court by knocking a civilian off his bicycle on his way into Salalah in a Land Rover. The man suffered no injury and his bicycle was undamaged, but Charki was worried about what might transpire in court and with good reason, for a few days later at the end of a short hearing he received a four-month prison sentence for his sins. I was horrified at the irrational savagery of the sentence and at once asked Johnny Gorman the Adjutant to persuade the Brigadier to intervene on Charki's behalf with the Wali of Dhofar, which he did. Charki was immediately excused the sentence, but it was an illuminating insight into how harsh and seemingly arbitrary the Sharia court in Salalah could be.

The time had come for David Bills to depart and we bade him farewell in one of the drunken, rowdy parties that KJ did so well. I had a very sore head the next morning, which added to my regret that Bills was going. We were like-minded people and things would not be the same in KJ without him.

The rains continued, causing amongst other things a spectacular blackout at Arzat one evening. We sat and watched with interest as huge blue sparks leaped and crashed their way along ancient cables strung on the gatehouse walls, dousing the lights in each successive office until they triumphantly leaped the last obstacle and plunged the Mess into darkness.

I ran regularly on the beach and watched as the sea grew daily more tumultuous until it was a grey, roaring waste of spray and mist like the North Sea in an autumn gale. Swimming was out of the question – the waves were powerful enough to fling a man onto the hard sand and break his bones and there was a fierce undertow which churned up the bottom attracting shoals of fish close inshore, immune in the thundering surf from the nets of the fishermen.

From time to time we enjoyed a little light entertainment at the regular conferences when Gordon-Taylor, who could not string three words of Baluch or Arabic together, would threaten to sack any officer who could not speak those languages fluently within a month. Thinking of his own failure in that field and the number of times he had made the same empty threat, it was difficult not to smile. Somehow it summed him up.

It was a year since an all-weather track had been built up the scarp to the east of the Wadi Darbat, but in the 1975 monsoon it had still been impossible to get wheeled vehicles to Tawi Atair, mainly because of the

Twin Tits low ridge a mile or so from the scarp. The track wound up to and over this feature and it proved to be impassable because of the nature of the soil in Dhofar which turned into a slippery, greasy goo when wet, effectively halting all wheeled transport on anything other than a horizontal surface. The idea was that C Company, in cooperation with the Jordanian sappers who had returned to Arzat, would spend a week or two breaking the white crystalline limestone of the Jebel to pave the steeper stretches of the road. I had my doubts about the effectiveness of such a method and I wondered whether the distance that needed to be paved could be completed in the time available, but recalling the misery of weeks without resupply in Tawi during the *Khareef*, I took the company up to the old familiar patch and we set to work. The Jordanians very quickly tired of such demeaning physical labour and we were soon left with a small cadre of them who were presumably unable to think of a good enough reason not to be there.

Still, the Jordanian squadron commander, who occasionally visited the work site, was an amusing fellow who enjoyed reminiscing about the time he had spent in London, most of which seemed to have been taken up with sexual adventures. Suppressing the irritation I always felt when Arabs chortled over the charms of Western women whilst affecting outrage if their own were as much as mentioned by a foreigner, I joined in the general merriment. The Jordanians would encourage me to speak Arabic as often as possible, for they delighted in the guttural, Omani idiom I had acquired and they would roll around slapping their sides with mirth when I came out with some particularly quaint solecism. I played along, for they were indolent, but charming people and I enjoyed their company.

It was getting hot and the back-breaking work progressed slowly, but there was a childish delight that never palled in smashing open a weathered chunk of grey Jebel rock to reveal dazzling white limestone shot with streaks of vivid pink. Within a few days we had a lengthening ribbon of dazzling white road in the wilderness, but I did not dare put it to the test yet by driving a vehicle along it.

Habib Ullah had been learning to drive for the past two and a half months and we both awaited the result of his test with trepidation. He passed.

The biggest single problem in mounting and sustaining a covert operation on the Jebel was water. We could carry three or four days' worth of the simple rations that we lived on – rice and a few tins of bully beef or mutton – but moving across the rugged terrain quickly exhausted the water we could carry and without an assured resupply, operations were very restricted. There were waterholes, but they were used by the tribesmen and their cattle and even if we visited them by night, their sharp eyes would detect the signs of our passing and secrecy would be lost. Helicopters clattering into a Jebel position compromised it even more surely.

26 May 1976

G Squadron of 22 SAS was in Salalah at that time and they decided to try a different method of resupply by night using a Skyvan to drop the large plastic water drums which we called burmails into a hidden position. The idea was that they would be parachuted from an aircraft which would fly over a drop zone marked by torches and continue on its way. Although the sortie would give notice that something was up, it was reasoned that there would be no way of telling what its mission was.

Daylight tests were to be conducted on the flat gravel plain not far from Arzat where there was a convenient airstrip, and I volunteered to provide some soldiers to assist in marking the drop zone and collecting the burmails and ammunition loads that were to be delivered. We turned out one Wednesday afternoon and after a short delay a Skyvan duly appeared from the direction of Salalah and made a few practice runs across the airstrip, flying so low that I could plainly see the faces of the air dispatchers in the gaping back door of the aircraft. G Squadron commander talked into his Sarbe and the Skyvan swung back towards us to make its first drop. Two black burmails tumbled out and fell under blossoming parachutes translucent pink against the bright blue sky and the soldiers gathered them up with whoops of enthusiasm. The second run was equally successful, but on the third time round we watched, transfixed, as a burmail slipped out of its harness and fell in a slow-motion arc, tumbling towards the rock-strewn, iron-hard surface of the plain. The soldiers began to scatter in all directions and a moment later the burmail exploded with a dull 'whoomp' and a spectacular plume of spray. We hurried over to ground zero but there was not a trace of water nor a shard of plastic to be seen. The enormous impact had blasted the soil and rocks into a star pattern, but the burmail and its contents had been atomised.

The Skyvan landed and we jumped aboard. The tail stayed down as we took off and climbed to 15,000 feet, giving us a magnificent, uninterrupted view for many miles across the plain to the hills beyond. At that height breathing was noticeably more difficult, but the air was deliciously cold. The G Squadron commander leaped from the door and swooped away, dwindling in a few seconds to invisibility against the dun-coloured landscape below and a few days later I persuaded him to let me join the Squadron in a series of fun jumps from Skyvans and Defenders over various parts of Dhofar. It was glorious, unstructured and informal and could never have happened anywhere else.

I visited Sumharam, the reputed city of the Queen of Sheba down by Taqah which we had looked down on from the Darbat picquet, we drove out from the town along a twisting track across the coastal plain, keeping our fingers crossed that we would not strike a mine like the one that had killed the unfortunate archaeologist in the same place a year before. The extensive ruins occupied a low mound overlooking a circular silted harbour formed by twin headlands jutting into its a narrow entrance and as I explored I wished, not for the first time, that I had a trained eye and knew what to look for. To me it was a collection of walls in varying states of disrepair, worthy of respect for their obvious antiquity and the craftsmanship which had gone into constructing them, but I wanted to know what was the purpose of this room, that open space, this chamber and there was no-one to help me. The Baluch considered the trip to be a complete waste of time and although I tried to explain the significance of the ruins, they remained indifferent and sat around chatting amongst themselves whilst I pursued my incomprehensible interests.

28 May 1976

Beyond the mountains on the edge of the Empty Quarter lay Mudhai, which was noted for the abundance of geodes to be found in the gullies and ravines there. Geodes are spherical lumps of volcanic rock between a golf ball and a football in size and they are caused by bubbles of gas in molten rock which cool to form spheres containing marvellous crystals of many shapes and colours. Peter, Ernie Marchant the Quartermaster, our Indian doctor and I decided to take a couple of Land Rovers and a radio and go and see the geodes for ourselves. We left Arzat early one Friday morning with enough water, beer and food to last the day and on 28 May set off up the Midway (Thumrait) road. It was a blindingly hot day and I was soon beginning to wish that I had brought some tinted goggles. As we started down the arrow-straight white road into the desert from Midway, the glare of the sun and a roasting wind began to take their toll and we started to suffer. The road seemed to go on forever across a featureless gravel plain, interrupted in the ruler-straightness of its course only once, where it wound down into and across a great wadi almost a mile wide and out the other side. Towards noon we reached Mudhai and climbed stiffly down to eat a sandwich and drink some beer.

We spent a couple of hours wandering around the wadi in the shimmering heat, collecting a good selection of geodes of various sizes and when we started back to Arzat, I was quick to get first place in our little convoy, so as to avoid several hours of eating dust. On the way back we kept the dust of Peter's Land Rover in view, for it was a lonely road and no help would be forthcoming in the event of an accident or a breakdown. Indeed, we had not seen another soul since leaving Midway.

In mid-afternoon we arrived back at the wadi and wound our way down the twisting road onto its broad floor, emerging on the other side after a mile or so. I looked back to check for the tell-tale column of dust from Peter's vehicle but could see none and so we turned back to look for them. As we recrossed the wadi I saw the other Land Rover by the side of the road with its two occupants sitting in the front seat, apparently resting, but as we drew nearer it became obvious that something was wrong. We stopped alongside to see Peter comforting Ernie, who was covered in blood and looking as though he was about to die. Whilst the doctor began fussing over Ernie, Peter told me that they were following my dust cloud at a distance so as to avoid being blinded by it, when they came to the sudden bend in the road where it descended into the wadi. As they went into the bend Peter touched the brakes, but there was no response and the next moment the vehicle plunged off the road and down a steep, boulder-strewn slope. Peter jumped out but Ernie was not so quick. He was tossed out onto the rocks and struck in the back by the Land Rover as it careered to the bottom. Although no bones seemed to be broken, he was badly knocked about and not a bit comforted by Peter saying 'Grit your teeth Ernie, and say "Scots Guards"' when he reached him.

Ernie looked in a bad way and he was already beginning to suffer from the heat, but fortunately I had noticed a white minibus tucked in under the cliffs on the far side of the wadi opposite where we now sat. It was the only other vehicle we had seen all day and it offered a chance to get him to hospital in more comfort than an open Land Rover, so we brought him as gently as we could to where the minibus had pulled up onto the road. The occupants were German employees of one of the construction firms in Salalah and they quickly agreed to drive Ernie to the hospital at Thumrait. On the way back to Salalah we called in at the hospital to make sure that he was being looked after and we arrived at Arzat late in the afternoon, somewhat subdued by the events of the day.

Whilst we were away, information had been received that some weapons were hidden in one of the tributaries of the Wadi Ethon called Tobruk. C Company was ordered to go there the next morning together with two ex-Adoo who were to show us where to search. Peter and I discussed the task and I decided that he would leave Arzat at midnight with a couple of platoons and head down the Taqah road. When he reached a point on the road below the wadi, he was to dismount from the vehicles, walk the five kilometres to the foothills and make his way up onto a picquet on Jebel Nashib overlooking the area we were to search. He and Hatim Ali, who was coming down from White City to occupy the high ground opposite with the reconnaissance platoon, were to be in position by dawn. I would move out in the early hours of the morning, bringing Jacks and the two ex-Adoo with me and go straight into the wadi to start searching.

Peter had invited the Germans who had succoured Ernie to dinner in the Mess that evening to thank them for their help and when they arrived, they were at once enfolded into the Regiment's lavish hospitality. They enjoyed themselves so much that it was impossible to get rid of them and at two o'clock in the morning, when I was forced to leave and go and change into uniform, they were still going strong. As I went out into the warm, clear night to join a small convoy of vehicles waiting silently by the gatehouse, the sound of laughter and music from the Mess followed me across the white, dusty square.

29 May 1976

Apart from an uneasy feeling that I had eaten and drunk rather too well, I had few worries about what looked like another routine operation in the hills and as we drove along in the darkness, my mind wandered back over the events of the previous day. A few kilometres from Arzat, we dismounted from our vehicles and began the long walk up a gentle slope towards the hills looming above us in the starlight. Grey glimmerings of dawn showed on the eastern horizon as we started up the first low hill and I realised with a start of alarm that I was in trouble. Even in the relative cool of the early morning sweat was starting out in sheets on my face and arms, blinding me and splashing down the front of my shirt. Soon I was struggling and gasping for breath on an easy climb that normally I would have taken almost at a run, and I knew it was going to be a very hard day indeed.

All the time we lived on the Jebel we were fit and hard, apart from the last month or so of the *Khareef* when the poor diet had taken its toll, but since we had come down to Arzat I had allowed myself to get idle. In the stifling humidity of April and May I had not kept as fit as I should have done and now I was paying the price. By mid-morning I was trembling, nauseated and dizzy from exhaustion and having found a shaded niche about halfway up the wadi from where I could see what was going on, I let Jacks control the search parties. If there was a contact I would need strength and wind, which at that moment did not seem to be there. I bitterly reproached myself for my stupidity and weakness, particularly as I compounded the error by eating and drinking to excess the previous evening instead of going to bed early and sober and I was beset by a feeling of uselessness and vulnerability which I did not care for at all.

Somehow I got through the day and evening found us on a small wooded spur called Jebel Khaspar in the middle of the main wadi complex. The smoke-blue shadow of massive Jebel Nashib chased the last of the sunlight across the wadi floor, bringing some relief from the furnace heat of the day and we refreshed ourselves at a spring gushing from the iron-hard red soil at the base of the spur. In that harsh, crackling dryness it seemed impossible that anything cool and green could survive, but the waters of the spring had created a soft, soothing oasis in the wilderness. Small birds flitted over the surface of the stream which shimmered in the slanting afternoon sunlight as it flowed down the wadi between banks of reeds.

During the evening we chatted to the two ex-Adoo and I mentioned some operations of the previous year and asked them if they had taken part on the other side. They smiled enigmatically in the way that *Jebalis* do when they wish you to understand that they have seen it all, but out of modesty do not wish to discuss it, but they gave nothing away. We settled ourselves on the hard earth in the shelter of our sangars above the waterhole, and spent an uncomfortable night being eaten alive by small brown ants which flatly refuted my comfortable theory that they retreated below ground at night. Sometime in the early hours of the morning our fitful dozing was interrupted by a burst of firing from a nervous sentry on Hatim Ali's picquet high above us which echoed eerily around the wadi. All the next day we searched high and low in the wadi, but we found nothing. Although I was still feeling weak and hung over from dehydration things were better than the day before and despite the ants and the gunfire I had managed to sleep a little. I still reproached myself for my feebleness and decided to put a rigorous programme of fitness training into effect as soon as we were back in Arzat. For the rest of my time in Dhofar I ran for many miles each day over the gravel plain or along the sea shore, pushing myself to the limit in the wet heat until I became fit and hard again.

The night we returned the Germans were back in the Mess, obviously determined to make the very most of their welcome and Ernie was back from hospital, covered in sticking plaster and looking very sorry for himself. Ernie was one of those people who rather enjoy their medical problems and we had been regaled for some weeks with details of his back problem. His latest woes dominated the conversation and I remember thinking rather unkindly that perhaps he would have enjoyed more sympathy if he had not kept on about them quite so much.

As the *Khareef* advanced there were days when the hills were hidden by low grey clouds which lay sultry and unmoving upon them and heavy seas pounded on the shore, booming like gunfire. On a dark and rainy evening in Tawi Atair the year before I had mistaken the sound for artillery and I recalled the light of laughter in Suleiman's eyes when he explained what it was.

1 June 1976

On the first day of June C Company spearheaded a move in strength into the Wadi Darbat from the scarp track and it was a measure of enemy's defeat that this place, which had been described to me as an awesome enemy stronghold when I first arrived in Dhofar, yielded to our advance without a shot being fired. We had been down on the broad flat floor of the wadi before, but each time it had been a small, short-lived foray often marked by a sharp skirmish. A year before the Adoo had repeatedly attacked our picquets on the heights above whilst the Tawi Atair track was under construction, but now we drove Land Rovers and a truck between abandoned fields and deep up into the valley where cattle grazed along the shores of a lake still filled with water even at the end of the dry season. Herdsmen watched us, their faces expressionless.

There was no sense of triumph that day, only relief that the thing was done and yet, paradoxically, a feeling of regret that a courageous challenge was no more. Peace would bring the dubious blessings of development to the Jebel, and there were those of us who would mourn the ensuing destruction of its innocence.

Ahmed Said and his cronies in the Firqa Jebel Ali at Mirbat had not been given a lot to do since their eviction from Tawi Atair and they were getting restless and stirring up trouble in the town. In order to keep them occupied and out of trouble we decided to use them on a search operation in the area of Qisais ad Deen around the headwaters of the Wadi Shuffloon. We flew up to Jibjat in a Defender and round in a great sweep over the Jebel to the east and south. We passed over the great sinkhole at Teyq and followed the course of an old vehicle track that wound its way through the desert hills of the Gatn beyond the monsoon belt, finally turning south and losing itself amongst broken, rocky knolls close to the scarp above Mirbat. Most of it looked fairly easy going for vehicles until we approached the great scarp, which dropped abruptly away three thousand feet to the coastal plain north of the town. Its precipitous slopes were thickly wooded and dark grey-green against a dense white carpet of monsoon cloud below which even now was surging up against the rampart of rock and spilling into the lower valleys and onto the plateau. A single narrow footpath zigzagging steeply up the cliff seemed to be the only way up and we noted its position carefully.

C Company, reinforced by a troop of Whimpy Waite's armoured cars and some of the Jibjat *firqa*, was to motor along the Gatn and rendezvous with Ahmed Said and the Firqa Jebel Ali who would make their way up the scarp from Mirbat. Peter and I were joined by Michael Jacks, Lofty Blackburn and Andrew Lundy, a new *firqa* officer fresh from England who had once been a brother officer in the Loyal Regiment. Mike Martin

From left to right, two *firqa* guides, David Freeman, Peter Willdridge, Baluch medic, Douglas McCully, Mike Jack. Standing above the clouds overlooking Mirbat, 1976.

also hitched a lift in order to look at ways of improving the track, so we were quite a crowd.

6 June 1976

The day before the operation was due to begin, we started up the Midway road early, turning off at Raven's Roost and grinding our way along the familiar Gatn track past Zeek and Ashinhaib, which was the first Jebel position I visited, Abdul Aziz, the old airstrip near the track to White City where I had carried out my first ambush and the spot where the water bowser had been mined. I was very much aware that it might be my last visit to that part of the Jebel so it was a nostalgic journey for me. We finally arrived in Jibjat in the late afternoon and for the first and only time I had Faqir Mohammed put up some new tents we had brought with us in straight lines on a flat piece of ground well away from the dilapidated old *murchas* on the east picquet. It all looked very North-West Frontier as the turbaned soldiers busied themselves about the tents preparing their evening meals and the sentries kept watch from high ground around the camp.

The next morning we were joined by the armoured cars and the *firqa* and we set off along the dusty track. We were well above the monsoon line, the morning was hot and clear and there was a magnificent view to the north over the whole of the central Dhofar highlands. I loved the empty sweep of the grey and yellow hills and deep canyons running down to the desert beyond and I wished that I could have spent more time there, but the Adoo were in the greener, richer lands on the south side of the Gatn and that was where the job was. There was no point in regretting a missed opportunity and so I relaxed and enjoyed the drive, trying to commit to fond memory as much as I could of the dramatic, wind-sculpted landscape around us.

We reached the end of the road not long before evening and an hour's reconnaissance on foot was enough to establish that there was no way forward for the vehicles without some engineer help. I selected a small depression in the rocks on the edge of the scarp as our base camp and we built sangars in an arc on high ground around it. Lalu the cook was with us and he immediately gathered up a few meagre sticks, lit a fire and began cooking chapattis for the evening meal. Every time one of the British officers came anywhere near him he would call out a cheery 'Hello Sahib' and of course for me he reserved his usual maniacal howl of laughter, rolling his brown eyes and hopping from foot to foot in helpless mirth.

ARZAT

The *firqa* arrived early in the morning, very disgruntled at having to climb the scarp during the night, for many of them were older men who had joined Ahmed Said in the hope of a quiet life spent commuting between Mirbat and Salalah and they were not at all taken with such unwonted exercise. I went across to greet them, but they were already in a thoroughly surly and uncooperative mood and they had few words for me. I shrugged my shoulders and turned away from them, leaving Blackburn to try and talk them into a more reasonable frame of mind. He had a measure of success and for the next couple of days we contrived some sort of cooperation whilst we patrolled the area and searched the rugged turrets of rock overlooking Mirbat. On one occasion the *firqa* even claimed a contact and we all became excited at the prospect of action, but it turned out to be a false alarm probably caused by a bored *firqa* loosing off a few rounds into the blue just for the hell of it.

It was too good to last for long and on the second evening, Blackburn came to me with a very gloomy face. The *firqa* were claiming that they hadn't been given enough food, that they weren't getting a fair share of the water and that they hadn't been properly briefed and they also wanted to know why the Jibjat *firqa* had been allowed to join an operation on their territory. It was all vintage Ahmed Said troublemaking and a cover for the fact that he and his men were tired and wanted to go home. The next morning I called off the operation, but Ahmed was in a very truculent mood and with characteristic nerve he demanded a helicopter to fly him and his men back to Mirbat. I refused and said that I would be submitting a report to Firqa Force Headquarters on the way the operation had gone. I had no intention of doing so because it would have been a complete waste of time, but the thought that I might would make Ahmed sweat a bit and I saw no harm at all in that.

We set off back along the Gatn, stopping to investigate a waterhole which one of the Jibjat *firqa* had mentioned to me on the way out. A short distance from the track we located the wadi tucked under a rock overhang at the bottom of a steep sided wadi. It was stagnant, green and slimy with age but it would do at a pinch if we came this way again and I marked this position carefully on my map. We returned to our vehicles and drove back along the Gatn, passing Jibjat without stopping and eventually turning hack onto the Midway road at sunset. It was the last time that I would look upon the hills of Dhofar.

The last days were beginning to slip by rapidly. The Germans gave a memorable return party and a few of us went to their construction camp to be confronted by a table groaning under the weight of dozens

FIGHTING THE SULTAN'S WAR

Lieutenant Charki, OC 10 Platoon, C Company, on the Jebel above Mirbat, during the *Khareef*, 1976.

of bottles of Lowenbrau beer and mounds of sausage. We ate and drank until our back teeth were awash and our stomachs ached and we sang 'Lili Marlene' (or the few words of it that we could remember) and toasted Britain, the Federal Republic, the Queen, the Sultan and anyone else we could think of and staggered blearily home in the early hours of the morning.

At the beginning of July Rajah Masoud came down from the hills to Mirbat and offered his services to the Sultan. After our meeting at the Hayeen waterhole I had come to understand the respect in which he was held by the al-Amri and I would have liked to have met him, but when he arrived in Salalah he was immediately surrounded by the establishment and lionised, and mere mortals like myself were excluded from the celebrations following his surrender. He was a man of fortitude and courage and his defection must have been a bitter blow to the dwindling band of Adoo in the Eastern Area.

As the campaign wound down other priorities began to impinge upon the straightforward business of defeating the Sultan's enemies. Into the simple organisational structure of SAF some bright spark decided to inject all the bureaucratic paraphernalia of proficiency grades, career structures, pay bands and suchlike nonsense, which largely accounts for the top-heavy structure of generals, staff officers and civil servants in the British Army. My soldiers, some of them veterans of years of campaigning in the hills, were now required to pass elementary weapon-handling tests and we began a dull, grinding round of basic training, beginning with Lesson 1 on the FN rifle. There was even talk of organising the *firqa* and controlling them more tightly, but how that was to be achieved was as yet unclear. It was all getting a bit 'heavy' and a far cry from my first days in C Company, when I took a census to see what weapons we held. I was glad that I would be gone before things coagulated into a rigid, stultifying system.

Peter and Michael Jacks disappeared in the direction of Bombay for a few days, clutching a bag full of pills prescribed by Spice and a copy of *Playboy* magazine containing an article entitled 'Bombay Duck – who lays what in the Indian city of vice'.

I was developing another theory and I wanted to try it out, so when Peter returned we made our last sortie onto the Jebel together. I reasoned that if we could get close to a centre of activity (and that usually meant a well or a waterhole) and remain hidden for long enough, there was a chance that we would catch the Adoo out. It would not be easy, given the extraordinary perception and sharp senses of the local tribesmen and there were not many waterholes that lent themselves easily to infiltration, but it was worth a try. Now that the Adoo were becoming an endangered species, we would have to work that much harder for a contact.

We were looking for a focal point within a night's march of a drop-off point on a vehicle track with woods close by to provide the necessary cover. It also had to be in an area where one of the dwindling bands of Adoo might be, which narrowed the area of choice quite a lot. These considerations began to focus my attention on the Wadi Hinna where the operation we had mounted six months before had come to nothing because it had been compromised at an early stage. I wanted to explore the lower part of the wadi where B Company had suffered the loss of one of its platoon headquarters because it seemed to fit the requirement almost exactly.

Just after sunset a couple of days later we drove out onto the Mirbat road and by ten o'clock we were approaching the spot where the track looped in close to the hills to cross a shallow gorge formed by the lower part of the Hinna as it crossed the coastal plain. As the dark hills loomed above us, the convoy slowed to a crawl and one by one we dropped off.

The vehicles ground on along the rough track, their tail lights gradually fading in a roseate haze of dust, and we silently organised ourselves and moved off in single file, Peter and I leading. It was not a healthy place to be in the order of march because we would be in the forefront of any chance encounter, but it was the only way we could control the rate of movement and ensure the stealthy approach that I wanted. Left to themselves, the Baluch would stride out at full speed, heedless of the noise they made. As we began to climb the narrow path leading up into the wadi, the moon came out from behind the clouds, glimmering on the pale rocks and illuminating the dark hillsides around us.

We climbed on and up, sweating in the warm night air and seemingly making a thunderous amount of noise and I slowed the pace still more. We stopped to listen and from further up the track I heard a twig snap. Adrenalin began to pump and blood hammered in my ears as I signalled to Peter and we began to move cautiously up the track, covering each other as we went. More snapping noises came from ahead, closer now, and I strained to see and hear. We crept forward, moving with infinite care, safety catches off and every nerve-stretched taut.

Suddenly there was a heart-stopping crash and a hammering of hooves as a deer, startled by our approach, flew off the path and crashed down through the undergrowth. I let out my breath in a rush and Peter and I began to giggle silently and uncontrollably. It was a repetition of the camel incident last December, but no less nerve-racking for that.

Further up the valley we came to a small wooded hill by the path overlooking the Hasheer waterhole which I had chosen as our target from one of the aerial photographs taken by Andrew Dunsire before the last operation in the Hinna. One platoon wriggled into the dense undergrowth at the lower end of the knoll whilst the other moved up to the top, from where they could see all the way up to the rim of the vast bowl where our positions had been in December.

The eastern sky began to lighten, etching the steep wadi sides black against a pearl grey sky. Gradually, light reached into the lower parts of the valley, touching our hill and resolving shapeless black forms into recognisable figures. An old man came slowly up the track below us leading a camel and singing a monotonous, tuneless ditty, his age betrayed by a quavering voice. We could hear the soft shuffling of the camel's broad padded feet on the rocks and its familiar grunting punctuated now and again by a loud, human-sounding belch which echoed up the valley on the still morning air. As they came up to our position the singing stopped abruptly and we held our breath whilst the moment drew out into seconds. Then the song and the soft shuffle started again and the pair of them passed on up the track and out of earshot.

It was possible that the old man had heard something or perhaps spotted a footprint in the dust of the track and now a decision had to be made whether we should stay or go. On the one hand, he might have seen nothing or if he had, he might decide to do nothing about it. On the other, he could pass the news of our presence at the next stop on his journey and the huts of Hasheer were not far from our hiding place. If that were the case, we would be wasting our time in the valley and we might even be subjected to an attack, although I considered that unlikely, given our numbers and the fact that we were prepared. I decided to stay and see what happened.

The sun rose above the rim of the wadi high above us and it quickly grew hotter. The air was still, the valley lay gasping in the baking heat and the only sound to be heard was the ceaseless metallic zinging of cicadas. Towards noon a shot rang out from far up the valley, followed quickly by two more. I inched my way forward to the edge of the thicket and swept the slopes with my binoculars, but I could see nothing. Stillness descended again. Nothing moved in the shimmering heat bouncing off the rocks and boulders on the valley floor and even in the shade of our hiding place it was becoming like an oven. Sweat trickled down my back and sharp stones dug into my stomach and thighs.

The sun passed directly over us and began its slanting descent towards the west. In the late afternoon we heard voices calling to one another higher up on the slopes, but again there was nothing to be seen and not a soul had approached the waterhole all day. As purple shadows began to gather in the deepest recesses of the valley I wriggled silently over to where Peter lay. 'What do you think?' I whispered. 'Well, this is usually a busy track and we know the waterhole is in use, but we've seen no-one since the old man went by early this morning. I reckon they know we're here and that's what those shots were about earlier in the day.'

I decided to pull out. It had been a long, tedious day, but it was not entirely wasted. It seemed to me that the biggest problem was not remaining concealed, at least not in thick countryside, but the near impossibility of taking a patrol into an area without leaving signs underfoot that would advertise our presence to the sharp-eyed herdsmen of the Jebel. The answer to that difficulty would require further thought, but it was a problem others would have to solve.

As we filed down the path in the gathering darkness, my feelings were curiously mixed. I was relieved to have survived and I was looking forward to going home but already there was a deep sadness in my heart that I was leaving the hills of Dhofar and would never look upon them again. It is a sadness that will be with me on the day that I die.

Stonecutters' Island,
Hong Kong,
August 1986

Epilogue

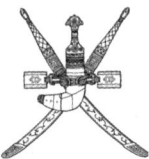

It is now ten years since I left the service of the Sultan, yet the memories of Dhofar and the faces of the men who were my comrades in arms and friends remain fresh and sharp in my mind.

Even as we drove up the Midway road through the teeming rain of the *Khareef* to rendezvous with the plane that was to take me to Muscat, I knew that a sense of loss would set in once the relief and joy of homecoming was done. In the years that have passed Dhofar has never been far from my thoughts and I often wonder what it would have been like to go back. I tried hard enough to return, but once the war ended opportunities for loan service dwindled fast and though I toyed with the idea of leaving the Army, a three-year contract seemed too insecure for the responsibilities that I had.

It was not easy to readjust to the routine and rituals of the British Army after Oman. On the Jebel I developed a strong and serious attitude to training with a corresponding contempt for the peripheral irrelevancies that are important to so many people in the Army and I made no attempt to conceal my feelings. The result was that whilst I was a happy company commander on operations in South Armagh after my return to the regiment, the tour in Cyprus which followed was an unmitigated disaster. I could not take the folderol of colonial-style garrison life with its fetes and parades seriously and I made no bones about it.

I worked hard to make my training a success but I was often frustrated by my inability to convince homesick young soldiers of the importance of shooting and fieldcraft. The image of Ahmed and his dead soldiers kept thrusting itself into my mind as I watched them playing games on the training area.

Within a year or two of my departure Brian Spice died of cancer, aggravated perhaps by a weary resignation to the injustices of life. John

Jerry Blatch and John Gordon-Taylor ('Black John'), the CO,

Gordon-Taylor is still serving in Oman at the time of writing and was promoted after a long tenure in command of the Southern Regiment. Karim Bux eventually found himself an easy billet in Northern Oman which he had earned after long years of service on the Jebel and Harry Fecitt drifted around the Gulf for a few more years before returning to England and getting back into the Army on a limited service TA commission as perhaps its oldest combatant captain. Yarpy Wardle found employment with a large brewing concern in England and was reputedly tamed at last by his wife, who thereby achieved something that neither the Rhodesian Army nor SAF had succeeded in doing. Despite all my lobbying on his behalf, Peter did not inherit C Company when I left Dhofar, but was obliged to wait until shortly before the end of his tour to be given command. He returned to the British Army where he experienced much the same sort of difficulties as I encountered.

The Sultan's Army has become more powerful and, no doubt, more bureaucratic with the passing years. It now possesses an array of sophisticated weaponry and impressive equipment, though what it is all for is less clear.

Tarmac roads link the old Jebel fortifications and close by the well at Tawi Atair stands a modern two-storey building symbolising the civil

— EPILOGUE —

development which has gone ahead as promised in 1975. The hillmen of Dhofar have become urbanised and organised and are presumably happier than they were, but they have paid a price which they will be slow in understanding whilst we, the British soldiers of the Sultan, cherish fading dreams of a way of life that is lost to us forever.

Appendix 1

Letter to Lieutenant Colonel John McKeown[1]

Major D. M. Freeman
4 QLR Kimberley Barracks
Deepdale Road
Preston Lancashire
17 June 1981

Lt. Col. J. H. McKeown
St John's College
Cambridge

Dear John,

I must apologise for not replying sooner. As you can see I have changed jobs, and in the interval I have been rather wrapped up in winding up the affairs of my mother who died in February.

To business. First, let me say where and when I served in Dhofar. I arrived late in 1976,[2] and was immediately sent to White City (Medina al-Haq) to command C Company of the Southern Regiment (KJ). At that point, the company had moved onto the Jebel after a month's rest and refit following a spell on Simba, and was to occupy White City (two platoons) Jibjat and Ashinhaib. The company commander, a contract officer named Harry Fecitt, had gone off on leave upon my arrival in the Regiment. In the New Year, I went on a joint SAS (BATT) SAF operation to secure a new position on the scarp above Arzat at a place called Medina al-San, where I stayed for about a week. From there, I flew to Hagaif (point 825) to take over from a company of the Jebel Regiment which was about to embark upon the disastrous attempt to take the Shershitti cave complex.

After a month or so in Hagaif, we moved to White City, handing over to a company of the Jebel Regiment. In April 1975, the Company was transferred to Tawi Atair, and half moved there whilst the other half under my command took up positions on the picquets overlooking the Wadi Darbat above Taqah. By this time Harry Fecitt had departed for Dubai, and I was confirmed as the company commander. The reason for the Darbat picquet was that Taylor Woodrow were bulldozing a track through to Tawi, and the working party had to be protected. We spent May and June on picqueting and operations in and around the Darbat, and from July to mid-March the following year the company was based on Tawi. In mid-March we were brought down from the hill to the Arzat camp, where we carried out basic training and mounted operations into the wadis debouching onto the coastal plain between Arzat and Mirbat.

Operations in the Eastern area fell into three categories. There were the routine patrols, searches and visits which resulted from low level intelligence (village gossip, to put it plainly) and the company commander's 'feel' for what might be happening. Next, there were the larger scale operations which escalated out of a contact on a routine patrol or ambush, and finally there were the large, rather more formal and preplanned ventures involving several companies and air and artillery support.

Routine patrols and ambushes were our bread and butter, and although they went off without incident more often than not, they undoubtedly played an important part in restricting the enemy's movements and generally making life difficult for him. There was also a better chance of a contact on these irregular, unpredictable forays, and almost all the contacts I was involved in, other than stand-off ambushes or shooting attacks on static positions arose out of an ordinary, everyday patrol. They arose out of chats with the *firqa* (see my remarks below) and from the knowledge of the area which came from living there for many months.

Although I must have mounted dozens of ambushes, I never had a contact on one, a fairly normal pattern for Dhofar and indeed, for most CI wars. There was one spectacular success in the Company, however, early in 1975. Medina al-San had become our responsibility, and at that time we had a platoon in each of four Jebel positions. Harry Fecitt looked after the Western two, Ashinhaib and Medina, whilst I looked after White City and Jibjat.

After an initial lull, Medina began to suffer sporadic stand-off shooting attacks, and despite a vigorous patrolling programme the enemy gradually became bolder, and eventually launched a rocket and mortar attack on the base. Harry Fecitt decided to move down there, and in the middle of March mounted an ambush around a waterhole about five kilometres west of Medina where the enemy were believed to gather. To Harry's astonishment an enemy patrol appeared in the wadi around midnight, and Harry detonated the Claymore mines lining the edge of the track. Four enemy were killed instantly, one was wounded and captured and one escaped. There were no casualties to our own platoon.

LETTER TO LIEUTENANT COLONEL JOHN MCKEOWN

If the Adoo decided to initiate a contact on a SAF patrol or operation, one could be fairly sure that he had recce'd his escape routes fairly carefully, and there was therefore little chance of trapping him. My philosophy on these occasions was to do as much damage to him as possible, using direct and indirect fire and manoeuvre to get him out of whatever spot he might be in. It was usually a waste of time to escalate the affair, as he would normally be off when things began to look doubtful. If on the other hand we surprised him, which happened surprisingly often, then we had a chance to cut off his escape routes and do damage. On these occasions I was always surprised by the Adoo reaction to our arrival in the area, and we always identified our targets, not by what they were wearing, which was usually the same as other tribesmen and the *firqa*, but by the fact that they started scattering. If they had remained in the village playing the part of innocent cowherds, we doubtless would have passed the time of day with them, chatting and drinking tea and milk, especially if there were no *firqa* around to identify them.

On these operations I grew to respect the Adoo as natural and formidable guerilla soldiers. They had a good feel for ground, across which they moved at great speed by day and night. Their fire positions were almost always well chosen, and I noticed more than once an ability to organise and mount area ambushes at short notice, almost instinctively. Other Adoo groups would 'march to the sound of the guns' especially if their comrades were in difficulty, and when they were trapped, they often fought to the death. All *Jebalis*, Adoo and *firqa*, were amazingly stoic, and two examples will suffice.

During the *Khareef* of 1975 I mounted the same number of patrols and ambushes as in the dry weather, a pattern which had not always been the case in past years. On both sides. I suspect there were those who regarded the *Khareef* as a time for truce from the exertions of the season's campaigning, and so it was that we surprised the enemy on a number of occasions in the wadi systems to the south of Tawi Atair. The first contact came when we surprised a small group resting up in the small hamlet around the Hayeen waterhole. We opened fire as they came tumbling out of the thatched huts, hitting their leader, Rajah Masoud, in the arm and leg. For all that he and his friends scampered up the wadi side and escaped in the thick mist. Despite his wounds and the lack of medical attention. Rajah was fit and operating again in a few weeks.

On another occasion we were subjected to a well-planned area ambush. Thanks to the enemy's poor marksmanship (which was his one very weak point) the only casualty we suffered was a young *firqa* lad shot in the chest. The bullet rattled around his rib cage, but again, despite his wounds he managed to walk three kilometres across some very rough ground before collapsing on the airstrip at Tawi Atair, close to death. He survived.

There was a good deal of rather muddled thinking about the *Jebalis* and the *firqa* amongst some of the expatriate officers in SAF, who tended to dismiss the tribes on the hill as all disloyal and collaborators with the enemy. This attitude rather missed the point, which was that the *Jebalis* had an ancient tribal and nomadic way of life which owed nothing to anyone outside the immediate family circle. It is expecting rather a lot to demand instant loyalty from a people whose concept of government was hazy, to say the least. Many remote villages had never experienced the influence of the state in any shape or form, and knew nothing of the ideological struggle being waged in the province between the Sultan's government on the one hand and the communist-backed rebels on the other. Thus brothers could be separated, one in the *firqa* and one in the local Adoo gang, and understandably enough, in those circumstances, some blurring of the political distinctions took place. I even heard of cases of men changing sides several times, each time being welcomed back into the fold without rancour or recrimination. Equally, a village might play host to an SAF patrol in the morning and that night welcome an Adoo patrol and give it shelter. In the circumstances, security was always a problem, and a balance had to be struck between not telling every detail of one's intentions to the *firqa* on the one hand, and telling them sufficient to retain their trust and cooperation on the other.

Colonel Tony Jeapes[3] has written at great length about the *firqa* in his recent book 'SAS Operation Oman', and I would bow to his greater experience in the province, but his view of them represents the opposite viewpoint. The *firqa* could be very good, and they knew their own areas very well. When they chose to be they were a match for the Adoo, and although they could be tiresome, I preferred to have them on my side. They were on occasion unreliable, and once or twice simply refused to do what I asked of them, but I found that if they were brought into the scheme of things and given lots [of] patrols, their morale and discipline improved by leaps and bounds. They were not good at ambushes, for example, which required lots of patience, because their make-up did not suit them to it, but in mobile engagements they easily outdistanced the slower moving soldiers, and were quite fearless about tackling the Adoo.

The tribal aspect of the *firqa* had always to be borne in mind, and I had a lot of trouble with the Firqa al-Amri in Tawi Atair, who had a leader from another tribe with a splinter group of outsiders. It was not until the minority finally went their own way and formed the Firqa Jebel Ali based at Mirbat that things began to go right. Despite some ups and downs I generally managed to maintain good relations with my *firqa*, although the never ending cry of *Anna ureed* ('I want') did occasionally get me down. I made a particular friend of Salim Musalim the leader of the Firqa Khalid Walid in White City, and we enjoyed a close working relationship. I had no hesitation in taking him into my confidence.

The British officers in the Sultan's Army were a mixed bunch. Although no-one could say that the seconded officers were the pick of the British Army, most of them had gone out there for what I believed to be the right reason, i.e. to get some adventurous soldiering. They had also been so used to looking after their men that by and large, most of them stuck to their duty as they saw it, and if things went wrong, it was usually due to misunderstandings, or a failure to make allowances for the customs and beliefs of the Arab or Baluch soldiers. I do not think it unfair to say that, in KJ at least, the seconded officers spent a much larger proportion of their time on the hill than did the contract people.

The contract officers varied widely. Many had come to Oman because they did not fit into society for one reason or another. Some were adventurers of the sort who are always attracted to places like Oman, and some were there because, like the seconded men, they were seeking a different type of soldiering. There were some very good, properly motivated men amongst them, but one of the criticisms that I would level at SAF was that it allowed itself to become too heavily influenced by the contract men at all levels. There was not enough sacking of dead wood, although to be fair, things were beginning to improve when I left. Some tenures of command were also far too long – five years in the case of one contract CO.

BATT, too, I thought were a mixed blessing. Credit must go to them for the way in which they set up and led the *firqa*, and it was largely due to their efforts that the Government forces were reestablished on the Jebel. I can only speak of them as I saw them in 1974 to 1976, however, and from that viewpoint several criticisms can be levelled at them. The most dangerous flaw was the way that BATT had never been integrated into the command structure. From the Brigadier downwards everyone was aware that they had a direct line to the UK which they would use if necessary. In the event, this split command system was never fully tested, because commanders on both sides had the sense to make it work, but in a real crisis the dangers of such a system are obvious, and it certainly made life difficult on occasions lower down the scale.

One example will suffice to illustrate the point. I have already mentioned my friendship with the leader of the Firqa Khalid Walid,

Salim. Over a period of months we built up together an agreed way of operating and, I like to think, solid mutual trust between us. So it was, that when we took part together in a large operation in and around the Wadi Ethon south of White City in March 1975, FKW and C Company were as one and working well together from the start. No sooner had we begun operating in the Wadi on the second day of the operation, however, than in flew a BATT team with all their goodies, neatly interposing themselves between Salim and I. Perhaps that was untypical, but it illustrates the problem that BATT teams caused in the later stages of the war.

Their soldiers were by and large very good as one might expect, but a mutual suspicion undoubtedly existed between SAF and BATT, and it was sometimes reflected in the attitudes of some of the less aware soldiers. It was also evident that not all of them had received what I knew was the firm SAS line on treatment of civilians, and I remember one occasion when I had to order a GPMG gun team to stop firing on what I could see was an elderly, unarmed villager going peacefully about his business. The temptation to introduce 'free fire zones' into the Dhofar war was always there for what I would describe as the cowboy element, SAF as well as BATT.

Finally, the Sultan's soldiers. I cannot speak of the Arabs as KJ in my time was almost entirely Baluch, and the only Arab soldiers I saw were Jordanian engineers (very bad) and the Oman artillery and armoured car squadron, who seemed reasonably competent. The Baluch were a joy to work with, and they looked naturally to us as the people who knew how to read maps, summon up air and artillery strikes and generally look after their interests. So we started with a natural advantage, and I am sad to say that even so, one or two people managed to provoke the Baluch to mutiny. Their principal handicap was a widespread lack of even rudimentary education, a product of the deliberate neglect of Baluchistan by the Pakistani government, but despite this, they were avid learners. I believe that, given a year and a team of good British instructors, a Baluch battalion could be made into a formidable fighting organisation with few equals. They remained cheerful throughout the endless dreary months of the *Khareef*, and were unfailingly generous and courteous. They had to be led, and except for a few legendary Baluch officers whose bravery was renowned, they rarely took the initiative. Once shown the way, however, they would follow faithfully, and were quite unmoved by casualties inflicted upon them. They would also work uncomplainingly for long hours, and during the month of Ramadan, they carried on with patrolling and ambushing without a murmur, although many of them stuck rigidly to their daylight fasting. The only difficulty I had with them was when they insisted on praying at stand to in the mornings and evenings, a practice which I eventually got round by stating that those praying (and that meant taking off all equipment and boots for ten minutes or more) on operations would henceforth be bound rigidly to the prayer routine, operations or not. The number of praying soldiers rapidly fell to what I knew was the hard core of the faithful.

I do not have a record of the names of the various operations in the Eastern area during my time. They were few and far between, and in my view, not very successful, mainly because of the cumbersome preparations which always seemed to be necessary, and which warned off the Adoo every time. I have mentioned the operation in January 1975 to put in Medina al-San which involved two platoons of KJ, a troop of BATT and about thirty *firqa*.[4] The next operation in which KJ was involved took place south of Ashinhaib in the early part of 1975, about March I think. The whole battalion took part with a number of BATT and *firqa*. There were no contacts on that occasion and very little equipment was recovered.

The next operation took place in and around the Wadi Ethon a week or two later, and again involved most of KJ, the Firqa Khalid Walid from White City, some companies from Frontier Force (FF) a battery of the Oman Artillery and the BATT. There were a number of contacts on that occasion, and some equipment including an RPG-7 and an 84-mm Carl Gustav were recovered. On that occasion the Adoo waited until most picquets had been flown off to base locations, and hit the last helicopter lifting off from a position on the Jebel Aram, causing a number of casualties amongst the passengers and crew of whom two were fatalities.

The next operation was the long-standing effort to protect the road building parties constructing the Tawi Atair track up the scarp from Taqah and over the Jebel. During the month or so that this work took to complete there were a number of engagements in and around the Darbat and one fairly large, but short-lived sortie into the wadi itself. By this time the enemy were beginning to give up their hold on the lower part of the Darbat, although further up it continued to provide them with a safe haven, and it was not satisfactorily cleared during my time in Dhofar. The most spectacular incident during this period was a mortar attack mounted upon the Taylor Woodrow plant park near Taqah which caused some problems amongst the Pakistani work force, but no casualties. Mining in that area also became a nuisance and it was at this time that the Government archaeologist was killed on the approach to the ancient city of Sumharam when his Land Rover drove over a TMN mine. The other occupants of the vehicle survived with injuries of varying degrees.

The next large-scale operation took place out of Tawi Atair after the *Khareef* in 1975, with the aim of establishing a SAF presence, albeit temporary, in the Wadi Shuffloon, an enormous feature which had its origins in the wild country east of Tawi Atair known as Qisais ad Deen. The operation involved KJ, FF and a great deal of helicopter and other air support, and lasted about ten days. In common with many other operations of that sort, it was too obvious from early on that an operation was in the offing, and although there were contacts, it was on ground of the enemy's choosing. The operation had little tangible result, but many of us were now familiar with the ground, and it was yet another area in which the Adoo could no longer move with impunity. I became convinced that this kind of large-scale operation was no longer relevant to the war we were conducting in the Eastern area, and advised strongly that henceforth we should rely on covert moves into an operational area on foot, and this tended to be the pattern from that point on. A number of smaller sorties were carried out on the scarp above Mirbat, notably in the Wadis Ghazeer and Hinna in the later part of 1975 and early in 1976, almost all being marked by short but fierce engagements with casualties on both sides. It was and is my view that these wadis, together with Qisais ad Deen, would be the last refuge of the rebels in Dhofar.

There it is. I could, and maybe one day will write a book, but I hope this will be of some help to you. For more precise details of other company and battalion activities during that period in the Eastern area I think your best bet would be Douglas McCully, who was the second-in-command of KJ at about the same time as I was there. He is now the Training Major of 5 Queens in Canterbury.

Please excuse the typing. I'm very much a two-finger man, and the poor typing also accounts for the occasional mis-spelling. I look forward to seeing the book, should you ever get round to it. Best wishes, and please do not hesitate to write if there are any supplementary questions. I have purposely left out the war stories, but can give you personal accounts if you wish.

David

---

1. Written in response to a request for information from Lt Col McKeown, who was researching a thesis on the origins and course of the war in Dhofar.

2. Should be 1975.
3. Now Major General.
4. Firqa Salah al-Din.

Appendix 2

Timeline: War in Dhofar

Phase 1 – 'Containing' – 1963–1967

1963
APRIL   Musallim bin Nufl and followers from the Kathir tribe attack an oil company truck on Salalah–Midway Road, killing an Omani escort; after carrying out two further attacks, Musallim travels to Saudi Arabia to seek support.
1 MAY   A Land Rover belonging to the RAF Station at Salalah is blown up on a land mine.

1964
Musallim makes a second trip to Saudi Arabia where he receives arms and ammunition from Taleb bin Ali al-Hinai. He returns across the Rub al-Khali Desert with thirty-four followers and caches the arms, which are soon discovered by Sultanate forces.
Another group of Dhofari dissidents begin training at al-Mansurah in northern Iraq.
AUG.–SEPT.   Several people are killed by mines laid on the Salalah–Raysut road and Musallim and his followers attack the oil camp at Raysut.
DECEMBER   The SAF is allowed to operate in Dhofar for the first time when a company from the Northern Frontier Regiment (NFR) travels overland from northern Oman to Dhofar to search for Musallim.

1965
Musallim returns to Dhofar, followed in March by another group of Dhofari dissidents led by Amir bin Ghanim.
MAY   Two companies of the Muscat Regiment (MR) deploy to Dhofar to stop dissident activities as part of Operation Rainbow.
MAY   A dhow intercepted by the Iranian Navy in the Shatt al-Arab carries Dhofari dissidents and arms.

1–9 JUNE   The various dissident groups meet in Wadi al-Kabir in Central Dhofar and agree to merge into the Dhofar Liberation Front (DLF).

9 JUNE   The new DLF attacks an oil company lorry at Aqabat al-Hatab on the Salalah–Midway Road and shoots the driver; the DLF regards this incident as the official start of the Dhofar War.

9 JUNE   Aircraft of the Sultan of Oman's Air Force (SOAF) fire their guns and drop bombs on an enemy for the first time, as Provosts support MR elements operating in the Nejd of Dhofar.

18 JUNE   MR carries out a cordon-and-search operation in Salalah, arresting 30–35 suspects identified by information from the May 1965 dhow capture.

JULY   A Company MR establishes the first UAG Tented Camp.

AUG.   Another group of rebels use al-Rub al-Khali Desert to enter Dhofar with eight vehicles and a supply of arms and mines. Their caches are found by A Company MR near Mudhai.

OCT.–NOV.   DLF attacks increase, including on the coastal towns of Taqah and Mirbat.

1966

External support for DLF begins to shift from Saudi Arabia to Egypt and Iraq.

FEBRUARY   Musallim returns to Dhofar with another convoy of arms and is wounded during an attack on an NFR patrol on 8 February.

The increasingly serious situation prompts SAF to send a second company of NFR to reinforce the company already in Dhofar, as well as the new Red Company, embryo of the new DR, elements of the Oman Artillery, air cover from SOAF, and the Coastal Patrol's dhow.

9 MARCH   Three soldiers from NFR die after their patrol base on Jebel Dhofar is attacked.

13 MARCH   A Company of NFR is ambushed in Wadi Nahiz and two soldiers and Captain A. W. Woodman are killed; Woodman is the first British officer to die in Dhofar.

APRIL   The DLF employ a rocket launcher against SAF for the first time.

26 APRIL   Dhofari members of the Dhofar Force attempt to assassinate Sultan Said during an inspection at Arzat Camp outside Salalah.

24 MAY   B Company of NFR is ambushed on Jebel Dhofar and eight soldiers, including the British company commander, and ten enemy, including Amir bin Ghanim, are killed.

25 SEPTEMBER   The enemy launch an unsuccessful attack on Mirbat and also ambush reinforcements on way from Salalah.

— TIMELINE: WAR IN DHOFAR —

OCTOBER   British forces in the Aden Protectorate conduct a cordon-and-search operation in Hawf, across the border from Dhofar, and capture a number of Dhofari fighters

1967

JAN.–FEB.   MR carry out operations along border in a temporarily successful effort to deny resupply to the enemy on Jebel Dhofar.
MAY   MR establishes a company position at Raven's Roost (Qairoon Hairitti) on the Salalah–Midway Road to prevent frequent ambushes.
AUGUST   John Mecom Oil Company announces their withdrawal from Dhofar.
NOVEMBER   Sultan Said orders construction of a fort on the border at Habrut.
30 NOVEMBER   Aden and the Protectorates, receive their independence; the People's Democratic Republic of Yemen (PDRY) is declared and the communists move in.

Phase 2 – 'On the back foot (losing)' – 1968–1970

1968

JANUARY   A series of enemy attacks, using mines, rifles, light machine guns and mortars, indicates that they are being resupplied from PDRY.
JUNE   SAF establishes forward bases at Janook and Defa in the Western Sector.
10 AUGUST   Salalah is attacked for the first time when mortar bombs fired from the mouth of Wadi Jarsis land near RAF Salalah. This results in the construction of the Hedgehog Positions.
1–20 SEPTEMBER   DLF's second congress is held at Wadi Hamrin in Central Dhofar, the radicals (mainly communist) gain control and oust the nationalists from the Front's leadership and the name is changed to the Popular Front for the Liberation of the Occupied Arabian Gulf (PFLOAG).

1969

China provides PFLOAG with arms, equipment, and training facilities, including some training in China.
25–28 MAY   MR launches Operation Lance to penetrate the Shershitti Cave complex in Western Dhofar but meets fierce resistance and suffer serious causalities.
AUGUST   Rakhyut falls to the enemy, eliminating the last Sultanate presence in Western Dhofar.

1970

6 JANUARY   PFLOAG fighters attack Taqah with mortar and rocket support.

17 MARCH   SAF (MR) regains control of Sudh after it is taken by the enemy, but the refusal of the Sultan to provide men to garrison the town results in its recapture.

APRIL   R. F. Semple leads a British military team to Oman to discuss the possibility of using the Special Air Service (SAS) in the Dhofar War.

MAY   SAF's last position on Jebel Dhofar, overlooking the Salalah–Midway road, is withdrawn, leaving the enemy a free run of the Jebel.

11–12 JUNE   The new National Democratic Front for the Liberation of the Occupied Arabian Gulf launches an attack on the army camp at Izki and fails to explode a bomb at the camp in Nizwa; an NFR party is soon able to capture or kill all the Izki attackers.

Phase 3 – 'Turning' – 1970–1973

1970

JULY   The first SAS elements arrive in Oman to train a bodyguard for the Sultan and to prepare the next SAF battalion due to move to Dhofar.

23 JULY   Sultan Said bin Taimur is replaced in Salalah by his son Qaboos bin Said, but the event is not made public until 26 July – Oman's renaissance commences.

30 JULY   Qaboos bin Said arrives in Muscat, and announces socio-economic development throughout the country, a truce in Dhofar, the expansion of SAF to allow it to deal with the Dhofar situation properly, and the incorporation of the Dhofar Force into SAF. Despite the changes, the Front continues to carry out attacks throughout Dhofar.

SEPTEMBER   Elements of the SAS deploy into Dhofar as the British Army Training Team (BATT).

12 SEPTEMBER   *Jebalis* in Eastern Dhofar attempt a counter-revolution against the Front but are brutally suppressed, which encourages defections to the government.

An enemy attack on the fort at Taqah is driven off by SOAF Strikemaster aircraft.

DECEMBER   Musallim bin Nufl surrenders to the government.

1971

JANUARY   SAF returns to the offensive, as the Desert Regiment (DR) recommences operations on Jebel Dhofar while SOAF and artillery strikes are carried out against enemy concentrations and supply points. Meanwhile, NFR establishes itself at Haluf in order to allow operations against the enemy from the north side of the Jebel. This is the first time a complete battalion is based on the Jebel.

A small headquarters for the Dhofar Area, the forerunner of the Dhofar Brigade, is established in Umm al-Ghawarif Camp at Salalah.

The first *firqa* is raised with the help of BATT and begins training at Mirbat under the name of Firqa Salah al-Din.

14 FEBRUARY   Colonel M. G. (Mike) Harvey arrives as first Commander, Dhofar Area.

21 FEBRUARY   The newly formed Armoured Car Squadron has its first contact with the enemy near Raysut, inflicting a number of casualties.

23 FEBRUARY   Operation Everest results in recapture of Sudh by the Firqa Salah al-Din and the BATT team, supported by a company of MR and Coastal Patrol dhows.

MARCH   The number of surrendered enemy personnel (SEP) reaches 201 from September 1970.

MAY   NFR move to a new base at Akoot (also called 'Karlsberg'), permitting them to mount the first battalion operations into the treeline of the Western Sector in two years.

8–9 JUNE   The Front celebrate the anniversary of the 'revolution' with multiple attacks on RAF Salalah, Awqad, Mamurah, Taqah and Mirbat, and follow up with more attacks on coastal towns in the following weeks.

1–3 SEPTEMBER   NDFLOAG are involved in demonstrations in Muscat, Matrah and Ruwi, but these are contained without major incident by the new police supported by SAF elements.

SEPT.–OCT.   With the end of the monsoon, the arrival of helicopters, an increase in the size of BATT, the expansion of the *firqa*, and improvements in administration set the stage for major offensive operations to be mounted on the Jebel.

2 OCTOBER   Operation Jaguar, led by a number of firqas and two squadrons of the SAS, is launched in the East to establish a permanent base on the Jebel and pacify the Eastern Sector.

NOVEMBER   Helibome forces are used in Operation Leopard to set up a line of picquets running from Mughsayl on the coast across the Jebel to the Negd in an attempt to prevent enemy resupply.

14–20 DECEMBER   A Front conference at Ahlaysh in Central Dhofar merges PFLOAG and NDFLOAG to form the Popular Front for the Liberation of Oman and the Arabian Gulf (also known as PFLOAG).

1972

EARLY   Soviet weapons and supplies appear on the Jebel as the Front's relations with China begin to deteriorate.

7 MAY   As a result of monsoon redeployments, the Tawi Atair and Leopard Line positions are abandoned but White City (Medina al-Haq) is reinforced, making this the first time that SAF is able to hold positions throughout the monsoon on the eastern and western Jebel.

25–26 MAY   Sultan Qaboos orders SAF to carry out Operation Aqubah in retaliation for Habrut: artillery and SOAF air strikes are carried out against Front targets in Hawf.

Successful operations are carried out in the east to consolidate gains and to clear Wadi Darbat of enemy.

8 JUNE   Operation Simba, an ambitious attempt to deny the enemy resupply from PDRY, begins with the seizure of Sarfait on the border. Bad weather delays the move down the escarpment and then a strong enemy response and other developments force a withdrawal to Sarfait.

9 JUNE   The Front celebrates its 9 June anniversary by firing rockets at RAF Salalah; one strikes the Officers' Mess and seriously wounds two people.

19 JULY   The Front launches its biggest-ever operation in an attack on Mirbat but is repulsed after several hours with heavy enemy casualties.

19 JULY   PDRY troops attack the Sultanate fort at Habrut and force the Dhofar Gendarmerie to withdraw, following which the fort is destroyed.

AUGUST   At least a thousand armed enemy have been killed, wounded captured in battle since July 1970, in addition to 570 SEPs, while SAF losses in all Oman during the same period total 90 dead and 266 wounded (including traffic accidents).

Brig. J. S. (Jack) Fletcher takes over as Commander, Dhofar Area, which is upgraded to Brigade status.

After the Commander of SAF (CSAF) briefs the Iranian Ambassador in Salalah, Iran sends some sixty loads of supplies on C-130 Hercules aircraft.

SEPTEMBER   The first Iranian helicopters with pilots and ground crews arrive in Dhofar.

22 SEPTEMBER   Operation Hornbeam begins by sending patrols onto the Jebel above Mughsayl as a preliminary step to establishing the Hornbeam Line as a series of picquets, linked by a barrier of barbed wire and mines, between Mughsayl and the northern side of the Jebel.

NOVEMBER   The first Iranian Special Forces Unit arrives in Dhofar and is deployed on the Hornbeam Line.

23 DECEMBER   Operation Jason begins in northern Oman and captures nearly eighty PFLOAG members who are preparing to open a second front in the north.

1973

26–27 MARCH   The first two Diana positions are established by DR on the Jebel overlooking Salalah plain to prevent rocket attacks on RAF Salalah.

30 JUNE   Sultan Qaboos lays down three priorities for Dhofar: defence of the coastal plain, especially Salalah; the continued maintenance of a position at Sarfait; and continued operations on the Eastern Jebel.

SUMMER   SAF remain in strength on the Jebel throughout the monsoon for the first time.

OCT.–NOV.   Katyusha rocket launchers are used for the first time against Salalah and the Diana positions.

18 NOVEMBER   A PDRY Air Force Il-28 Beagle aircraft drops eight bombs near Makinat Shihan in north-west Dhofar, in the only instance during the war in which SAF is bombed from the air.

4 DECEMBER   Construction of a permanent Hornbeam Line begins.

19–29 DECEMBER   The Salalah–Thumrait (Midway) Road is re-opened permanently by Government forces, the bulk of whom are provided by an Imperial Iranian Battle Group, moving simultaneously from Salalah and Thumrait.

Phase 4 – 'Winning' – 1974–1975

1974

JAN.–MARCH   The success of Operation Jason in the north leads to further arrests and arms discoveries in other Gulf States.

4 APRIL   The first squadron of Royal Jordanian Engineers arrives at Thumrait.

10–12 MAY   An Arab League mediation committee visits Muscat but is refused admission to PDRY; PFLOAG insists that the committee comes to 'liberated Dhofar'.

29 JUNE   The Hornbeam Line, to stop enemy resupply between Western and Central Dhofar, is finished.

JULY   A PFLOAG congress, marked by disputes between Dhofari and other Gulf members, ends with the shortening of the Front's name to Popular Front for the Liberation of Oman (PFLO) and the decision to concentrate military activity on Dhofar.

AUGUST   Brigadier J. B. (John) Akehurst takes over command of forces in Dhofar.

OCTOBER   Hammer positions are established midway between the Hornbeam Line and Salalah–Thumrait Road.

29 OCTOBER   A Land Rover with five PFLO members exchanges fire with a SAF picquet near al-Rustaq and one enemy is killed and the others are captured; additional arrests prevent a PFLO attempt to disrupt Omani National Day celebrations in what becomes the final PFLO-related incident in northern Oman.

14 NOVEMBER   The Iranian Task Force is increased in size from battalion to brigade strength and is deployed to Manston (Aydim) in preparation for a major offensive in Western Dhofar.

2 DECEMBER   Operation Nadir begins with SAF diversions prior to an Iranian attack on the Shershitti Caves complex in the West. When Iranian forces suffer heavy losses in the face of strong resistance, their objective is redefined as the capture of Rakhyut.

1975

JANUARY   The Civil Aid Department is established.

4 JANUARY   Operation Dharab is launched by SAF to relieve pressure on the Iranian drive on Rakhyut and to renew the attempt to capture the Shershitti Caves complex.

5 JANUARY   Operation Dharab forces suffer a serious reverse not far from Shershitti and plans to capture the caves are abandoned, however, Operation Dharab continues until 20 January and results in the establishment of key positions at Stonehenge and Gunlines.

6 JANUARY   Iranians succeed in capturing Rakhyut and commence establishing the Damavand Line.

21 FEBRUARY   Operation Himaar is launched under command of Frontier Force (FF) to engage the 9 June Regiment in the Wadi Ashoq and is followed by major operations in the Centre and East

1 MARCH–15 SEPT.   Jordan's 91 Special Forces Battalion relieves Omani troops guarding the Salalah–Thumrait Road. On 8 March a patrol is ambushed in Wadi Nahiz, losing one soldier killed and two wounded, and three more Jordanian soldiers are killed when their Land Rover is ambushed on 3 July.

9 AUGUST   A fierce skirmish in the Eastern Area leaves 4 soldiers from the Southern Regiment killed, 1 enemy killed and 1 wounded and captured, 1 *firqa* wounded.

13 AUGUST   Operations Wagid Bagri and Badri are mounted as the opening diversionary moves of the final push in the West to capture all remaining enemy-held territory in Dhofar.

19 AUGUST   The enemy fires a SAM-7 missile for the first time, shooting down a Strikemaster. Another Strikemaster is brought down on 29 September and an AB-205 helicopter is downed on 31 October.

11 SEPTEMBER   Jordan's 91 Special Forces Battalion hands responsibility for the Salalah–Thumrait Road back to SAF and returns to Jordan.

OCTOBER   The Sultan of Oman's Air Force begins receiving thirty-one Hawker Hunter combat aircraft as a gift from Jordan.

15 OCTOBER   The first of two diversionary operations is launched in preparation for Operation Hadaf, the main thrust of the final push, the move down the escarpment from Sarfait (Operation Kahoof) is so successful that the entire plan is quickly and drastically revised.

17 OCTOBER   Operation Said, the second diversion prior to Operation Hadaf, is launched by Iranian forces to the north and west of Rakhyut.

SAF uses Hawker Hunter aircraft and 5.5-inch guns to attack enemy bases at Hawf and Jadib in PDRY in retaliation for heavy shelling of Sultanate territory; the attacks are called off on 21 Nov. after two Hunters are lost.

22 OCT.–18 NOV.   Operation Hadaf by FF succeeds in clearing the treeline along the north side of Wadi Saiq and capturing the Shershitti Caves, which are then handed over to the Iranian Task Force.

28 NOVEMBER   Operation Hilwah to capture Dalkhut and clear the Darra Ridge begins.

1 DECEMBER   Dalkhut captured by FF.

2 DECEMBER   The Frontier Force troops clearing Dara Ridge meet up with elements of the Muscat Regiment coming from Sarfait just off the Dara Ridge at Magsayl waterhole in the Wadi Saiq. This marks the end of organised enemy resistance in Dhofar and permits the Commander of the Sultan's Armed Forces to inform him that Dhofar is secure for civil development.

11 DECEMBER   Sultan Qaboos declares that the Dhofar War is officially over.

Post-Victory Mopping Up

1976

10 MARCH   The Sultan announces a ceasefire along the border with PDRY.

APRIL–SEPT.   A number of contacts are made with scattered enemy in Eastern Dhofar, these are accompanied by the surrender of the principal Front leader still in Dhofar in July.

30 APRIL   The Front fires its weapons across the border at Sarfait for the last time.

SEPTEMBER   The Front's Special Force crosses the border, but as the result of captures by SAF and surrenders, in operations that ends on 16 October, only two members achieve their objective of infiltrating Eastern Dhofar.

SEPT.–DEC.   Major operations are launched in the East to round up the fifty or so remaining enemy.

14 SEPTEMBER   Operation Storm, the codename for SAS activities in Dhofar as BATT, ends after recording twelve SAS deaths during the six years of its operation.

24 NOVEMBER   An Iranian F-4 Phantom aircraft is struck over PDRY territory by a SAM-7 missile and crashes into the sea off Jadib; one crew member is killed and the other captured; with the help of Saudi mediation, an Iranian merchant ship is able to recover most of the aircraft in December.

1977

APRIL   RAF Salalah (along with RAF Masirah) is turned over to the Sultanate for dual use as SOAF Salalah and a civil airport.

1 MAY   The last squadron of Royal Jordanian Engineers departs Dhofar.

5 JUNE   An enemy group launches a stand-off attack against a KJ platoon position in Eastern Dhofar; there are no casualties and all the enemy escape.

1978

31 JANUARY   A SOAF helicopter is fired upon by PDRY positions but is not hit.

2 JUNE   The bodies of five British employees of Airwork Services are found at Khawr Rawri, near Taqah; they had been shot dead by an enemy group

7 JUNE   An SOA convoy on the Salalah–Thumrait Road is ambushed by an enemy group, two soldiers are killed and eight are wounded.

1979

9 MAY   An operation on Jebel Aram in Eastern Dhofar results in a contact with the enemy; three are killed but the fourth retreats into a cave and kills an SAF company commander before surrendering.

19–20 MAY   A soldier and one enemy are killed in a skirmish north of Mirbat, while another enemy is killed on following day in a separate contact.

8 AUGUST   A soldier in the KJ sector is killed by an enemy group.

21 OCTOBER   A soldier from the KJ is killed in a contact with an enemy group near Wadi Darbat.

1980

28 MARCH   In the final contact of the war, a KJ ambush in the east results in one enemy killed and a second enemy probably wounded.

Index

Ahmed Dur Mohammed (SSgt, Pl Comd)
    Tawi Atair operations 78, 91
    Hayeen contact and KIA (9 Aug. 1975) 101–8
Ahmed Said (Firqa leader)
    arrival in Tawi Atair 99–100
    Hayeen contact 101–7
    money-belt accusations 108–11
    Tawi Atair operations 119–29
    Mirbat area operations 190–3
Akehurst, John (Brig, Bde Comd) 18, 161
Ali Matook (Adoo paymaster, KIA 9 August 1975)
    Hayeen contact 104–8
Andreydod (village) 85, 162, 171
Anshaam (village) 71–2, 114, 135, 156–8
artillery 54, 97, 107, 117, 121, 170, 190
    25-pounder guns 10
Arzat (HQ KJ) 7, 9, 12, 21, 36, 41, 42, 48, 56, 57, 62, 68, 124–5, 136, 141–2, 151, 168, 170
    command 50, 51
    helicopter shooting 55
    Christmas party 165
Ashinhaib 9–10, 15, 19, 31, 33, 41–2, 48–50, 55–6, 192, 203–4

BAC Strikemaster aircraft 13, 40, 107, 109, 132, 158, 170
Badil Mohammed (Lt, Pl Comd 11 Pl)
    White City operations 15–17
    Mirbat 117–27
    Tawi Atair operations 127–69

B Company KJ
    contacts 40, 62, 164, 195
    Tawi Atair 175
    operations 179
BATT (SAS) 60
    Jibjat 11
    Medina al-San operation 19
    Point 825 25
    CO 22 SAS 26
    Raven's Roost operation 42–5
    Tawi Atair 150–2
Bills, David (Maj, OC B Coy)
    contact 41
    Tawi Atair 65–9, 112, 124, 128–9
    Arzat and Salalah 124–5
    departure 183
Blatch, Jerry (Capt, Trg Offr) 172
Blackburn, 'Lofty' 128–9, 191, 193
Brett, Keith (Maj) 47
Britten Norman Defender aircraft 12, 118, 127–8, 186, 191
Burls, Tim (Capt) 127–8

Charki Faqir Mohammed (WO2, CSM, then promoted to Lt, Pl Comd 10 Pl)
    Medina al-Haq/White City operations 16–17
    Hagaif 25
    discipline 35–6
    Tawi Atair operations 132–63
    Adoo contact 169
    Arzat Sharia law 183
Creasey, Tim (Maj Gen, Comd SAF) 24, 118

D Company KJ
 operations 54, 73–4, 93–4, 109–10
 contacts 172

Fecitt, Harry (Maj, OC)
 meeting 1–7, 15, 31
 contact Darbat 41
 Ambush 47, 137
 Dubai 140, 200–3
 joint command with DMF 204
Firqa 10–13, 25–9, 81, 89, 92, 93, 96, 114–16, 123, 136, 141, 150, 159, 168–9, 171, 176, 195
Firqa al-Amri 90–1, 170–1
Firqa Khalid Walid 34–40, 50–3, 63, 207–9
Firqa Jebel Ali 100, 190–1, 207
 operations 42–4, 94, 128, 131, 135, 160–4, 191–3
 challenges 67, 80, 82, 85, 99–100, 109, 119, 120–1, 128–34, 137, 151
 contact 86–7, 101–7
 donkeys 98
 training 110, 148–9
 Surrendered Enemy Personnel (SEP) 119–20
Firqa Sala al-Din operations 19–21

Gatn, The 9, 11, 17–,18, 25, 29, 33, 42–6, 50–1, 67, 98, 115, 128, 191–3
Ghaday (village) 93–94
Gordon-Taylor, John (Lt Col, CO)
 and DMF 8, 36, 48, 50, 77, 78, 118, 124, 140, 141, 150, 152, 165, 170, 180–2
 contacts Darbat 41–4
 wounded soldier 61
 Arzat 175
 Kizetakhayf operations 179–80
Gorman, John (Capt, Adjt) 147, 170, 183
GPMG 43, 101, 164, 208

Habib Ullah (soldier, C, Coy) 53, 79, 156–7, 165
Hagaif 23–32 *passim*, 40, 57, 203
Hajji Bilal (CSM Bilal)
 prayer & Ramadan 18, 120–3
 Tawi Atair 74–5, 112, 168–71
 donkey racing 97, 130
 posted 176
Harris, Peter
 Company 2iC 77–8
 Tawi Atair 179–80
Hatim Ali (Capt, OC Recce Pl) 29, 188
Hawker Hunter aircraft 125
Hayeen 113, 132, 172
 Tawi Atair operations 84–8
 contact August 1975 100–10, 119
 John Akehurst shot down 165
 Rajah Masoud shooting 205
Horgan, James (USA) 152

Ibrahim Abdullah (Cpl, Section Comd, 12 Pl) 30, 35, 69, 124
Imam Din (Sgt, Mortars) 62–3, 70, 169
Iran/Iranian 169
 Shershitti operation 23
 mortar ammunition 44, 46
 aircraft shot down 132

Jacks, Michael (Capt) 177, 191, 195
Jebel ash Shawr 63, 68, 138–9, 172, 179
Jebel Harr 171–2
Jelal (Pl Sgt/Comd 10 Pl) 15, 42–4, 122, 127
Jibjat xxvii, 9–12, 15–17, 25, 33, 61, 191–3, 203
John, Ionnestu 167

Karim Bux (Maj, OC HQ Coy) 172, 200
Kizetakhayf (village) 89–90, 178–9

Lai Bux (Pl Sgt, 10 Pl)

INDEX

donkey racing 97–8
Hayeen contact 101–5
Loxton, Ashley (Capt, FOO) 133, 162
Lundy, Andrew (British Firqa officer) 191

Marchant, Ernie (Capt, QM) 186
Martin, Mike (Taylor Woodrow) 49, 191
McCully, Douglas (Maj, 2iC) 10, 41, 46, 65, 68, 99, 150, 188, 192
  arrival 47
  2iC 73, 94, 112, 116
  Salalah 142
  Raysut 148
  Tawi Atair 159–62
Medina al Haq (White City)
  operations 33–6, 39
  BATT 44
  road building 49
  Firqa contact 50
  company search operation 51–3
  admin 55–60
  mine injury 61
Midway *see* Thumrait
Mohammed Daan (Firqa)
  Hayeen and Adoo intelligence 82–7
  Tawi Atair operations 90–9, 128, 137
Mohammed Said (Firqa) 99
  contact Hayeen 101
  command 109
  Tawi Atair 137–160
Mohammed Salim (Lt, Pl Comd) 15, 47
Mohim Khan 156
Moody, John (Capt 2iC/Maj, OC B Coy) 131
  meeting 55
  2iC 68, 77
  donkeys 130
  Tawi Atair 160–4
mortars (60 mm)
  faulty ammunition 44–6
mortars (81 mm) 9, 28, 46, 54, 62, 137, 148
  registration 27, 62–3, 69, 148
  blue-on-blue incidents 20, 31
  contact 47–8, 70–1, 73
  BATT 25

Point 825 *see* Hagaif

Qaboos bin Said al-Said, His Majesty, Sultan of Oman
  coup in his favour xxv–xxvii
  declaration of victory xxix
Qairoon Haritti *see* Raven's Roost
Qisais ad Deen 67, 98, 115, 121–2, 128, 148, 159, 170, 178, 191, 210
Qunf 121–2, 127–8

Rajah Masoud al-Amri (Adoo)
  sister in Andreydod 86
  contact Hayeen 86–7
  surrender 194
  contact 205
Ramsey, Wally (Halcrows drilling engineer) 153
Raven's Roost (Qairoon Haritti) 9, 25, 31, 33, 42, 192
Ritson, Geoff (Maj) 65, 68
Rose, Mike (Maj) 60

Saladin armoured cars 55, 71–2, 114, 164, 191–2, 208
Saleh Mohammed (Cpl) 53, 71, 106
Salim Musalim (Firqa) 10–11, 35, 51, 107
Shahbaz Khan (Pl Sgt) 27–8, 173
Shepherd, Jim (Lt Col) 144
Sher Mohammed (Capt, QM) 14, 84, 140, 177
Sherrington, Peter 153
Shershitti xxiv, 23–6, 31, 161, 203
Shervington, Patrick (OC) 31
Shipley, Michael (Capt, Coy 2iC; KIA March 1975) 31

Short Skyvan aircraft 185–6
Spice, Brian (SNCO Medic) 79, 92–9, 195, 199
  Tawi Atair 88–9, 127, 128, 132
  casualty handling 107
Suleiman (Lt, Pl Comd)
  White City 15
  Jibjat 25
  Tawi Atair 83, 127, 132–6, 151, 162, 169
  contacts 86–7, 157–8
Sumharam 13, 61, 186, 210

Tawi Atair
  Khareef 77–122
  operations 77–176
  takeover 65
Thumrait (Midway)
  road 9, 186
  hospital 187

Wadi Darbat
  contact 39–40, 157–8
  BATT 44–5, 90, 136, 139, 164, 165, 170, 183, 186, 190
  mines 61, 156
  Darbat picquet 65–76
  operations 93–9, 114
  ambush 136
Wadi Ethon
  BATT and mortars 44–6
  battalion operation 51–2
  operations 208–9
  weapons hide 188
Wadi Ghar 170
Wadi Ghazeer
  picquet 100
  battle of Mirbat 117

  operations 131
Wadi Hayeen
  Adoo 110
Wadi Hinna 84
  air photos 160
  company operation 162–4, 171, 172, 195–6
Wadi Nahiz 25
  sniping 27
  helicopter shot down 31
Wadi Shufloon 67, 85, 122, 128, 162
  battalion operation 129, 169–72
  search operation 191
Waite, Whimpy (Sgt) 71, 191
Wardle, Ian (Yarpy) (Capt, IO) 96
  contact 50
  contact Hayeen 87, 109
  marriage 141
  Arzat briefing 170
  post Dhofar 200
White City *see* Medina al-Haq
Willdridge, Peter (Capt, 2iC C Coy)
  arrival and Tawi Atair operations 94–9
  Hayeen contact (9 Aug. 1975) 101, 107
  training 110
  Tawi Atair operations 113–14, 130–6
  Khareef 120–8
  contact 139–40
  M16 rifle 148–50, 160–2
  well drilling, 167–170
  Arzat operations, 178–97
  command, 200
Willoughby, Hugh (Maj, OC D Coy) 94, 110

Zeek 42–3, 50, 192